IMPERFECT

IMPERFECT

AN IMPROBABLE LIFE

Jim Abbott
and Tim Brown

BALLANTINE BOOKS · NEW YORK

Published in the United States by Ballantine Books,
an imprint of The Random House Publishing Group,
a division of Random House, Inc., New York.

BALLANTINE and colophon are registered trademarks
of Random House, Inc.

Library of Congress Cataloging-in-Publication Data
Abbott, Jim
Imperfect : an improbable life / Jim Abbott and Tim Brown.
p.   cm.
ISBN 978-0-345-52325-9
eBook ISBN 978-0-345-52327-3
1. Abbott, Jim.   2. Baseball players—United States—Biography.
3. Pitchers (Baseball)—United States—Biography.   4. Athletes with
Disabilities—United States—Biography.   I. Brown, Tim.   II. Title.
GV865.A26A3 2012
796.357092—dc23   [B]   2012001917

Printed in the United States of America on acid-free paper

www.ballantinebooks.com

2 4 6 8 9 7 5 3 1

First Edition

Book design by Jo Anne Metsch

To Maddy and Ella, so they may know the courage
and sacrifice of their grandparents;
and to Dana, my best friend.

— JIM

To Kelly, my strength; and to Connor and Timmy,
may you always know my pride.

— TIM

"So, what are you going to do about it?"

—HARVEY DORFMAN

Introduction

Ella is my youngest.

She has my hair and eyes and her mother's smile. The timing is distinctly hers. She was five when she asked, quite publicly, "Dad, do you like your little hand?"

My *what*? Do I *like* it?

I had come to her preschool's Career Day bearing baseball cards for her classmates. In the morning rush getting the girls through the front door and into the car, I'd packed into a gym bag a couple familiar baseball caps, an Olympic gold medal, and a baseball glove.

I had come first as a dad, and then as a former baseball player. I'd pitched for the local team, the California Angels, and for the team everybody had heard of, the New York Yankees. I had come because I wasn't pitching anymore, and because Ella's mother, my wife, Dana, wryly pointed out that preschool Career Day wasn't really for fathers who no longer had careers. The query, posted on the door of Ella's classroom weeks before, read: "Do any of the dads have an interesting job they could come and speak to the children about?" When I arrived one afternoon to collect Ella, the answer beside her name on the door, in Dana's handwriting, read, "No." Calling her on the playful taunt, I'd scratched out "No" and written "Yes— baseball"—presumably precisely as she had intended.

Ella had been excited. The classroom had hummed, curiosity over the stranger in the room sparring with the early-morning Cap'n Crunch joggling.

I'd seen hundreds of similarly occupied, similarly distracted schoolrooms, and every one of them put me back at my own tiny desk in my own childhood in Flint, Michigan.

At any age, I was the kid with the deformity. At Ella's age, I was the kid with the shiny and clunky metal hook where his right hand should have been.

Thirty-five years later, classrooms remained among the few places where I was conscious of my stunted right hand. I would enter and later find I had slipped it into my front pants pocket, tethered against unconscious gesturing, signaling to the room that the details of its story would come at my choosing, if at all.

In this particular room, its walls lined with finger-paint art and construction paper trimmed by tiny round-tipped scissors, I was introduced first as Ella's dad and second as a guy who once pitched in the major leagues. Every eye in the room went to the place where my hand should have been. They always did, no matter the demographic.

I started, slowly.

Who knows their Angels? The Yankees? Who's your favorite? Does anyone play baseball?

I was getting to the subject of my hand, building toward it, the courteously unasked question even among preschoolers. The baseball glove was on the desk before me, awaiting the demonstration, how I threw it, caught it, threw it again. I scanned the room for a kid who looked athletic enough for an easy game of catch, so that Career Day didn't end in a broken nose and Emergency Room Day.

A five-year-old hand went up. "My brother plays baseball."

Another. "Do you have a dog?"

A third. Ella's.

Do I *like* it?

I had never thought of my birth defect in terms of liking it. I'd disliked it some, found it a nuisance at times, hardly thought about it at others. I didn't remember it being called a "little hand," and certainly not by Ella.

We never called it that at home. We never called it anything.

Mostly, my relationship with my hand and its various conse- quences was blurred, and often complicated. Its permanence bobbed in a current of all it might have taken from me and all that it offered. It carried me where it would, to frustration and reluctance, and to fear, but also to the resolve to thrash against its pull. From the mo- ment I could understand I'd been so cast, my parents had champi- oned my opportunity to thrash. Special people, they said, endured against the disability, the child born imperfectly. As significant, spe- cial people endured against what the disability incessantly drew: the self-pity, the ignorance, the rationalizations of a life less fully spent. I didn't know about special, but I knew I wanted to endure, and I knew it pleased them—and me—when I did, when I was up to the fight.

I've wondered from time to time if I was carrying it, or it me. Mostly, I think, I did the heavy lifting. My parents—Kathy, my mother, returned to school and became an attorney when I was in my teens, and Mike, my father, was a sales manager for Anheuser- Busch—generally declined to stand as shields. As far as I know, they weren't at my schools asking for favors, or whispering to the youth-league baseball coach to keep me out of the infield, or standing in an upstairs bedroom window, making sure the kids in the yard played nice. I really sort of found my own way through.

Baseball helped. It leveled the playing field, then placed me above it—ten and a half inches above it, on the pitcher's mound. The rest was about results, and not about who learned to tie his shoes first or who could button his shirt fastest or who looked like what. I remember once feeling dissatisfied with a professional career in which I lost more than I won, and that ended sooner—and with far more heartache—than I hoped it would. My mother reminded me of the journey I had taken, how at every step I had longed for the next one, and *only* the next one. In the Flint youth leagues, I had simply wanted to be good enough to play with the next age group. Soon, I aspired to be good enough to pitch at the big public high school. Then in college, the Olympics, professional baseball, the big leagues. Every level, she said, was, in its moment, a gift, every experience grander and more rewarding than the last. There was no rehearsed progression. It just happened. I think that's the way my parents thought of it, too. And I liked it just fine.

Did I like this hand, though? Could it be as simple as a child's curiosity, all black and white and no gray? I wondered if that really was what she was asking.

Do I like what I have been? How I have been looked at? The battles I chose? The ones that chose me? Those I evaded? What I became?

Do I like who I am?

It was a lot to consider standing in front of a dozen five-year-olds, the morning frivolity undone by my desire to be truthful, and then to reexamine a life spent at the blunt end of inspection, followed inevitably by introspection. The teacher, Ms. Roberts, white-haired and not typically indulgent, held her gaze from the rear of the room. This, she could be reasonably sure, was going to be more interesting than last week's stockbroker.

What I honestly felt was that my hand had put me here, with my daughter and her friends, in a place where I could touch my own childhood: my mother's hand on my cheek, other boys' taunts on my shoulders. My little hand was my motivation. It was my pride and my insecurity, my antagonism and my empathy.

I looked at Ella. I would not go back to that age again. A new school, a new classroom, had always meant new kids with the same questions. I cringe still. I'd look forward to recess back then, an hour to show them I could do what they could.

"Do you know your hand looks like a foot?"

"Why do you have only one finger?"

"Can you move it?"

"Does it hurt?"

"Did you know you are giving everyone 'the finger'?"

And me, longing to fit in, going along, answering as if it were the first time the subject had ever come up, then going home to the brick wall on the side of the house. I was always comfortable being by myself, even if I didn't prefer it.

There, I'd throw a rubber-coated baseball at a strike zone outlined in chalk. I would imagine myself a major-league pitcher, and I'd throw the ball and catch it and throw it again, often for hours. I'd switch the baseball glove—a Dusty Baker model my father had bought at the corner drugstore—back and forth so that I hardly thought about it anymore.

Just like any other kid, I thought.

Like Ella.

Do I like my little hand?

I rolled her question in my head for a second time and nearly laughed at its genuineness, its path from the clear blue.

"I do, honey," I said. "I like my little hand. I haven't always liked it. And it hasn't always been easy. But it has taught me an important lesson: that life isn't easy and it isn't always fair. But if we can make the most out of what we've been given, and find our own way of doing things, you wouldn't believe what can happen."

So this is the story of me and my little hand. And of a life in baseball. But, first, of a life.

IMPERFECT

CHAPTER 1

I spent two baseball seasons in New York and enjoyed them most on Saturday mornings, when the city composed itself with a long, slow breath.

Maybe it was a sigh.

Either way, on this particular Saturday the sidewalks twenty-seven floors below the apartment window were less cluttered, the taxi hailers appeared in a hurry but not altogether panic-stricken, the dog walkers smiled and nodded at passersby as their little city pooches, pleased not to be rushed, did their morning business. Across 90th Street, a broad patch of emerald green—conspicuously so against the old brick and brownstone and grit—hosted a game of soccer, filling the neighborhood with cries of encouragement, whoops, and applause.

The sky was gray, a leaden touch to a yawn-and-stretch morning on Manhattan's Upper East Side. The idle observations from the uniformed lobby doorman and the waitress four blocks away at Gracie's Corner, where the wait was manageable and the pancakes were reliably fluffy, were about afternoon rain, the prospect of which further softened the jostle of the expired workweek.

I liked it there.

Dana and I had carved something like a routine from our first year east. What began as an exercise in survival became almost comfortable. We'd rented a one-bedroom apartment with a sofa, a coffee table, and a couple chairs, bought a few things for the kitchen, and mostly ate out. We were in our mid-twenties, a good time for exploration and discovery and a semi-furnished life. At first we walked the neighborhood within a few blocks of 90th and York Avenue, browsing the shops and studying the menus taped to the windows before widening the radius to include Central Park and the museums that run practically side-by-side along Fifth Avenue.

We began to smile at familiar and friendly faces: the people with whom we regularly rode the elevator, the guy behind the deli counter a couple doors down, the woman who pushed quarters across the top of a stack of tabloids, change for our newspaper. Amid its swirling rhythms and every-man-for-himself pretenses, New York was becoming a good place for us. We were learning about each other, fending for ourselves, accumulating the scrapes and bruises that come with the outsiders' clumsy entrance.

I'm not sure the transplants among the city's millions ever believe that life there can be done quite right. There's simply too much one can't know, there being so many wonderful layers of people and cultures, so many siren blips and impulses. And yet, many find their spots. There is a life to be had in the spaces of stillness amid the commotion, and that's where we generally succeeded in hosting it.

The job wasn't going as well.

I walked with Dana that morning with *The New York Times* under my arm and work on my mind. A man pushed buckets of fresh flowers to the sidewalk, far enough to be tempting to passersby, not so far as to be out of sight. The paper carried the story of the Yankees' loss last night at The Stadium, a Cleveland Indians rookie named Manny Ramirez—raised in New York's own Washington Heights—hitting his first big-league home run in front of scores of friends and relatives down the left-field line, and, two innings later, his second. The Mets had lost in Chicago. The Angels game had gone too late to make the early edition. There may have been a mention of me somewhere within those pages, which I'd chosen not to read.

It was early September and beginning to feel like it. The weather was turning and the Yankees were in the race, in second place, a couple games behind the Toronto Blue Jays in the American League East. Life and baseball were moving fast, each jostling the other to take the lead as Dana and I stuck to our recent game-day habits: me feeling the anxiety and freshness of a new five-day cycle, eager for the ball and another shot, her fretting that I'd lose again and we'd have to relive the previous four days.

As we walked, we spoke of that afternoon's start against the Indians, what it might bring, then left the conversation as a pile of half-finished thoughts. We ate breakfast, the two of us crammed in the way people so frequently are in that massive city, shoulder to shoulder with strangers, yet feeling mostly alone. Dana, I could tell from her clipped sentences, felt the gravity of the day keenly even as she stirred her coffee. What we didn't talk about I felt in my stomach: the ballgame—*my* ballgame—hours away, too near to allow me to ponder anything else, too far off to do anything about. We returned to the apartment and I left Dana there. "Good luck," she said with a hug. "Thanks," I said. "We'll see what happens," thinking, *Sorry to have dragged you into this.* I gathered my pre-packed duffel bag, and returned to the streets to summon a metered ride to Yankee Stadium.

Even at mid-morning on a Saturday, the mere four miles from the Upper East Side to the Bronx—York Avenue to FDR Drive to the Major Deegan Expressway and up to 161st Street—seemed long. I wanted to be there, into my routine, burying myself in a pile of scouting reports, awaiting game time, a clock that wouldn't start until the heavy metal door to the clubhouse swung open. Taped to the other side of that door would be the lineup, me on the bottom, pitching against a team that, five days before, had hit almost everything I'd thrown, and hit it hard.

I stared from the rear passenger window across the East River, made dreary by the skies, and considered exactly where it was I was going.

What would come that afternoon, I did not know. But I sensed that something would, something well within the boundaries of glory and ignominy, those sorts of extremes, but something important to me. I'd come from the Angels nine months before to lead the Yankees' pitching staff, or so the papers said. I'd cost the Yankees three players everyone thought were pretty good, the thinking being that given a little Yankee-like run support and granted Yankee Stadium's expansive center and left-center fields, I could be the ace they'd needed since, I don't know . . . Ron Guidry?

I won the home opener that year, 1993, going nine innings and beating the Kansas City Royals and David Cone, 4–1, in front of almost 57,000 people. It was an incredible experience on a fantastic stage, a great rush. I was sure I'd found a new home, and surmised I was okay with leaving behind the big contract offer from the Angels and life in Orange County, which included Dana's family.

The Angels had raised me in the ways of professional baseball, straight out of the University of Michigan, straight from the draft, straight from the Olympics, and straight into their starting rotation. Four years later, after I'd had the best ERA of my career (as it turned out) but 15 losses in 1992, they traded me. Maybe these are the rhythms of Major League Baseball, but they weren't my rhythms, not at all. Suddenly I'd been transplanted from an ocean view in Newport Beach to a city view on the Upper East Side, from the mom-and-pop Angels to the pinstriped, corporate George Steinbrenner Yankees.

There was more, of course. There was always more.

I'd gone without a right hand for nearly twenty-six years. The doctors said it was a birth defect, which, in my case, was what they called something that was less an issue at birth than in life. The birth actually went fine; the complications came long after. The best I can say is I managed them. When I was young my father put a baseball in my hand, and it made sense, and eventually it put me in a place where, maybe, I was a little less different.

Baseball, to me, was validation. And sometimes leaning on baseball like that was a good thing.

The cab bounced north. I held the approximate fare plus a couple dollars in my hand to avoid any holdups at the ballpark. Best to just slam the door and be off, over the slate-gray cobblestones, past the grinning, blue-coated security, down the curling flight of stairs.

Other cars accompanied my cab. They were driven by strangers with their jaws set, starched shirtsleeves buttoned at their wrists, people working on a Saturday morning just as I was. I loved my job mostly, but sometimes got to wondering why it didn't always love me back. Often on these drives, or on bus rides through unfamiliar cities, I'd look at people in their cars, people in the streets, and mentally frisk them for the symptoms of their lives. What would they give to be in my place, to be a big-league ballplayer, traveling the country, making millions, regular paychecks on the first and fifteenth, win or lose?

Probably the same I'd give.

Five days before I'd felt like I'd lost, and lost badly. The start had come at the old ballpark in Cleveland and I hadn't gotten out of the fourth inning. I'd hit just about every bat in the Indians' lineup, a few twice, always on the barrel, and trudged off the mound having allowed ten hits, four walks, and seven runs. While Dion James and Paul O'Neill and Don Mattingly rallied for 14 runs and a win in spite of me, I returned to the clubhouse, tore off my road grays, and put on a pair of shorts and a T-shirt. Without a thought, I went for a get-it-all-out run, straight through the Municipal Stadium parking lot and into the streets of Cleveland, which seemed a good idea at the time and only ended up further annoying our manager, Buck Showalter, a by-the-book baseball man who hadn't read the chapter on get-it-all-out runs.

Still, rather than stew in the clubhouse, gauging the relative flight-and-crash capabilities of folding chairs, I dashed into the steamy afternoon toward the blinking lights of what looked like an airport, away from the anger and frustration, away from the expectations. All of which, it turned out, tailed me out of the clubhouse.

In the dugout I'd left behind, Showalter turned to an assistant trainer who'd returned from the clubhouse.

"How's Jim doing?" Showalter asked.

"I don't know. He's gone."

"What do you mean, 'gone'?"

"Just, 'gone.'"

I hadn't exactly been Ron Guidry in my first season as a Yankee.

To that point, I'd won nine games and lost eleven, and was about to
be bailed out of a twelfth that was pretty well deserved. My arm felt
fine, though I'd gnawingly lost some velocity on my fastball. My
signature pitch—a cut fastball, which ran inside on right-handed
hitters and had always left my hand reliably—seemed in the throes
of a mid-life crisis. Sometimes it darted in on the right-handers, hard
and late. Other times, it dawdled across the plate, practically begging to get hit, and, generally, major-league hitters don't have to be
asked twice. I was inconsistent, pitching well at times and winning,
pitching well and losing, pitching poorly and losing, and making all
the in-between stops, leaving me right at mediocre. So, I stomped
across the pavement, killing the five-plus innings I'd left to the bullpen, sweating out the disappointment, full of anger and having nowhere to put it. It's funny: As a starting pitcher, you'd spend four
and a half days training your body and your mind for those three
hours, and when it ended abruptly and ingloriously, the preparation,
adrenaline, and made-up images of pushing onward just sort of hung
there while the game went on without you. What were you supposed
to do with all that stuff? Put it in a sandwich bag and carry it around
for another four and a half days? Some of the most grounded pitchers
I ever knew had the toughest time assimilating back into the team
model for those fifteen or thirty minutes after they were out of that
competition mode. I was one of the worst at it. Instead, I'd throw
things and yell and hope not to harm anyone.

By the time I'd circled back to the ballpark, composed myself, and
fell back into a folding chair, the rest of the guys had the Indians
whipped. They were happy. I was trying to be. I felt like I'd personally spit the bit. I felt like they—okay, *we*—deserved to be satisfied
with the win, but damn if it wasn't hard to screw on that smile. The
good news was the Indians on Saturday afternoon at Yankee Sta-

dium. I'd have another shot at them. They probably viewed it as another shot at me.

A couple days later, back in New York, Showalter informed me I had been out of line for leaving the clubhouse in Cleveland. First, I had no idea how he found out. Second, I was surprised it was an issue, though I guess I shouldn't have been. Steinbrenner didn't always treat his players as adults—you'll wear your wool cap running in the outfield before games, whether it's April in Chicago or August in Texas, and take your heat exhaustion like a man—and Showalter minded those dictates. I'm not sure the Yankees' playbook specifically bans mid-afternoon jogs in Cleveland, but, honestly, I hadn't read the whole thing. Additionally, my start in Cleveland was getting a pretty good run in the papers, complete with speculation I'd be removed from the rotation if I didn't pitch any better, and spend the rest of the season in the bullpen. These are the trials of playing in New York, of course, and for the Yankees, in September, in a division race. The new guys, of whom I was one, found it a bit more trying, so my disposition darkened.

I'd actually get five days between Indians starts because of a day off in the schedule, just in case I needed another twenty-four hours thinking about how important the game was to me. What I really needed was a cold beer with some good friends. Fortunately, the Chicago White Sox came through New York, splitting up the Indians series. Kirk McCaskill, primarily a reliever for the White Sox, had been a young starter for the Angels when I had come up with them in 1989. Robin Ventura had played at Oklahoma State when I was at Michigan, had been the third baseman on the Olympic team when we won gold medals in 1988, then had spent the last four years as the White Sox's third baseman. The White Sox were on their way to winning the American League West, so the boys were in good spirits, and one night after a game we took off for Elaine's, the Upper East Side saloon, where I was struck by one thought and dragged into another. Sitting with two trusted friends, it occurred to me that I had few—if any—of those kinds of relationships with the Yankees, where an every-man-for-himself climate precluded much in the way of deep alliances. There were guys I respected, guys I liked, and guys I wanted to befriend—it just hadn't happened. Considering my last start in Cleveland had been so brutal, and that the end of the season was only weeks away, leaving little time to save it, the dearth of friends felt especially sharp. Anyway, it was good to be with a couple of them, particularly those who remembered when the baseball was good. Then, the bartender at Elaine's, whom I knew a little, politely interrupted our stories and laughter to request an autograph. I accepted the baseball he offered and turned it in my hand. It had been signed by one other player, in faded ink. The name: Pete Gray. I sighed.

Gray played seventy-seven games in the outfield for the St. Louis Browns in 1945, a war year. I'd heard about him since I was very young and admired him greatly, though quite independently from my own disability. Gray played despite having no right arm. Respectfully, I'm reasonably sure, I declined to sign the bartender's ball. I had endeavored to uphold a life above brands that began "one-armed" or "one-handed," and detested the notion of someone displaying or hawking the Jim Abbott/Pete Gray Two Good Arms Between 'Em ball. How awful. With Ventura and McCaskill watching stiffly, I told the bartender I'd be happy to sign anything else, which he refused in a huff. I wondered if Pete Gray would have gone along.

These were the encounters that embodied my relationship with my hand: personal until it wasn't, forgotten until it couldn't be.

When I was most comfortable, presumably most vulnerable, there it had been. *Sir, your hand. Mr. Abbott, your hand. Jimmy, your hand.*

All in all, it was turning out to be quite a week.

THE TRAFFIC NEAR the ballpark picked up. As the cabbie slid to the right, cars streamed past on the left, heading north into Westchester County and Connecticut or west over the George Washington Bridge and into New Jersey. Looking through the window, I found myself envious of the men and women in their cars, as I often did, the people who worked their jobs and were able to go home at night and leave that part behind. I daydreamed of jobs in which you worked hard and the reward followed. I mean, I wouldn't have traded who I was or what I did. But, in so many ways, their lives looked so appealing. My parents' lives. My brother's life. Nobody kept score, at least not in the newspaper, not where a man might as well have his ERA stamped on his forehead, so he'd walk into Gracie's and know everybody was thinking about how he had gotten knocked around in Cleveland six days ago. Mostly, maybe, I just wanted the ache to go away. It was fine when I won. When *we* won. But success didn't swing nearly as high as failure arced low, when the explanations were seemingly beyond extra laps or longer bullpen sessions or more time studying hitters. Two years before, I'd won 18 games and was third in the American League Cy Young Award balloting, behind Roger Clemens and Scott Erickson. A year before, though I lost 15 games, I was fifth in the American League in ERA. I didn't feel that different. I'd changed uniforms, changed ballparks, changed coasts. But, this was still the same arm, and those were still the same hitters. It made no sense. And it hurt. It really did.

The driver made his left, casting Yankee Stadium massively on the passenger side, his car clattering on the narrow, pocked road. Setting up my exit, I noted the square red numbers on the meter, organized the bills, stuffed the unnecessary ones into my pocket, and pulled the duffel bag closer. A book—*Lincoln* by Gore Vidal—and a couple Billie Holiday CDs clunked together inside my game-day survival kit. I liked calm before I pitched. Yankee Stadium generally didn't dispense tranquility, so you had to bring your own.

Already, hours before the first pitch, people lined the steel barricades that formed a broad path from the cab door to the players' and media entrance. Dressed in their navy blue caps and jerseys and windbreakers, holding out balls and cards and photos to be autographed, they shouted, and I smiled the best I could and waved, conscious that I might need a few supporters out there today. Depending on how you were going, the walk through that gauntlet could feel like the stroll of affirmation or the trudge of shame. NYPD officers and Yankees security stood casually nearby, an eye on the gathering crowd and another at the sky, which couldn't seem to decide whether or not to let loose with the rain. I hoped it wouldn't, but its color was beginning to match those dark Mattingly road jerseys outside the gate.

For such an old ballpark, The Stadium—as every Yankees fan in New York referred to it—felt fresh every day. The sight and smell of the place on the morning after a night game was especially remarkable, given how it bounced back, no matter what, win or lose. The trash was gone, along with the people, and any lingering regrets. Workers in galoshes hosed it all away, from one end of the stadium to the other. Aided by my own game-day regimen of an anti-inflammatory pill and a few Advils, fending off the normal late-season wear, I felt a bit like the ballpark must have: scrubbed and ready for another day.

Just inside the building, a narrow staircase descended from the main concourse two flights to a dark, low-ceilinged hallway. A left led to the visitors' clubhouse. Straight ahead were two doors—one to a room where news photographers and radio broadcasters worked, the other to the media dining room and, beyond that, the writers' workroom. My route took me past those rooms, a door to the manager's office and eventually, after another right, the clubhouse.

When the door swung shut behind me, I dragged a finger down the batting order: Boggs 3B, James LF, Mattingly 1B, Tartabull DH, O'Neill RF, Williams CF, Nokes C, Gallego 2B, Velarde SS, Abbott P. The Indians' lineup would arrive by clubhouse attendant later, but I knew it well enough anyway.

It was ten o'clock. The clubhouse smelled clean, insomuch as any clubhouse can. My locker was on the right side of the room, not far from the short hallway that led to Showalter's office, and across from the bathroom and showers. Don Mattingly was in the corner locker, the one reserved for Yankees royalty. And, yes, he could have been *in* it. The locker was large enough to pull a folding chair into, allowing Mattingly to sit almost completely out of view, a handy thing when the clubhouse was at capacity. Downtown, people were paying thousands a month for studio apartments only slightly larger and with less of a view. Fellow pitchers Jimmy Key, Rich Monteleone, and Bob Wickman occupied the same wall.

Then it was 10:10. I was constantly checking the clock. I'll grow old waking up to the same dream, I'm sure, the one where it's time to pitch and I'm madly searching for my glove while a tight-faced pitching coach is screaming my name and then, huffily, asking for volunteers to take my place.

I got comfortable in a pair of shorts, a T-shirt, and shower shoes, CD player in my hand, Billie in my ears. I listened for the emotion in her voice, the crackle when she really meant it, the patience she had for the song. I tapped in to her pace, the tempo I'd seek on the mound. Lined end-to-end, every note became the song, like every pitch could become a game. A win.

She sang:

> *Might as well get used to you hanging around,*
> *Good morning, heartache, sit down.*

Yes, yes.

The trainers' room was homey and clean, but without the sterile feeling of a doctor's office. The guys in there—Gene Monahan and Steve Donohue—kept it that way. The mood was soft lights, the aroma was strong coffee, and the conversations were friendly but muted, unlike the clubhouse, where the loudest wins. We'd chat, but I'd be there for the comfort and the quiet, to clear my head and body for the day, and soon I'd again don the headphones. The trainers would go about their routines, patching the wounded and bringing old bodies back to life. My routine was about visualization. I'd lay a towel over my eyes and begin the sequence, gently flexing and relaxing my feet, working upward until I reached my shoulders and neck. I saw only darkness and felt only awareness. So few times would players actually focus on how, say, their calves felt, unless one hurt.

My eyes closed and my body awakened, I'd see my warm-up in the bullpen, my fastball hitting the corners, staying down, the baseball jumping out of my hand, the ball pulled toward the catcher's mitt. I'd experience the walk from beneath the dugout roof to the mound, something loud on the stadium speakers, the crowd getting excited, breathing strength. I'd pitch the first inning, Matt Nokes lowering his mask from the top of his head, plate umpire Ted Hendry jabbing a finger at me, Kenny Lofton, Felix Fermin, and Carlos Baerga taking their turns, then nothing but the mitt.

By then, the clubhouse had first cleared out and then was filling again with teammates, those in the starting lineup coming in from batting practice. Pitching coach Tony Cloninger, Nokes, and I met as a group for the first time that day. There was some gravity to this, a strategy meeting when the last start went so poorly, and against the same team. On the bright side, Indians manager Mike Hargrove swapped out a third of the lineup that had hit me so hard, including three guys—Paul Sorrento, Alvaro Espinoza, and Sandy Alomar Jr.—who'd combined for six hits and four RBIs against me in those 3 2/3 innings.

Sometimes these discussions were about how to attack the hitters, other times they were about how to stay away from the hitters. That was always the philosophical debate, and it varied from pitching coach to pitching coach, from catcher to catcher. I didn't really have enough different pitches to have a say. At some point—and this definitely was one of those times—I had to let go of all that and trust what it was I did best. Albert Belle's strength might indeed have been an inside fastball. And, by "strength" I meant he might hit it five hundred feet or line it off my forehead. But, I was most effective throwing inside fastballs. In fact, to right-handed hitters, that was about all I threw.

I was asking myself, as I often did, to trust it. When the world started spinning and wobbling, when the newspapers speculated about my job security and the ballpark leaned in to gauge the fight in me, I had to remember to trust what I did, to simplify when the game sped up, to throw every pitch with something even more than conviction. I'd fallen at times into a spiral of hoping for a result I had no control over, though that understanding wouldn't come free until the result was long over and settled. It was a career-long struggle, actually, forgetting the immediate past and concentrating on the immediate future—that course existing only in the ball in my hand, thinking of only the next pitch. But on that dreary Saturday in the Bronx I was not going to get beaten trying something different, or get beaten throwing a pitch the catcher wanted but I wasn't sure of. I was going to carry the game or get carried off, either way, because of me.

It made sense at the time.

The T-shirt I'd worn beneath my road grays in Cleveland had been sacrificed to the baseball gods, left in a trash can at Municipal Stadium. Others had paid the same price over the years, so it was not a particularly solemn occasion. The new one went on under the Yankees pinstripes. I wore old-style stirrups, but only on the days I pitched. They felt like baseball, the way the uniform was supposed to be worn.

Cloninger, one of the most genuine men I'd ever met, who always was squarely in my corner, accompanied me to the bullpen. Directly across from the clubhouse door, a narrow, sloping tunnel led to the dugout and then the field. That walk, from the moment I cleared the dugout and stepped onto the pebbly warning track, was the symbolic start of my game. That walk was a daily renewal. It stopped me every time, in fact. It was magical. I ran some in the outfield, enough to get my legs under me, then picked up my glove and found Nokes waiting in the bullpen. He was in full gear, set up on the inside part of the plate to an invisible right-handed hitter, my right side as I faced the hitter. That was my foundation, pitching inside, and the act of generating the arm and full-body mechanics to reach out and deliver the ball to that spot. If I could get there with the fastball, everything else—curveball, slider—would follow. I felt good. My body felt good. My head was pretty clear.

When I walked from the bullpen across the field, flanked by Cloninger and Nokes, I vaguely heard my name shouted from the stands, vaguely took the tone as encouraging, vaguely understood that Yankees fans felt the urgency of the pennant race. In my head, the drumbeat of the start began.

In the tunnel outside the clubhouse, Tony Kubek, who did Yankees television, asked Showalter about me, and my imprecise August, and what that might mean for September, and Showalter said, "We think Jimmy's going to pitch very well in September. We need him to. It's as much wishful thinking as confidence in Jim."

Probably just as well I hadn't heard that then.

Dana, I knew, would be in her seat in the family section by then, somewhere just to the left of home plate on the field level. These days could be rougher on her than they were on me, and lately they hadn't been much of a joy for me. And yet, when the anthem was done and my warm-up pitches were done and the baseball eventually came back to me—delivered with a sharp throw and a nod by Wade Boggs from third base—all of that was gone.

I liked pitching at Yankee Stadium. It was fair for left-handers, even if the fences down the lines crept in closer than I'd like, and I seemed to give up balls down the lines. I had a good feel for the park, and it for me, seemingly. It helped that the grass was high and the field was crowned, the drainage design making it appear Nokes was two or three feet closer than he was in other parks. From that vantage point, it seemed there was nothing behind him but the stands, a different perspective given how quickly the ground fell off behind the plate.

Banks of lights were on above the top deck even for the afternoon game, and the stadium was about half-filled—both elements reflecting the weather. Mattingly led us out of the dugout and onto the field. The mound was pristine, another attribute of a stadium reborn overnight. The dirt was fresh and almost gummy, but firm just beneath the surface. My own cleat marks followed me to the rubber.

The recorded voice of the baritone Robert Merrill burst from the speakers in center field. I held my cap to my heart, over the interlocking NY, and I listened to the anthem just attentively enough to know when it was over. My mind was on Kenny Lofton.

As I took one last look around, I noted the flags were blowing to right field. Short out there. I cleared the small globs of muddy dirt from the rubber with the toe of my right spike, licked my lips, readjusted my cap.

I squared my shoulders and brought the glove and ball to about chin level, briefly met eyes with Nokes, and looked for his fingers. He wanted a fastball. I knew he would. As I initiated the delivery for my first pitch, I felt the hardness beneath my feet, a pitching rubber that, in twenty-four hours, would be unearthed and delivered to my locker.

CHAPTER 2

My first pitch skittered to the backstop.

Just took my four-seam grip, went into my windup in front of all those people, let go of the baseball and yanked it past Matt Nokes on the glove side. It hit the backstop on two hops, which wasn't so bad; the wall is back there a good ways and to reach it I knew I must have my decent fastball.

One pitch in, I'd cleared out the catcher and the umpire, scared the bat boy off his stool, and drawn a light groan from fans still stuffing their ticket stubs into their pockets. Or maybe that was just Showalter, as he was still stuffing the lineup card into his pocket. Maybe he was thinking it wouldn't be long before I was running through the streets of the Bronx—this time with his permission.

In that last start against the Indians, I'd left, oh, a pitch or two over the plate. Maybe this was my body's unconscious effort to correct that. You know, aim for the inanimate objects—pine tar rags, helmet racks, backstop padding, whatever—and reduce the professional risk.

Kenny Lofton was the batter and in 11 at-bats against me he'd had seven hits. I did the smart thing and walked him on five pitches, which wasn't so smart because he also led the league in steals. When you walked Lofton it was like throwing a double, because sooner or later you knew he'd be standing right behind you, calling for time and brushing the dirt out of his sliding shorts. All you could do is get the ball back from one of your middle infielders and wait for him to tidy up so he could steal third.

Six days before in Cleveland, in part because I'd walked four Indians in 3 2/3 innings and in part because of the 10 hits that came with the walks, I'd allowed seven runs, as many runs as I'd given up in a start all season. We'd won only because we scored 11 runs after I'd left.

The baseball back in my hand, I needed to get my legs under me again. I needed to pitch away from my last start, almost as much as pitching into this one. I needed to get back to throwing strikes and to work to the extremes of the Indians' bats. After ball one to the next hitter—Felix Fermin—I did gradually find the strike zone, and my legs. I broke Fermin's bat with a cut fastball near his hands and the weak grounder that spun off his bat became a double play, expertly turned, Wade Boggs to Mike Gallego to Don Mattingly. Carlos Baerga, a switch-hitter who batted left-handed against me to keep the cutters off the neck of his bat, flew to left-center field on the third pitch, a nice cutter down and away he hit off the end of his bat.

It was good—really good—to have the first inning behind me. I'd been banged around in the media for close to a week, after being banged around by the Indians for better than an hour, after being banged around by the American League for about a month. Every inning, every out, every pitch mattered, even more than usual. It's not a great way to survive, living on every pitch, but it's what I had at the moment.

So, it was with some sense of achievement that I left the mound after what most would consider a fairly routine 11 pitches. In the best of circumstances, an uneventful first inning is nothing more than that, but I arrived in the first-base dugout feeling, I guess, buoyant. In any situation, but mine in particular, I felt like I'd broken the ice, getting through that first inning, getting past that last start, getting through part of the order, throwing a few pitches, getting a feel for Nokesy again. The momentum gathers, confidence starts to build. You know, the first inning is really one of the toughest for a starting pitcher. To get through that without giving up a couple hits or a run, I wasn't thinking I had it made by any stretch, but there is a bit of settling in, physically and emotionally.

I took my usual route from the mound to the dugout, took my usual seat (often, for no real reason, near the medical kit), placed my glove beside my left thigh, zipped my jacket to my throat. I checked my shoes, again for no reason. I got new ones all the time. But, the routine of cleaning my shoes with a tongue depressor—come to think of it, maybe this explains my persistent proximity to the medical kit—was my way of letting go of the last inning, good or bad, of clearing my head, a kind of psychological cleansing.

Funny how the week had gone, all the chatter about whether my pitching had become a hindrance to the Yankees, and whether I might not be better suited for the bullpen, which would have been nothing more than a plan to get me out of the way. As uncomfortable a time as it was, I'd reached a significant place in my life. Since I could remember, I had ached to be just another something. In a sandbox, I wished I could be just another kid on the playground. At a desk, just another kindergartner drawing the alphabet. In a gym, just another point guard learning to dribble with either hand.

But I wasn't, and couldn't ever be. So, I handled the pail and shovel the best I could, and tried not to tear that flimsy grayish paper with the hook at the end of my right arm, and tried to go to my right on the basketball court, and left every situation as the little boy who did very well, you know, considering.

When I was pretty good on a baseball field—any field, actually—it was thought to be remarkable because, well, look at what the one-handed kid did. As the years and seasons passed, "One-handed-pitcher" might as well have been my first name, as it always preceded "Jim." So, I came to believe all but one pitcher in the game were judged by the usual standards of stuff and ERA and wins and value to the club, while I was judged on a scale that modified those measurable qualities with the leniency of, "Hey, look at what the one-handed guy did."

Now, toward the end of my fifth big-league season, after trying so hard to be great—and therefore a pitcher without modifiers—I'd discovered equality in failure. Oh, the irony. Buck Showalter, the Yankees, the press, New York—they wouldn't have cared if I spit the ball out of my mouth—so long as I could keep Carlos Baerga in the yard. And, in the speculation as to whether I would continue in the rotation, the question was whether I could get hitters out or not. There was simplicity in that, in a backward kind of way. I'd have preferred a win and I'd have chewed the knob off a bat for a few more miles per hour on my fastball. But it struck me that, going on twenty-six years old, I'd back-doored into exactly what I'd desired my whole life.

CHAPTER 3

The journey from Flint to the Detroit suburbs, diagonally across much of the thumb of the Michigan mitt, is fifty miles of Interstate 75, the landscape leafy, flat, and unremarkable. Run it often enough and the neighborhoods lapping against the highway become too familiar to be anything but a couple two-story rectangles in another grove of trees, the occasional child swinging, pumping his legs against gravity in a backyard edged in chain-link. Southbound, the drive bends east through the outskirts of Grand Blanc, Waterford, and Auburn Hills, sags due south past Pontiac to Bloomfield Township, and darts east and then south again to Troy, Birmingham, and Royal Oak, maybe an hour from end to end.

If, say, one were headed to a hospital in nearby Southfield, Interstate 696 curls west toward Lansing just as you'd start looking for the high-rises in downtown Detroit.

On a Tuesday afternoon in mid-September 1967, Mike Abbott drove this route as fast as his borrowed silver Chevrolet Impala would take him. His girlfriend, Kathy Adams, lay in the backseat, trying not to be frightened, her eyes urging Mike to please go faster. They'd spent the day in Flint, where she had picked out a wedding dress—a silver-hued shift that cascaded over her belly to her knees. They were eighteen. Kathy was in labor. They'd left the dress behind.

He was three months out of St. Matthew High School in Flint, six months removed from scoring seven points in St. Matt's Class D state championship basketball game at the end of a 23-0 season. The year before, she'd graduated salutatorian at St. Agnes High School in Flint. She was pretty and smart, a cheerleader and a member of the Future Teachers of America and Future Nurses of America clubs. He was a strapping football and basketball star, a halfback and a small forward whose teams hadn't lost a game in either sport all year. She was studying to become a teacher, over on Kearsley Street at UM-Flint, rather than at Nazareth College all the way out in Kalamazoo, where she had a scholarship but wouldn't have seen Mike often enough. Farther down Kearsley Street, he was roofing the new GM plant, laying large tiles, then paper and hot tar, through a thankfully cool summer, putting money away for Kathy and the baby, then saying good-bye to friends and teammates who went off to play college ball on scholarships he might have had, too. She was two semesters toward a teaching degree, three trimesters into motherhood. They were preparing for a life together, one that had sneaked up on them and which they dealt with out of love and naivety.

Mike gripped the steering wheel and blew down I-75. He was about to be a father. He would have been a husband, too, in just a couple days, had the baby not come so soon, two weeks early. So he raced into adulthood at eighty miles per hour on the back of that Chevy small-block V-8, counting the mileposts between contractions, Kathy's moans cutting across the clatter of air that forced its way over the windows.

This is it, he thought, and clutched the wheel tighter, keeping his hands from trembling. He'd only had a father himself for seven years, and then Joe Abbott had died of a heart attack. Six months before that Mike had a brother, Jim, die in Greece while in the Navy. Everyone who knew Joe was sure it wasn't the weak heart that killed him, but the grief of losing his eldest son.

Joe and Frances Abbott had raised their seven children in a three-story Tudor house on East Fourth Street near downtown Flint, a couple hundred feet from one of the three Abbott family-owned meat and grocery stores. Joe was company president. Frances volunteered for many of the charities in town, and doted on her children, and proudly held herself as Mrs. Joe Abbott. The day Joe died, a little boy from down the block rang the doorbell and waited on the porch. When the door opened, he held out a bag of candy for Mike, hoping it would make him feel better.

They'd never buried Jim. He'd joined the Navy, been stationed on a battleship in the Mediterranean Sea, and disappeared in 1957 while on furlough in Greece. The Navy told Joe and Frances Abbott their son had drowned off the island of Rhodes. Jim's body, however, was not found, nor were his clothing or belongings. At Frances's urging, Joe hired a private investigator, who reported that Jim had met a girl while on leave in Rhodes. Accompanied by the woman at the end of his leave, Jim was late to the dock, missing the boat that would ferry him to his ship. Local police said a woman had come to them, frantic about an American sailor she'd left down by the water. She told them he was agitated and threatening to swim for his ship. When the woman returned to the dock with the policemen, the sailor—Jim Abbott—was gone. After a short search, the police—and eventually the Navy—presumed him drowned.

Frances didn't believe it. For years she would tell Mike, "Your brother is going to walk in the door someday." For a while, Mike believed her, too.

First Jim and then Joe, and the house was impenetrably sad. Three of the older children were married and no longer living at home. The rest—Tom, Betty, and Mike, the baby—were sent away: Tom to a military school in Wisconsin, Mike to a military school in Kalamazoo, and Betty to a boarding school run by nuns.

The name, Jim, like the memory of him, stayed with Mike. Indeed, had his brother walked in the door one day, like his mom promised, maybe none of it would have happened. Maybe his dad doesn't die from heartache and his mom doesn't wither away, and the family stays together in one house and none of it gets so hard. At Barbour Hall Junior Military Academy, Mike figured he spent almost as much time in the brig as he did the classroom and, when Frances consented to bring him home after a year, it seemed to Mike that the officers there were as happy to be done with him as he was with them.

KATHY'S MOTHER, ALSO named Frances, sat in the backseat of the Impala with Kathy, stroking her hair. Frances Adams knew the drill; she'd had six children herself. Mike caught glimpses of them in the rearview mirror, reflexively looking up when a new contraction seized Kathy, then back down the highway that didn't seem to ever end. He met Kathy's eyes and wondered where the damn exit was.

His own mother was back in Flint, waiting for word of the birth. By then she'd been widowed more than a decade and wore just about every day of it. She'd done what she could with Mike, who came back from military school and hit the streets of Flint with a chip on his shoulder. The life he'd had—the full, warm house, the sturdy father and mother, the comfort that tomorrow would be just like today—was gone. In its place was anger, and an unwillingness to stand with the others and take orders with the others and conform like the others.

Katie, one of Mike's older sisters, called him "a heller on wheels," and it fit, because Mike had an engine that wouldn't stop and a taste for recklessness. He wasn't a bad kid, just an unbridled one, and it wasn't long before the family adopted the maxim "Only Mike," a phrase often accompanied by agreement that it was a good thing everyone had escaped unharmed once again.

Meanwhile, as Mike found his way in it, the neighborhood was changing. After perhaps its most prosperous decade ever, Flint pushed through the 1960s dogged by signs of an economic downturn, white flight, and plain neglect. The city was beginning to fray, both in its structures and its relationships. While the community seemed to be lingering more and more on its differences—primarily along economic and racial lines—one of its strong commonalities was sports. Flint might have been known for its auto industry, but it was in its heart a sports town. The merging races and incomes and personalities generally put aside their territorial suspicions for a good game. And Mike was in, whatever the game, even as a young teen. He cared little for Flint's economic direction, as long as the rims stayed mostly unbent on the Flint Central schoolyard, just a few blocks from Mike's back door. He and his buddies played basketball in gyms all over town. Flint was the birthplace of community education, a plan to make the city's schools centers for neighborhood activity and growth and vitality. One of the by-products of community education was unlocked gymnasium doors into the night and a well-lit place to play five-on-five. On their driveway, the cement chipped and cracked and untrue, Mike's brother Tom taught him to go to his left and to box out and to take an elbow without running inside to Ma. They'd bolted a backboard and rim to the garage, and they'd play Around the World until the sweat chilled their backs and it was time to go inside. These were the skills and attitude Mike took into the schools, usually against boys and men much older. Skin color and economic condition were meaningless. You could ball or you couldn't. You could hold the court or you couldn't. On other afternoons, Mike and his buddies would lay claim to a backyard and play tackle football until dinnertime and the shrill voices of mothers up and down the block thinned the teams to almost nothing. Often, the games played under the moon on one side of the field and a porch light on the other required more courage and toughness than anything going on at Memorial Park or Central High. Boys endeavored to become men out there—bloodied and scarred, pissed-off and having the times of their lives.

Mike stood in there every day, every night. Still, it would take an exceptional person to help Mike focus himself. The battle was most often within Mike. His older brothers were checking in on him from time to time, ensuring he didn't stray too far. Outside the house, though, he was on his own. He was soon old enough and talented enough to play for Jack Pratt, part coach, part philosopher, and, in this part of Michigan, part deity. He coached every season of the school year. If you were an athlete, you belonged to Coach Pratt, body, mind, and conscience. By eighth grade, Mike was practicing with the varsity football team, playing halfback and defensive back for Pratt's scout teams. By ninth grade, he was starting both ways. Mike, like the other boys, heard the sermons, sometimes in a group with his teammates, sometimes with Coach Pratt's eyes boring into his own.

Believe in yourself and believe in your teammates. Believe in who you are, believe in who you can be, believe in becoming more.

Pratt's teachings extended well beyond the football field. He taught history, political science, and foreign relations. Yet, if you asked any of the boys who played for him, they would tell you his classes were about life. The way he talked, things made more sense when Coach Pratt said them.

Mike, above all else, was ready to believe again.

The thing about the kids at St. Matt's was that most of them weren't great players. They were a little on the small side, some even a little on the slow side. Yet they won games, lots of games, because Coach Pratt convinced them they would. When the boys filed into church every day, Coach Pratt would already be there, on his knees. But he didn't talk a lot about God. Maybe he figured he didn't have to, that God and church had religion covered, and that he'd take the other areas. When Mike was a sophomore, Coach Pratt's wife died of cancer. Mike and his teammates, his friends, knew Coach Pratt was devastated. He could hide his pain in his work, in the way he conducted a practice and then ran a game, in his insistence that they believe in themselves. But his eyes told them he hurt, and then he'd put that to use, too. When the bad stuff happened, he'd always told them they had a choice of what to do next. Coach Pratt's choice was to keep coaching his boys.

IN THE BACKSEAT Kathy gasped and Mike pressed the accelerator another half-inch. Strange, but all those years at St. Matt's, Mike never missed his father at a basketball or football game. They were big events at St. Matt's. His buddies' families were in the stands and afterward they'd all come down to visit, the dads all talking a little too loudly among themselves. His mom was there and that was enough. She'd rarely attended any of his brothers' games, but knew it was important for Mike, so she'd bundle up and sit with the other moms and cheer when they did. Maybe there had been too many kids or not enough time, but now it was just her and Mike. Well, and sometimes Joe.

A portrait of Joe hung in the living room since shortly after his death. It was life-sized. Maybe bigger. And when Mike did something she knew his father would approve of—received a good grade, played a big game, anything—she'd grab Mike by the collar and march him to the foot of that portrait. She'd smile and get that look, and Mike would know exactly where they were headed.

"You come look," she'd say. "Wouldn't your father be proud of you!"

They'd stand together at the foot of the portrait until Frances was done staring. The older Mike got, the more he liked those moments.

Late in the summer before his sophomore year at St. Matt's, Mike heard Sam Ragnone pull up to the curb in front of the house. Sam was a little older and had one of those cars that rumbled when it idled and roared when it left; you only had to hear it to know it was him. They were headed that evening to north Flint, then across town to a driver's training class at Southwestern High, by which time there'd be at least six of them in Sam's four-door Chevy. Sam did the picking up and dropping off, because the girls needed a ride and Sam had a car and an opportunity was an opportunity. The car was nearly full when Sam braked in front of a modest house on the north end to add his final passenger. A couple honks, the front door opened, and a

brunette slipped out and closed the door behind her. Pinning her
hair back and pulling a sweater over her shoulders at the same time,
she arrived at the car, smiled, and squeezed into the backseat.

It was the first time Mike Abbott had ever seen Kathy Adams. He
didn't talk to her all night.

KATHY WAS THE oldest of Frank and Frances Adams's six children,
five of them girls. Her father and mother grew up ten miles west of
Flint, out near Flushing and Swartz Creek, an area to which their
parents—Kathy's grandparents—had immigrated from Czechoslo-
vakia around the turn of the century. On both sides, her grandparents worked small farms that grew corn, wheat, and soybeans, and
raised cows and chickens. Amid the close community of Central Eu-
ropeans, Frank and Frances met as teens, waited out Frank's World
War II service as a navigator and bombardier based in Italy, and were
married shortly after he returned. Frank was twenty-four and Frances
nineteen. They moved to Flint to find work. Frank took a job at Flint
Home Furnishings on Kearsley Street downtown, and they started a
family and a life that would be quite different from Mike's.

Frank Adams sold furniture every day of the workweek from nine
in the morning until nine at night and again on Saturdays. He was
the kind of man who took a job and worked it until the day was
done, and worked it until retirement, however long that was. Eventually he was reassigned to a store on Flint's north end, in the suburbs, which wasn't much of a drive, but when Kathy was eleven,
Frank moved the family to the north end so he could continue his
habit of coming home for lunch at noon and dinner at six, and then
returning to work.

The first five children Frank and Frances conceived were daughters. The boy arrived when Kathy was sixteen. Frank and Frances, their five girls and their son shared three bedrooms, two girls in one of the rooms and two sets of bunk beds in another. Frances kept the house pristine. She did the laundry on Mondays, the ironing on Tuesdays, and the baking on Wednesdays. She didn't have a car, so she'd give Frank a list of items to pick up at the grocery store, and that's what she had for the week. They worked hard and didn't miss a day and that was the example they set for their children, who generally followed the same path of diligence and purpose.

EVEN IN HER present state—heart pumping, contractions building, wind blowing her hair this way and that—Kathy could read Mike's anxiety from the backseat. When their eyes met in the rear-view mirror she tried to settle him with her coolness, but knew it probably wasn't working. His neck was taut, his eyes panicky. Truth was, though the drive and the drama weren't exactly how they'd planned it, Kathy was as hopeful as Mike was skittish. While Mike felt he was falling off a cliff into fatherhood, Kathy already felt connected to motherhood. As irrational as it sounded to others, she trusted Mike. She adored him. If it was time for a family, then she believed they would make it work, maybe because she believed enough for both of them.

Mike was cute and cool and fun and had all these friends. Because of the driver's ed carpool, and in spite of his attending St. Matt's and her attending St. Agnes, they were running in some of the same crowd. One of Mike's buddies had taken a liking to Kathy and began to call her. She'd be polite for as long as she could and then ask a lot of questions about Mike. Even when she saw a *Flint Journal* story about St. Matt's football team, discovering with some horror that

Mike was a sophomore and so a grade behind her, she showed up to a St. Matt's dance one Saturday night hoping he'd be there. When the Righteous Brothers song "You've Lost That Lovin' Feelin'" began to play, she asked him to dance. Years later, her sister Maureen with whom she shared a bedroom, would tell her she came home that night in love. Mike was the one, and would always be.

Mike, too, was beginning to be convinced. They were spending a lot of time together. One Friday night after a football game, Mike and Kathy had come back to Mike's house. Mike, by then captain of St. Matt's football team, and Kathy, in her St. Agnes cheerleader uniform, were alone in the laundry room and in full embrace when the light came on. Mike's mother had caught them kissing.

"Michael?" she said.

"Yeah, Ma?" he answered.

"Don't call me Ma," she said.

"*Mother,*" he said.

"I want to talk to you for a minute."

Mike headed toward the kitchen, shooting Kathy a glance on his way out the door. His grin said he would take his mother's scolding, indulge her, and be right back.

"Michael," she said, "I don't ever, ever want that girl in this house again . . . wearing that uniform."

Mike smiled and hugged his mom. See, Frances Abbott was first a St. Matt's girl.

Early in their relationship, Mike saw that Kathy was what he was not. Where he was impulsive, she was thoughtful. He lacked direction. She was earnest. He wasn't sure what was next. She had a plan.

Kathy graduated from St. Agnes and, after considering nursing, went to college to become a teacher. Mike was nearby, finishing high school, considering whether he'd play ball in college, as Coach Pratt hoped he would, or go to work for the family. The college coaches were making sense. Maybe he'd stay in the area, play football or basketball or maybe both.

By December, early in Mike's basketball season, Kathy suspected she was pregnant. She didn't immediately see a doctor and kept her fears to herself. A little more time, she thought; maybe she was wrong. In January, having kept her secret for nearly a month, Kathy went to her doctor and he confirmed what she knew to be true. She— and Mike—would have a baby. It was due in October. They had that much time to figure out what to do.

There was no wedding planned, nothing like that. Mike had six months of high school still. Kathy had barely started college. They had been raised in conservative families, educated in Catholic schools that held services every day. This wasn't supposed to happen, certainly not to Kathy, who was so smart and had such a promising future.

Her father, who had been so very proud of her, said nothing, but stared through her. Kathy knew he was terribly disappointed and was thankful he kept it to himself.

Her mother was not so restrained. Kathy would have to move out. She could not grow pregnant in front of her impressionable sisters, and in a neighborhood where people would talk, and in a town where people would judge. She would have to give up the baby for adoption, because she was so young and Mike was even younger and abortion was out of the question.

"That's what you should do," she told Kathy. "You're not married."

That was that.

A little unsteady governing the smaller details that made up her typical day, Frances Abbott nonetheless was quite sturdy when the occasional major issue arose. Mike, her baby, of "Only Mike" notoriety, had gotten his girlfriend pregnant. Frances did not ask why, did not tell him how irresponsible he'd been, did not allow him to feel alone. Instead, they turned to Katie, the oldest of Joe and Frances Abbott's children. She lived with her husband, Mac, and three children in a small brick house in Bloomfield Township, not far from Detroit. Through the years, Katie had become accustomed to the breathless calls from Mike, the sound of him describing some crisis or another, asking what to do with Ma or this or that. Katie was cool and had a wonderful sense of humor and an adult's perspective. This was big, Mike told her. He didn't know what to do, where to go. Kathy had nowhere to live. Everybody was upset. Katie told him to stay calm and she'd call back in an hour or two. When she did, she told Mike to bring Kathy down, that she and Uncle Mac had cleared out a bedroom, that Kathy could stay there, and that he—both of them—should start thinking about keeping that baby.

So Kathy packed her things and left her sisters and her year-old brother and her mother and father in the little three-bedroom house in north Flint. She moved in with Katie and Uncle Mac and their children, introducing herself on her way in the door, Mike trailing with her two suitcases. Kathy was there for six months, out of the way. Being the oldest of six, Kathy knew a little about mothering, and through spring and summer in Bloomfield Township read to Katie's small children, knitted them sweaters, and made them mid-afternoon snacks. Every month Katie or Uncle Mac drove her into Detroit to see Dr. Kenneth Trader, who'd delivered Katie's two daughters. Mike chipped in with a few dollars when he could and visited on the weekends.

St. Matt's hadn't lost a football game in the fall and then didn't lose a basketball game in the winter. There would be a parade and convertibles and bands for an unbeaten basketball season, a state championship. Mike was finishing his fifth year playing for Coach Pratt. Over the final weeks of the basketball season, however, their relationship grew cool. Mike had tried to keep Kathy's pregnancy to himself. On the final bus ride of the season, Coach Pratt walked the aisle, got to Mike, and lowered his eyes to meet Mike's. Coach Pratt knew.

"You know," Coach Pratt said gravely, "you're flunking foreign relations."

"Coach," Mike said, "I've got more on my mind than foreign relations."

Coach Pratt returned to his seat. That was the last conversation they'd have about Mike getting his girlfriend pregnant.

Meantime, Katie, still advocating for Mike and Kathy to keep the baby, took them to her church—St. Hugo of the Hills in Bloomfield Hills—to meet a clergyman about a holy union. A young priest, Father Jim, told them no, he would not marry them, not with Kathy being pregnant, not in his church, not like this. Mike and Kathy left the church confused. Mike had not actually asked Kathy to marry him but had arrived with Kathy on the idea that it was the most responsible path. They did love each other. And they were, after all, trying to do the right thing. Katie left angry and stayed angry at the church for some time. As fall neared, Kathy convinced a priest at St. Agnes, her alma mater, to marry them. They set a date for late September. Kathy would be pregnant still, but that seemed a minor detail all things considered. What was important was they be together officially, because just like the wedding, they'd not ever actually decided to keep this child; it simply came to be.

They also had decided they'd eventually live in the house on East Fourth Street. Frances had moved to an apartment, leaving the old place empty. Where there'd once been nine, there'd be two—Mike and Kathy—and their baby. Decaying when Mike was a boy, the neighborhood had continued its slide, but the house was comforting to Mike. And it was free. He'd joined the Michigan National Guard, which would keep him out of Vietnam, but, ironically, not Detroit. The same summer, with Kathy in Bloomfield Township and Mike mopping hot tar in Flint, Detroit police raided an unlicensed bar at the corner of 12th Street and Clairmount Avenue on the west end of Detroit. The police action sparked an uprising—soon called the Twelfth Street Riot—that lasted five days. Nearly fifty died, more than 7,000 people were arrested, and some 2,000 buildings burned down, Kathy watching it all on the black-and-white TV. In Flint, the 125th Infantry of the Michigan National Guard, Mike's unit, was called in. Mike was only newly sworn, however, and so lacked the training to march into a smoking Detroit. He was left behind to build his life.

Kathy telephoned Mike on the afternoon of September 19, breathless. She was in Flint for the first time since she'd been sent off to become more pregnant and have her baby. She'd come back to be married. Two days before, she and Mike had walked hand-in-hand into a Flint jewelry store, pointed out two eighteen-dollar gold bands, and paid cash for them. And then, in the kitchen of her parents' house in north Flint, six months since she'd last been there, days from her wedding, Kathy went into labor.

"My water broke," she told Mike.

MIKE WAS SILENT, though not yet from anxiety or fear. He didn't know what she meant. Water? What water?

Life was moving fast, so much so that Mike could barely keep up in that old Impala. He prayed a state trooper would haul him down from behind and lead them into Bloomfield Township, through all those potential delays. But they were on their own, barreling toward a new life and a new child, parenthood and marriage, racing first to Katie's house—she stood anxiously in the driveway, and it killed Mike even to slow down and kick the door open—and then to Providence Hospital.

"Name?" the nurse at the desk demanded.

"Mike Abbott," he said. "Kathy Adams. Me or her?"

"Address?"

"Thirty-one hundred Miller Road West in Flint," Mike said, his mother's address.

"Insurance?"

"I don't have any," Mike said.

"You don't have insurance?"

"No, I don't," Mike said, hoping they wouldn't be sent away. "I don't really have a job, either. Well, maybe I do, maybe I don't. I don't know what I have."

The nurse looked over the top of her glasses at the soon-to-be father.

"My mother will pay," he told her.

IT WASN'T LONG—two hours at most—before a doctor came through the door of the hospital room and stood at the end of the bed. Mom had given birth quickly. Dad had taken care of the administrative details, those he could, and killed time in the waiting room, sweating. He was nervous, a little frightened of course, but forcing himself to breathe. He cared a lot for Mom, as different as they were, as they'd always be. They shared a great attraction for each other. He had the long legs of a basketball player and the thick waist and shoulders of a football player, and a generous, gregarious spirit. She was thin, magazine-pages pretty, and adored Dad. He was loud and so sure of himself. She was shy, liked books, and came to think life might be kind of boring without him. He needed stability. She wanted some color. Now they had wedding bands . . . somewhere. They'd had a baby. They smiled to each other, then looked to the doctor.

He smiled thinly, as generously as he could. "You have a fine baby boy," he began, "but . . ."

Dad's sister, Aunt Katie, sat beside him, Mom's mother, Grandma Frances, next to her, all to Mom's right. At "but," they'd reached for each other's hands.

". . . he was born without one of his hands," the doctor concluded.

For Dad, the next minutes clicked and clattered like an old silent movie unspooled by a projector. He listened but did not hear. He tried to hold the words in his head, align them exactly, but they wouldn't stay in order. Instead, other words came, other questions. *I don't know what I'm going to do about this,* he thought. *Who do I turn to? Can I handle this responsibility? Can I be the father to do that? Am I man enough?* He had been deeply unsure; now he was afraid.

Aunt Katie turned first to Dad. She saw defeat on his face and in his shoulders. He was sure right then that this was his fault. God had punished him for this whole mess, for Mom getting pregnant and her having to move away and them not being married, all of it.

A nurse arrived holding James Anthony Abbott, cleaned up and wrapped in a blue blanket. Wordlessly, she lifted one corner of the blanket and revealed the place where my right hand should have been. Mom raised her arms, accepting this tiny child.

She refitted the blanket around my right arm and held me tight.

DAD SAT THAT night at the kitchen table in Bloomfield Township. Aunt Katie sat across from him. Mom and I were together in the hospital room. Dad was inconsolable. He couldn't be this little boy's father. He was barely responsible enough to provide for himself and Mom. He had six months to serve with the National Guard. Who would take care of Mom and the baby then? It was all his fault, he kept saying. Maybe they should put up the baby for adoption, give him to people who could do this. Aunt Katie told him he was wrong, that no one was to blame, that the family would pitch in and help, that Dad was man enough to raise the boy.

Dad returned to Flint and to his mother, still emotionally spent, still unsure of what he should do. His mother grabbed him by the shirtsleeve. This time there would be no trip to his father's portrait.

"Michael," she nearly shouted, "you remember this: God takes away once, he gives back *twice.*"

Dad shook his head. Just words, he thought. This wasn't what he wanted. He should be off in college, playing ball like his friends, being eighteen. He shouldn't have a girlfriend in a hospital bed, a disabled child to raise, bills starting to come, a report date for the National Guard looming. The weight was unbearable. He turned away from his mother, who wouldn't let go.

"You listen to me!" she shouted this time. "You can do this!"

He turned back and she said, quietly, confidently, reassuringly, "You have to."

It was true. Dad nodded. He'd have to.

Mom and I were in the hospital for four days. In that time, doctors came, asked a few questions, and went. No, Mom told them, she hadn't taken any medication, didn't drink, didn't smoke. There were no accidents. There was no history of it in either family. The doctors nodded grimly. Mom didn't have a lot of questions, which was fine, because the doctors had no answers anyway. During the pregnancy there'd been no complications, and no indications of complications. The doctors shrugged and shook their heads. They didn't know why.

Really, it wouldn't much matter why anymore. It just was.

CHAPTER 4

Albert Belle missed a curveball by eight inches and I knew I might be on to something. Matt Nokes thrust his mitt toward me and whipped strike three to Wade Boggs at third.

The second inning brought Belle, Randy Milligan, Manny Ramirez, and Candy Maldonado, all right-handed hitters, all protecting against my cut fastball. But, here I was, changing speeds, flipping a curveball that dove short of and under Belle's swing, and on a full count.

Nokes knew we were on to something, too. I could tell by the way he sprang from his crouch after that breaking ball carried him toward Belle's back leg. I was only four outs in, and I was throwing a lot of pitches, but getting Belle—one of the most ferocious hitters in the American League, he would hit 38 home runs and lead the league in RBIs that season—on his front foot, looking for something else, thinking he'd measured the cutter, was important.

I'd shown the Indians' lineup, which had hammered me earlier that week, not just a second pitch, but an effective second pitch. And better than *them* knowing I had a curveball that day and would throw it for a strike, *I* knew I had it. Nokes could ask for it. I could throw it, if not always for a strike, then so it looked for a long time like a strike, or so it looked like a ball and became a strike. At a time when I needed it, that pitch gave me the confidence to breathe a little. I asked for it, and it was there, almost perfectly so.

Also, I was counting on something to go well. I was getting outs, but they were a lot of effort. The ball had life, but I couldn't establish enough command to really get rolling. Some of it was self-inflicted; I knew I had to change speeds more than I had in Cleveland, and the results at times were choppy. Part of it was just the natural process of me getting acquainted with the game. The feel of the ball in my hand. The feel of the mound under my feet. And part of it was trying to pitch back from failure, which was becoming more familiar to me than I would have liked.

I could see Nokes was enjoying this. The curveball was like a fun, new toy, and he wanted to pull it around the block a couple times, particularly against the Indians' sluggers. After getting only 11 outs against the Indians in Cleveland, maybe I now had the stuff to get through the order a couple times, and not have the offense work so hard, and get me and the team to win a ballgame again. So, as the ball toured the infield after the strikeout of Belle, I pounded my glove, eager to get the ball back, happy to get after Milligan.

I walked him on a 3-and-1 curveball. Yes, the game rises and falls and rises again. Then Ramirez, a skinny rookie with close-cropped hair, took ball one and ball two. Nokes stood, asked the umpire for a moment, and in a few seconds arrived at the mound. I knew what he was going to say. The enthusiasm from a few minutes before hadn't dissipated, but I was going to have to throw a strike for any of this to work. The night before, Ramirez had homered off right-hander

Melido Perez and again off lefty Paul Gibson. Not only had Ramirez's three hits—he'd also doubled—and three RBIs helped beat us, but they had set off George Steinbrenner, who'd demanded to know from his baseball people how Ramirez had managed to grow up in the shadow of Yankee Stadium and somehow elude all of his well-compensated scouts. As the game progressed, Yankees brass was of course pleased at the result, and even more so because it temporarily distracted the Boss.

Nokes never took off his mask. He showed up to let me know he was back there waiting on strikes, and to be sure a handful of pitches wasn't going to change our strategy. Mike Stanley was our regular catcher, and was mine twenty-four times that season. Nokes caught me eight times, most toward the end of the season, and I loved his passion. I appreciated the extra nod after a clever pitch, the extra emphasis with the target, the all-for-one kind of attitude. He showed a good low target, and he glided around easily behind the plate. Looking in, getting the sign, and then believing in it, I trusted Matt. As the innings passed, that relationship would become critical.

Before the game, he'd admitted to being baffled by my recent results. I'd won once since the end of July and Matt was the kind of guy, the kind of teammate, who'd take that personally, even if it wouldn't reflect in any of his stats. He wanted to be the catcher pitchers wanted to throw to. As desperate as I was to perform well, I knew Matt felt at least that strongly about it. In fact, it was Matt who first suggested we "pitch backwards"—by that, meaning we'd set up the cutter with the curveball and changeup rather than the other way around, which is how I'd pitched most of my career. Somehow we needed to get the Indians off my cutter and get into their heads a little. So Matt arrived at the mound and we stood there only briefly as the occasional raindrop bounced off his helmet. He said nothing more than, "Hey, the stuff is good. Let's go after the strike zone a little more aggressively here," then returned to the plate.

Ramirez, whose stance was closed and therefore—I hoped—more vulnerable to the cutter, took one of them for a strike on the inside corner and another for a strike on the outside corner, a pitch I figured might get a double-play grounder. No such luck, but I'd take the strike, and then bounced a curveball for ball three. Though he'd been in the league about seventy-two hours, Ramirez had shown himself in the scouting reports to be a free-swinger, and with great bat speed, so he'd bite on anything around the plate, and maybe hit it a long way. Nokes wanted cutters under Ramirez's hands, and with a full count I threw a pretty good one. Ramirez fouled it off and spent a few seconds examining his bat handle for cracks. He'd seen plenty of cutters so far and I hoped he figured on another. He flied to center field on a changeup he hit off the end of the bat but pretty well, which brought more good news: The ball wasn't carrying well to center or right-center, opening up more possibilities. In Yankee Stadium, pitchers survived by pitching to left-center, which kept the ball out of the right-field bleachers.

Two outs, Milligan on first, and Nokes, I knew, was worried about Candy Maldonado, a veteran guy who could handle the off-speed stuff and still catch up to a fastball if he guessed right. He wanted to stay firm with Maldonado, maybe set him up for the hard, inside cutter, because Maldonado was guarding against anything there. After falling behind 2 and 0, I rediscovered the strike zone, got a couple foul balls, and then convinced Maldonado to swing over a cutter. Six outs in, I was okay. I felt good. Nothing disastrous had happened.

I headed for the dugout.

CHAPTER 5

I daydreamed a lot, so that childhood was in there somewhere, tucked between the things I could do and the things I couldn't, the friends I had and the loneliness I felt, the inspiration and the doubt. While Mom and Dad found their paths, we moved from neighborhood to neighborhood; four times I'd become familiar with an elementary school—those friends, those teachers, those ends of town—then pick up and settle into the next. Before any of us knew it, we'd traipsed through our early years together, my younger brother, Chad, following four years behind. I never traveled alone, of course. At times it propelled me along, other times I dragged it; my condition was a relentless companion.

Not that the relationship didn't change.

Initially, as we were becoming acquainted, my thoughts were, "Oh, I'm missing a hand."

After several years, that developed into, "Hmmm, this makes me different."

Then, to, "Well, I can play ball, so I must be okay."

Maybe the last part was a little unsteady as far as a life philosophy, given my self-esteem balanced on those words. But if I could keep my head up, if I could make it to recess and win often enough, if I could laugh along at jokes pointed at my hand, if I could bury that hand in my pocket and wish it gone—or whole—then I must be okay.

When it didn't seem fair and I wondered why I must bear such a burden, I was always and immediately ashamed, like I'd given in. Like I'd quit. I couldn't quit. Not on my parents. Not on myself.

FIFTEEN DAYS AFTER I was born, Mom and Dad married.

She wore a gray wool suit instead of the silver dress—which would have required tailoring—and with it a pale lace chapel veil required by the church. She held a bouquet of white roses. Dad wore a dark gray suit. Mom had pinned a white carnation to his left lapel. The eighteen-dollar rings were in his left front pocket. I was with a baby-sitter.

St. Agnes's chapel was empty when they arrived. When Mom half-shouted an elongated hello, there was no response other than the *ohhh* that returned to her from the walls and high ceiling.

Her sister Maureen and Dad's friend, Steve Manville, stood behind them. Maureen, who'd shared a bedroom with Mom until the pregnancy, was maid of honor. Steve, the best man and a point guard at St. Matt's rival St. Michael's, tugged at a light gray suit that had fit him better a year or two before.

It was a Wednesday morning, about the time Fenway Park would roll up its gates for Game 1 of the 1967 World Series. Bob Gibson was pitching for the Cardinals. Dad's beloved Tigers had finished a game behind the Red Sox for the American League pennant. The Tigers had fallen out of first place for good the day I was born, which probably only helped to further stir up those hours. Like most of the guys in the neighborhood, Dad liked Willie Horton and Norm Cash and Bill Freehan and the pitchers Denny McLain and Mickey Lolich. But he loved Al Kaline, No. 6, the Tigers' powerful and elegant right fielder.

For those two weeks, however, Dad hardly had given baseball a thought, and then he was only vaguely aware the World Series should be starting any day. Instead, he was standing in the church, ready to be married, except there was no priest. They'd scheduled for ten o'clock in the morning so Dad could get to the Chevrolet plant on time, but ten had passed and still the room was quiet except for the hollow sighs. The doors to the church opened and when everyone turned, expecting the priest to walk in, Mom's parents entered, and then Dad's mother with Ed, one of Dad's brothers. Cheri, Mom's younger sister, arrived. She was still in high school, attending St. Agnes, and so was in the neighborhood.

The marriage having been put off once because of my premature arrival, the wedding party spread across the St. Agnes campus in the hopes of finding someone in a stiff white collar to perform the ceremony. Since it was a Catholic school, the odds seemed good. Father Maurice Olk, a big man whom Mom adored for his warmth and spirit, was on the football field, pacing between the 20s, breviary in hand, waving his free arm, rehearsing the day's services. He'd forgotten the ceremony. Flushed, he led Mom back to the chapel. Dad had a job to get to, Mom a baby to feed, Cheri an English class to get to, so they'd barely gotten everyone together when Father Maurice was introducing Mr. and Mrs. Michael Abbott. The walk from the chapel's front steps to the parking lot wasn't especially long or scenic or romantic, but it would have to pass for the honeymoon.

Dad had quit his job putting the roof on the GM plant. Actually, he'd been asked to leave and he'd surrendered. As was sometimes the case with Dad, it was complicated. While slopping around tar, he'd witnessed a coworker fall from the roof, then be taken away by ambulance. Dad kept reporting for work, but found it gradually more difficult to screw up the courage to get up on that roof and keep his legs under him. The job foreman grew weary of talking Dad up the ladder and suggested a new line of work. A couple weeks later, Dad was on the Chevy assembly line. He stood by as the engines crept past; if there was a yellow mark on an engine, he'd put a yellow part in it. That was the whole job. Later in life he would learn it was a crankshaft, but at the time he had no idea what the part was. If the part fit, great, he'd done his job. If not, he'd wait for the next engine to roll past and examine it for a yellow mark. The work was dirty; the shop smelled bad; he was dirty and smelled bad. He lasted thirty days before returning to a less hazardous position at GM.

On the day he was married and for that month, he worked the second shift on the assembly line, clocking in at two, clocking out at eleven, putting in his time. Sometime after Dad left for work, Mom would report with me to a second-floor bedroom of the big family house in downtown Flint, lock the heavy wooden door behind her, and wait for Dad to get home sometime before midnight. Up there, we were safe from the neighborhood, from what Flint was becoming, and from Mom's imagination, which had been roused by Dad's protective instincts. When the three of us had moved in, Dad had walked Mom through the house, pointing out the door that had been broken down during a burglary, then the door a stranger had burst through one night while the whole family was in the living room watching *The Donna Reed Show,* and the windows that faced the busy road where people and cars passed. "You've got to be careful," he told her. "Lock all these doors and windows behind me." Instead, she scooped me up, went to the bedroom, locked *that* door, and read me stories and sang me songs.

When Dad returned, the rest of the house was in play again. We went more than three months like that, killing hours in the Flint panic room. When Dad, as part of his National Guard commitment, reported to Fort Polk in Louisiana, Mom and I lived in her parents' house. He was gone six months—the first two were infantry training, the second four medical training at Fort Sam Houston in San Antonio. They spoke often and Mom sent envelopes stuffed with photos, many of them of me staring blankly into the camera.

In the months that led to his time away and then while he was in the service, Dad yearned to be home. He hoped not to be called to Vietnam, but that wasn't the reason for his petition to return to Flint before his required six months were over. From the afternoon in the maternity ward when he was sure he was being punished for confusing the church's preferred order of marriage, *then* conception and childbirth, Dad had grappled with the new uncertainty in his life. School, basketball practice, and work had been replaced by family and job, by paying bills, protecting his wife and son, and making a future for them all. The questions that chased him out of bed in the morning and kept him from sleep for hours at night seemingly had no answers.

How would he take care of this little boy? And who would fix him? What would happen when he found out he was different? What's a boy's life without a hand? Without sports? How would he defend himself against all the cruelty out there?

The worries that his son would grow up vulnerable, frightened, and alone hounded him. He'd carry those grinding insecurities for years, but never were they more relentless than in these first months, when he, too, was vulnerable and frightened. Dad became deter-

mined to make it all right, starting with moving us into the house
he grew up in, where he was comfortable, and then holding a job. Six
months later, upon his return from the National Guard, we became
a family. If you didn't look too close, I was enough like most babies.
Dad chose to be the provider and the doting father. Where he once
carried apprehension and could see only obstructions, he smiled
when I did, and when Mom did. It was a start, Dad's first move toward searching for hope and recognizing opportunity. As downtown
Flint teetered toward unpredictability, we soon moved into an apartment on Flint's north side, and a year later Dad bought our first
house. Through the usual baby stuff, all the while we were creeping
up on the greater problem of my right arm, which was small and
weak and wouldn't do much. Worse, of course, it ended at about the
wrist. As I grew older, the structural condition of that arm and hand
became less important—as far as my parents were concerned—than
the condition of my self-esteem, particularly as I came to realize all
the other boys and girls had two fully developed hands. Then we'd
deal with what I was going to do about it. There would be daily
physical dilemmas, daily obstacles and daily triumphs and failures,
which never did disappear. But there was always tomorrow.

Mom and Dad were consumed by preparing me for the world outside our living room. That meant frequent trips to doctors and specialists and physical therapists, frequent examinations and X-rays,
followed by the process of sorting through the results, opinions, and
recommendations. As I neared kindergarten, they wondered if I'd be
allowed into the public elementary school in the neighborhood and,
if I was, if I could cope with it. With that approaching, we spent a
little more time on the structural side of my handicap, which meant
more time at the Mott Children's Hospital and consultations with
the Crippled Children's Fund, which, in spite of its ghastly name,

did ease the financial burden on the family—now a family of four with the addition of Chad. By then, while Mom made some money teaching and prepared to go to law school, Dad was working long days as a meter reader and meat cutter to keep the lights on, the furnace lit, and everybody fed. Yes, a meter reader. I wasn't even sure there were parking meters in Flint. Like I said, complicated.

In each doctor's office, the initial consultation began the same way: a long look at my right arm and a question, posed inoffensively: "What happened here?" Of course my parents had no answer. After more inquiries, all of them predictably about the nature of the pregnancy, what Mom may or may not have been exposed to, whether there was a traumatic event and if there was a family history of birth defects, the responses to which did nothing to explain my condition, they'd get around to considering what to do about it. The consensus among specialists was that I'd function better with a prosthetic arm and a mechanical hand—a hook. Before long, I was in the backseat of the family car, headed west on Interstate 69, bound for Grand Rapids and Mary Free Bed Hospital, Mom and Dad not too sure about it but earnestly honoring the opinions of the experts. I was five. I'd spend a month there, most of it by myself. I think it was harder on Mom than me. She cried most of the two-hour drive back to Flint. They'd come to visit on the weekends, but otherwise I'd trudge along with the program, which seemed to have as much to do with the doctors and nurses learning about me as it did with me learning to live with one good arm and one not-so-good arm.

The experience was somewhat frightening. While the staff did wonderful work and was quite kind, for a five-year-old on his own the hospital was cold and sterile and not at all like my room and bed back in Flint. These beds had nets over them. I couldn't decide whether they were there to keep me in or other people out. I spent a lot of time on that conundrum. I'd not considered myself before to be at any great disadvantage, since I managed to get most things done with some effort. Here, I saw children near my age with no legs, or no arms and no legs, or various combinations thereof. A decade had passed since doctors discovered the effects of thalidomide on women and their unborn children and withdrawn the drug, yet the consequences remained evident at Mary Free Bed. I was lonely and shy, but made a friend in a little girl with a big, friendly smile. She had remarkable spirit. At the hospital to master the daily tasks that everyone outside the hospital thought nothing of, that little girl had learned to open a tube of toothpaste, squeeze the toothpaste onto a toothbrush, and brush her teeth on her own. This was considered a great victory, and she happily shared it with visitors. She had no arms, but she had two legs and two feet, and she used those.

While my friend the little girl learned the mechanics of dental hygiene, I was measured for a new right arm and educated in its many clunky benefits. It was bulky and heavy and had two steel pincers at the end, all of which was strapped to my tiny body by a harness. The clamps, operated by a cable, opened when the arm was extended and closed when the arm was drawn back. Despite the stump sock—they really called it that—even short periods wearing the artificial limb left my arm raw and sweaty and, right away, left me wondering if it was worth the effort. Even at five, going on six, I admired the kids in the hospital for their determination and encouraging outlook. They were nice to me. Their challenges were beyond anything I could have imagined. I wasn't sure I belonged there with them. I mean, I was practically whole. My parents, it turned out, were sure I did not belong there.

Unable to stay in Grand Rapids because of work, school, my baby brother, and the fact that they could not have afforded the hotel room, Mom and Dad visited on weekends. What they saw convinced them they'd made a mistake. There were children at Mary Free Bed—strong and brave children—who would always need the good people at Mary Free Bed. Their little Jimmy wasn't one of them.

One Saturday afternoon, a woman pushed her wheelchair-bound son into the hospital lobby. She was dressed in expensive furs. Jewelry shone from her ears, fingers, and wrists. An orderly approached from behind the reception desk. She gave the wheelchair one more gentle push and before it stopped rolling, she had pivoted on her high heels and was on her way back through the front doors. The aide caught the wheelchair on the glide. She had not said good-bye to the boy, had not given him one last hug, had not told him she loved him and would see him next weekend. She'd simply dropped him off, like he'd been a line on her to-do list. *Deposit alimony check, get nails done, dump kid.* Watching from a chair in the lobby, Dad was appalled. He filled out some paperwork and we walked out that same front door. On the drive back to Flint, me in the backseat again and ready to wield my unwieldy new arm, he spoke quietly with Mom. He'd had an epiphany, the kind that would carry him—and me— through much of my childhood, and help coax him out of his. The children we'd left behind, they'd need tending to, regular care, separate rules. The kid in the backseat, he'd be fine. Their heartfelt and perhaps desperate intentions—to have their child grow up with an honest shot at routine, at normalcy—hadn't gone as planned. As Grand Rapids disappeared behind them, they couldn't shake the suspicion they'd been swinging sledgehammers at butterflies, trying to solve the unsolvable.

"We don't have a problem," he told Mom. "We've got a blip on the screen. We can handle this. We could make it a problem if we want it to be a problem. But, it's no problem anymore."

I was just happy to be with Mom and Dad again, happy to feel the wind and hear the whistling through the crank-down windows, happy to have the hospital behind me, happy to have that smell out of my nose, happy to be going home. It was an important ride for all of us. We'd done our time on that side of the world, where the days were long and earnest, the people were committed to helping and healing, and tomorrow, frankly, would look a lot like today. I didn't want to be poked and stretched and then sit around staring through the windows as nurses wrote notes on their clipboards. Nobody did, of course. Mom had known as much before she'd said good-bye a month before, when on her way home she'd sorted through conflicting ideas of protecting me and going along with the doctors, having left me to the white-coats. She cried because she'd miss her little boy and she cried because it seemed like overkill. She wished no one would have to be there, that no child would sleep under a netted bed, have to push around institutional food with institutional silverware, and wished the roof would blow off so the sun could come in. But, for the moment, her sadness was intended for one child only: hers.

On that two-hour trip to Flint, we'd get our strength back. Mom and Dad felt hope, even optimism, for the first time beginning to focus not on what I lacked but what I had. The children who would stay behind—and many of them had arrived long before I had—were to Mom and Dad amazingly resilient. They'd show up in the therapy rooms in leg braces, or on crutches, or on legs in general appearance but not function, and take one more step than they had the day before, then burst into gritty smiles when the nurses cheered. There was more heroism in an afternoon at Mary Free Bed than there is in a decade of baseball games. Those kids figured it out, took a breath and, needing a mile, sweated through another inch.

Mom was right. I didn't belong. I was taking up space. I'd figure out my own way. As it happened, the chances for that came fast.

It was one thing to strap into a prosthetic arm in a hospital room, sit with a therapist and, on the twenty-third try, grasp a now scarred wooden block from a desktop. It was quite another to pull that off in a kindergarten classroom with twenty-five other five-year-olds whirling about, all of them—it would seem—staring. I didn't want to be that kid.

On a morning in the fall of 1973, at nearly six years old, I would be that kid, officially. I rolled the stump sock up my right arm over my elbow and slid my old arm into my new arm. Mom cinched the harness over my shoulder and across my back. That summer I'd smashed bottles in the backyard, broken wooden planks in Uncle Mac's basement, and boldly flipped steaks on the grill without a spatula, much to the uncomfortable amusement of our cookout guests, because my hook was, of course, one serious and indestructible weapon/utility tool and also a reasonable way to lift a wooden block. By the winter, with the release of a new television show, *The Six Million Dollar Man,* my hook would even have its cool moments. I'd slip away and become Col. Steve Austin, the bionic action hero, complete with rebuilt arm and covert missions that inevitably would end in the garage with me karate-chopping a Coke can I'd found under the workbench. I saved the world over and over, one Coke can at a time. On that morning of the first day of kindergarten, however, I wasn't feeling so indestructible.

I was feeling different and I hadn't even left the house. For six years, I'd figured out enough things: I could work a fishing pole, though tying the barbed hook and then baiting it was out of my reach; I crushed a lot of worms. I could ride a bike just fine. I could punt a football a good ways. My dad had gone down to the drugstore and bought me a baseball glove, handing it over like it was a piece of crystal, and I'd found my way around that. The glove was a Dusty Baker model, tanned and leather and about as pliable as a new arithmetic textbook.

School, however, seemed different. My curious head was excited. My plastic arm was on the sullen side. After I dressed in my new Toughskins jeans—straight out of the Sears catalog—and ironed shirt Mom had laid out, picked at breakfast, stood out in front of the house on Copeman Boulevard and got my first-day-of-school picture taken, and started the half-mile walk down Copeman, along Seneca Street, and up Mackin Road toward Anderson Elementary School, my arm became heavier and more obtrusive with every step. Mom, walking alongside, brightly pointed out my friends' houses, the small rectangular structures with their aluminum awnings and neat lawns that sat just off the sidewalks along the way. She greeted the crossing guards on every corner and chatted reassuringly about the day that lay ahead.

As we walked, and she talked, and kindergarten came to be only a block away, what I thought about was being that kid. I wished I could hide my fears like I always did, but Sears didn't make pants with pockets deep enough for a store-bought arm. Maybe it wasn't on the first day, but soon after I recalled a little girl crying at the sight of my prosthesis and its steel tongs, so sinister and threatening that Mrs. Mitchell told my parents she was worried about the other boys and girls in the class. She asked them to talk to me about being careful, so we had a serious conversation one night about that, how this thing that I hated wasn't so popular with anyone else, either.

The thing about a disability is, it's forever. And forever might not end, but it has to start somewhere.

For me, it began with the realization that I was different, except it did not arrive with a single unpleasant thunderclap. It arrived in nagging episodes over the course of every day, and what followed was the routine fight back from them, and the desire to be accepted.

That's how baseball—all sports, really—grew for me, from the Wiffle ball games in the backyard to the pretend games off the brick wall to the bike rides through the neighborhood and Little League games and then to the high school games.

I wanted to play. I loved to play. But there was more. I sought acceptance beyond what my appearance told people about me. Their eyes, the way their voices softened, their subtle acts of protection, it was pity I didn't want and couldn't stand. Of the surviving qualities of Flint, parts of which were otherwise creeping toward ruin, there were plenty of games to play. By fifth grade I was being carpooled across town to play flag football on muddy fields lined by parents. The murmuring about that kid, the one people stared at, usually would start in the parking lot. Those doing the whispering must not have thought so, or didn't care if I did, but I could always hear them. I could see them. They'd hold their conversations through our warm-ups, and then when I was the one playing quarterback, and then whenever the thought struck them. Even then I'd shut it out, or try, put my head down and play through the noise. Conflictingly, the games I loved brought me here, to these places that could be so uncomfortable in front of all these new people, and then they would make me the equal of their sons, or allow me the chance to be.

In the years that followed, only the crowds changed. They got bigger and louder, but the reaction was always the same.

There was a story about me in the local paper, *The Flint Journal,* in 1979. I was twelve. The headline was JIMMY ABBOTT: SPECIAL IN MORE WAYS THAN ONE. The black-and-white photo showed me running off a dusty infield, wearing Toughskins, Jox sneakers, a mesh shirt bearing the name of a local real estate company—Grant Hamady—and an Anheuser-Busch cap, courtesy of my dad, now an Anheuser-Busch salesman and still complicated. My friends teased me for weeks after that, calling me "special" and all, but the short article and the photo that ran with it are still in a frame in Dad's office, and Mom can still quote from the text.

I had told the writer, Chuck Johnson, "I look at major leaguers and I wish it was me," and the quote ran near the bottom of the story. My mom loved that sentiment, that I could have such an improbable dream. That I would dare to. It's true, sports had a spiritual and therapeutic place in my life, functioning to comfort and strengthen me. And to distract me. I could always throw. I won the softball toss in third grade and, I won't lie, that was a huge deal for me. In fact, I thought it was so important that I won first and second place. I'd left the prosthesis home that day.

But, you know, there was no grand plan for sports to rescue me from a lifetime of bullies and insecurities. My father was a good high school athlete and still quite young, so naturally we'd wrestle around and we'd figure out a way to play catch and he'd talk about growing up playing stickball, so we'd try that, too. But, it was no different from the day he presented me with my first fishing rod with the Zebco reel, the kind where the whole thing would work with one hand and one thumb. And it was no different from working scissors for a class project. Or letting the line run free on a kite, then gathering it all back in. Or doing the dishes.

Nobody pushed me to become an athlete—a ballplayer—because they hoped it would make me one of the guys, and certainly not because they believed I'd someday make a living doing it. I played sports because that's what the boys in Flint did. When Sammie Phillips and Chris Cole were led by their moms down Copeman Boulevard, past the porches and the waving neighbors and our yellow Volkswagen station wagon, it was to play ball, some kind of ball. And when years later the older boys went hand-over-hand on a bat to see who could pick first, and they chose their teams, and I was the leftover kid standing there, I'd go home dispirited, only to have my dad tell me to get back out there and find a way into the game. So much of my childhood seemed to be spent riding my bike to the playground, my baseball glove looped through the handlebars, knowing I wasn't going to be the first pick or even the last, but yearning for a way to prove myself.

It seemed like a lot to hope for, but I had plenty of hope, and plenty of help.

DONN CLARKSON WAS born not far from my neighborhood in 1925. The family doctor came to his parents' house to deliver him, and when Donn resisted the doctor insisted, pulling him with forceps into the world and to his first breath. Donn used to say with a worn laugh that the doctor was in a hurry to get home for supper, because as it turned out those forceps crimped a nerve that led to Donn's skull, so that he'd forever have limited use of the right side of his body. He walked with a limp. He grew up and went to work for NASA as a Space Science Education Specialist, lecturing in schools, churches, and to service groups about the space program. Eventually, Donn—Mr. Clarkson, by then—became a teacher, my third grade teacher at Dye Elementary School, the kind who'd hand out cookies and posters of rocket ships and every Friday afternoon turn down the lights and show a movie. I'd sit next to Mr. Clarkson while he ran the films, close enough to the projector so I could feel its heat against my face.

Mr. Clarkson knew what it meant to stand out in a room of kids. So, him with his limp and me with my arm, we shared a bond we almost never talked about. When he was young, he'd been told he'd probably never ride a bike and certainly never drive a car. He spent half his childhood on a bike. By the time he retired from NASA, having spoken to small gatherings in small towns all over the Midwest and beyond, he'd driven maybe two million miles, then became a licensed pilot and flew at least that far. I knew none of that. His wife, Jean, was a local occupational therapist for forty-four years, twenty-five of them working with handicapped children at another elementary school in Flint. They spoke often of me and my challenges. I knew none of that.

What I knew was when a girl in class looked me dead in the eye and told me she didn't like my hand, I ran near tears to Mr. Clarkson, whose advice was, "Next time you tell her you don't like her face, because she can't change her face any more than you can change your hand." Different era, you know.

And what I knew was that Mr. Clarkson had an eye for detail, for the sorts of things that might not be bothersome for most, but perhaps would have been for him, and therefore might be for me. Every morning before school I'd stand mostly still while my sneakers were tied, this being one of those learned skills that, at eight, I hadn't quite gotten around to yet. Mom or Dad would double-knot, triple-knot those Keds so they'd be all but soldered on. I really hadn't thought much about it, but Mr. Clarkson greeted me one morning with a great smile and a hand on my shoulder. "I've got it!" he said. "I figured it out!" And I had not the slightest idea what he was talking about. "I know how you can tie your shoes," he said, and I looked down at the tangled messes of laces piled atop my shoes and thought, *This could take a while.* Seems Mom had mentioned something to Mr.

Clarkson about the daily shoe-tying experience, and he had gone home and worked on a strategy that night. The following morning he turned on the projector, occupying the rest of the class, and dragged two chairs into the hallway. Through open classroom doors, other kids in other classes watched what surely must have been some disciplinary drama going down.

Mr. Clarkson was a tall man with big hands. We sat across from each other, knees to knees. He untied his shoe and mine. It took him longer to untie mine. He then clenched his right hand into a fist, nearly mimicking mine, pinned the right lace to his shin with his right hand and nodded for me to do the same. With the right lace taut, he curled the left lace with his left hand around the right lace and looked at me. I was following. By looping it under and through, it made a loose knot. His did. Mine sort of did.

He repeated the process, this time with loops. With his left hand he pulled at the right lace, then slackened it, allowing the bottom of the lace to fall into a circle. That, then, he held against his leg while he drew a second loop through the first. With a little tugging, it all became a knot. He looked at me and smiled. His shoe was tied. Mine could have passed for the nest of a small sparrow. He laughed and we started over again. After a couple days, I could tie my shoes.

This certainly wasn't brushing my teeth with my feet. My victories were so much smaller than that. But, they were mine, just as the insecurities were. I'd left Mary Free Bed in Grand Rapids and within days was in elementary school down the block. Had I been capable of broader perspective, I might have wondered why I could find my way in both places, but felt I belonged in neither.

My place seemed to be in the desperation to stand alongside everybody else, in that area in boys' brains where we kept score, and in that corner of our hearts where we knew when we were being tested.

Because of that, for a long time, maybe forever, I would view myself through the things I didn't want to be.

I didn't want to be that kid.

I didn't want to be different.

I didn't want to be pretty good, you know, considering.

I didn't want anyone feeling sorry for me, or treating me special, or looking past me.

And I didn't want to wear that thing on my arm.

So, I stayed at it, whatever it was. That was my whole plan—to show up. Nearing the end of elementary school, I'd undergone surgeries that were supposed to expand the range of motion in my right arm but didn't. And I'd fought the morning battle with my parents over whether I'd really have to wear that arm again, when all the other kids were calling me "Captain Hook." We'd moved more times, my young parents seeking their footing, better neighborhoods and school systems, and for a time settled into the end unit of a townhouse. Outside, a brick wall wrapped around the bottom floor. There, out of sight, away from the world, I was free to dream. With no one staring or judging, I'd stand in front of the brick wall, a rubber-coated ball in my left hand, my Dusty Baker glove hooded over my right wrist, and I'd throw, and catch, and chase, and switch the glove back and forth. The yard was quiet except for the thump against the wall and my footfalls and thick breaths that followed, all in pursuit of the baseball. When the glove transition grew more comfortable and I became better at it, I'd move closer to the wall, throw the ball harder, test myself. Then I'd retrace the chalk rectangle on the bricks, step off the distance to a pitcher's mound, and throw at that.

Inside the house, Mom was becoming a lawyer, working through her studies to the tune of the *thump-thump-thump* from behind the far wall. From down the block, Dad would drive up in the Volkswagen van, his workday done. Chad and I would play our games, our backyard baseball and football, and I'd keep throwing. It felt right, even in the dark, even in the cold, even when Mom had already announced dinner, twice, and then Dad had to stick his head out of the door.

They were encouraging and instinctual as parents. They never pushed, but they never said, "Don't, that's not a good idea." There was never any dissuasion. Mom was an optimist. She sort of had this "Well, if that doesn't work we'll do this" attitude. Dad was a why-not guy. He sometimes didn't see the consequences of things. Where I was a worrier, he'd buy the rubber boat with the motor next to the side of the road and say, "Let's put it on the beach, it'll be great." And I'd say, "Dad, where are we going to store it? What are we going to do with it?" He'd look at me and say, "Why not?"

Dad loved Al McGuire, then the Marquette basketball coach and one of the great personalities of the sport. Well, McGuire told this story on TV one time about going to Marquette's basketball practices, day in and day out, for more than a decade. And every day, when he came to an intersection near campus, he would turn right. Left was a part of town he'd never seen, because he always went right. The basketball court was right. One day, out of curiosity and restlessness, McGuire went left. His quote, according to Dad, was, "Sometimes you gotta take a left." Dad sort of lived by that. Dad went left quite a bit.

By the time I was nearing high school, Dad worked for an Anheuser-Busch beer distributorship. He was in sales and drove a route. He was an on-premise manager, meaning he was in the bars, slapping hands, making sure everybody had what they wanted and making sure Budweiser was well-placed.

Mom had gone through University of Michigan–Flint, then to

law school at Cooley College in East Lansing. Many nights I went to bed listening to her tap at a manual typewriter and awoke to the same sound. She commuted one hundred miles a day, earned her law degree, and became a civil counsel for the City of Flint. She also was in private practice.

While they worked, Chad and I became independent. I'd come home from school to an empty house, make myself some lunch, and then go back to practice for whatever sport was in season.

Our folks, meanwhile, weathered the storm that many do not. They went through what people go through when they marry at eighteen, not really having the chance to experience their own adolescence. They lived apart for short periods, never more than a month or two. We'd live with Mom. And there was always reconciliation, happily.

Dad was a free spirit, but there were times when he was the most responsible person I knew. He instilled solid values; made clear the family was important. In words, he never confused his priorities. But sometimes, he did like to get out and see the world. He is, as I remember him saying a million times, someone who burned the candle at both ends. Maybe it goes back to his dad dying. He's always had a hunger to see the world, to be a part of it, a part of what's going on. My mom was almost the complete opposite of that. She was a homebody, very quiet. So there was always that clash.

And then, more often than not, they'd come see my games.

I was no prodigy. I was cut from the freshman basketball team at Flint Central High School. I made the freshman baseball team, but didn't get a hit the whole season. It was a long time before I separated myself from boys my age on athletic fields, beyond the occasional softball throw. Partly as a result, those early teenage years were perhaps my most difficult in terms of accepting my disability. Yet even then using it as an explanation for failure held only fleeting re-spite. Mostly, any thoughts about my hand were private, and when I brought them up it was more often to hide some other pain or anxiety—the typical pains and anxieties of a teenager—and so even then it seemed dishonest.

Meantime, I remember points along the way. I remember the faces, the events, the casual observations of classmates. I remember the long stares. And being glad my jeans had pockets. I remember the kids who took one look at me and said, "Your hand looks like a foot," observations that amused them to no end and yet for me had become part of the routine. And I remember baseball coming to find me, pulling me along.

My parents were supportive and challenged me and allowed me to bruise, if that's where the day was headed. Dad sent Chad and me off to school every morning with some variation of the same message: "You're the best," he'd say. Or, "Be a leader." Or, "Don't let anybody get you down." Something that would make me feel loved and safe no matter what I was headed out into.

Sometimes, the real tests came in the places where there was not a single spectator. Places like Whittier Middle School came alive many winter nights in a city where basketball—not baseball—was the one and only game.

In my early teens the guys from the neighborhood—Mark "Shark" Conover, Danny Nathan, David "Crame" Cramer, Alex Green—would bang on the front door just after dinner. They'd stand there in their heavy coats, sweat pants, and wool caps, their cheeks already red from the walk down the hill, laughing and pushy to get going. I'd grab my winter gear, leave behind the aroma of one of Mom's specialties—pork chops, stuffed peppers, cube steak—and the dirty dishes, for the junior high gym. The walk was about a half mile, a lot of it along Burroughs Creek, which ran through a park that separated the black and white neighborhoods on Flint's east side.

Dozens of us would wait in the parking lot, often enough breathing steam and bouncing lightly on our toes against the cold, for the community school director to unlock the door from the inside. The games were exactly what you'd expect. All over Flint, city leaders opened gyms in hopes that basketball would be the alternative to all the other nighttime options. The lights were dim and the balls, slick and swollen from use, were dark leather. The courts were dusty except on the edges, where they were damp from slushy footsteps. My first job was pushing a broom from end to end on those courts and collecting one-dollar bills from the folks who came to watch the adult leagues, but what I preferred to do was play. So, we played. Depending on the turnout, we'd go five-on-five or three-on-three, full- or half-court. This was pure pickup ball, rough and loud and sometimes intimidating. Some of the best players in the city showed up at these gyms and, until I was cut from my ninth-grade team, I thought of myself as a decent player who could hang with them. Granted, I had a hard time going right, and everybody knew it, and there wasn't a kid on that floor who wouldn't overplay my left side. Oh, I'd fake an unsure dribble or two with my right hand, try to give the impression I'd go right if I had to, but without fail I'd end up on the left side of the floor looking for a teammate or a shot.

The games were unforgiving. If I hadn't already figured it out, nobody was going to feel sorry for me. More likely, they were going to force me right, and that was true in basketball and in life.

While I'd always felt different and knew I'd have to live with it, I began to stand up to those feelings in high school, sometimes in those gyms, but mostly on the baseball field. I was never completely comfortable or free of uncertainty, but I had my protected place.

When I was unsure, baseball would tell me I was all right, that I'd done something well. It was my self-image. Hey, I'd been in the newspaper. I'd been on TV. The doubt would come and go, but I could lean on my parents, all they'd instilled in me, and I could lean on the game, and what it meant for me. There was always another issue, it seemed, no matter how I tried to outrun it. But I'd done stuff on the field, been better at something.

And I'd won my share, no matter what my hand looked like.

CHAPTER 6

By the time he was done, Jim Thome would be one of the great home-run hitters in baseball history, right there with Mickey Mantle and Reggie Jackson and Frank Robinson, pushing 600 home runs for his career.

On September 4, 1993, he had five.

In 285 at-bats, he had struck out 64 times. He had turned twenty-three eight days before, and at that age was what you'd call a swing-hard-in-case-you-hit-it guy. It wouldn't be long before he swung hard and hit it a lot, but for the moment he was a young man with a puncher's chance of completely ruining an otherwise promising afternoon.

Thome was a big, strong hitter who had a long swing from the left side, meaning my cutter—if I wasn't careful—was generally running into the path of all that barrel. The strategy was to throw the cutter at his right hip and maybe have it catch the inside corner, then go away with the cutter off the plate. Even at that age Thome could keep the inside fastball fair, so if I missed, I wanted to miss in on his hands.

Yankee Stadium was a wonderful ballpark, particularly for a left-handed pitcher. Guys like Thome, however, made that right-field fence feel very close.

On a bit of an uppercut swing, he flied to Bernie Williams in center field.

From one hitter to the next, you couldn't get much more extreme than Thome to Junior Ortiz, the Indians' catcher who, in thirteen big-league seasons, would hit five home runs. In fact, by the time I saw him, he hadn't hit one in four years and wouldn't ever hit another—that fact alone was reason enough to pitch around Thome if it came to it. Ortiz was smallish, right-handed, and could be pesky, in that way where you didn't want the number 9 hitter extending an inning, getting on base for the top of the Indians' order or making you work any harder than you had to.

He grounded out to second baseman Mike Gallego.

So, I was through the order once. I'd walked a couple, struck out a couple, and generally stuck to the plan—Nokes's, pitching coach Tony Cloninger's, bullpen coach Mark Connor's, mine. It wasn't spectacular—we weren't even winning yet—but the ball was coming out of my hand pretty well. I'd given myself over to Nokes and our plan entirely, throwing what we wanted, hopefully in the area we wanted. His intentions were exactly mine, so I almost could see his fingers call for pitches before they uncurled from his fist.

By comparison, at this point six days before in Cleveland—two out in the third inning—against a similar batting order, I'd already given up nine hits and seven runs. The only difference for the day game after the night game was that Indians manager Mike Hargrove had subbed out Sorrento, Espinoza, and Alomar Jr.

Maybe I'd worked the Indians' lineup to overconfidence.

I finished the third inning by getting another ground ball, this time pitching more aggressively to Lofton, this time trusting my cutter and Nokes's feel for it. I followed the ball to Gallego and then to Don Mattingly, and made my way to the dugout, by then allowing myself the notion that this would, indeed, maybe, quite possibly be a better day.

CHAPTER 7

The brick, mortar, and soaring gloom of Central Community High School stood four stories above Crapo Street in Flint's East Village, commanding the sort of stern consideration a medieval fortress would against its sprawling fiefdom. The campus covered forty-three acres, spanning at least four blocks on each border. Better known as Flint Central or simply Central, the school opened in 1923, twenty years after Buick Motor Company began building engines in a single-story plant in town and nineteen years after William Crapo Durant took control of Buick.

Bookended by a public library to the north and Whittier Middle School to the south, Central was distinguishable for its capital E structural design, bell tower, solemn architectural details, and stately carriage. The place had heft, as though it had risen from the earth of its own diligence. Sixty years after its first graduating class, there was little one would consider fanciful about the place; not the low ceilings, not the broad concrete steps at the main entrance, not the tall windows painted shut, not the people in its locker-lined hallways, and not the neighborhood it dominated.

Once, as many as two thousand students over three classes—tenth through twelfth—walked over the lawns, along the cement sidewalks and past the flagpole into its classrooms each morning. By the time it closed in 2009 from neglect and economic circumstance, the school's population was closer to one thousand over four classes. People were leaving Flint and taking their kids with them.

I arrived in the fall of 1981, having graduated from across the parking lot at Whittier and now just another of the faceless hundreds endeavoring toward something like adulthood. My family lived by then in a house on Burroughs Park, a tree-lined meadow that broadened as it curled north and west over three hundred or so yards toward the middle and high schools. Gilkey Creek skirted one side of the park, which served many purposes for the boys who lived on its perimeter. Depending on the season, the park was a football field, a hockey rink, a baseball diamond, a snowball battleground, a wrestling mat, a cover for a few secret minutes of a budding romance, and a place to kill time before the sun went down. Every summer night, clumps of dirt and smears of grass from the park went home on the knees and elbows of every kid who ran it, no exceptions—not the middle-class white kids from the east border or the lower-income black kids from its west side. The distinctions in our park were not drawn from race, however, but from the final scores of the games we played, and from the courage shown in those knock-down-drag-outs, and from the hospitality of moms who poured Kool-Aid from the porches closest to the park. This is where we scored the first significant touchdowns of our lives, and learned to drag the bat head to go the other way. We practiced our hockey stops on the frozen creek until our knees and elbows were raw. It's where we threw and took our first punches, leaving us breathless and sad.

Some of the early founders of Flint once lived along Burroughs Park, but, like so much in Flint, things weren't what they once were.

After a lot of bouncing around, settling in neighborhoods and then—for one reason or another, often because of the schools—moving on, the Abbotts and their two boys moved into the middle of three houses at the end of a short road overlooking the park. By then, some of those big, beautiful homes were showing their age. The lives of many of the breadwinners in the cul-de-sacs and verdant streets near Burroughs Park would change in the 1980s, just as they would all over Flint, when General Motors began boarding up its manufacturing plants. For decades a man in Flint could chart his course from the playground to high school to an assembly line or management job at GM, the path their fathers and grandfathers had taken to middle-class stability. When the jobs disappeared, so too did Flint's hope, and the street corners that had been edgy in my father's youth became strictly off-limits in mine.

We settled there when I was in fifth grade, between an elegant old couple on one side and a professor and his wife on the other. Gardens colored their backyards. Our house, by our previous standards, was huge, with spacious rooms and fireplaces that heated them. A furnace dominated the basement. Running it was expensive, so Dad bought a wood-burning stove, attached it to the furnace, and fed the stove with the wood from pallets he'd collect from the family meat business. One afternoon he called me over to the stack of pallets in the backyard and said, "Jim, lemme show you how to take these things apart." Then, with a grin, he cranked up a chainsaw. I swept up the sawdust. In spite of its size and the large property it sat on, the house was affordable because the streets that led to ours had begun to reflect the coming economic recession. Chad and I walked to school—through the backyard, over Gilkey Creek where once a wanderer's dead body had been discovered and dominated our conversations for weeks, across the park, and up a hill, where we'd turn back toward the house. Mom and Dad would wave from the front door—*Everything all right?*—and we'd wave back.

Some of the best friends in my life were made in the Wiffle ball games in that backyard, and in the trees scaled in that park, and at the ends of the bike rides that would deliver me to pickup games that might or might not accept me. After all the moving around, it was good not to be the new kid, the different kid, and better to be the familiar kid. It was good not to answer the questions. And it was especially good to be simply one of the guys, no better or worse. It took a few beatings to get there. The neighborhood mirrored a diverse city, one that was hurting in a lot of ways. So when dusk came and the games thinned out, the white kids and black kids would wave their good-byes and head to their neutral corners until tomorrow, just like the skinny kids and chubby kids and the one-handed kid.

By the time I tromped across Burroughs Park for my first classes at Flint Central, the city's unemployment rate paralleled those of crime, inflation, and despair, each racing to determine which would sink Flint first. As GM was planning the celebration of its seventy-fifth anniversary and the United Auto Workers its fiftieth, nearly a quarter of the city's working-age population was idle. Downtown, Montgomery Ward, J. C. Penney, and Smith-Bridgman closed. When the local food market advertised to fill a couple entry-level positions, applicants stood two-deep around the block. Some brought sleeping bags, coolers, and lawn chairs. Crack cocaine became the new industry, homicide and arson the new hobbies. As the decade wore on, *Money* magazine surveyed three hundred major U.S. cities for their livability; Flint was three hundredth. Few who lived there were surprised, though they cloaked their reactions in outrage.

We were okay. Dad was selling beer. Folks always had money for beer. Mom was an attorney. Folks always needed a way out of trouble. We had food to eat, clean clothes to wear, and plenty of pallets to carve up and burn.

Years before, I'd worn down my parents on the subject of the prosthetic limb, so by my freshman year I couldn't have said whether it was in a box in the garage or in a hospital storeroom or in a city landfill or on some other kid's arm. As I'd neared the end of elementary school, the last place I saw it was on the floor of my bedroom closet, there with five sneakers that were too small or tattered, toys I'd outgrown, a pair of snow pants, and a plastic bat split along its seam that one day could be brought back to life with duct tape. "I haven't worn that in a long time," I thought, "I don't think I ever will again." While I was glad to be rid of it, that arm held more than cables and bands. It symbolized my parents' efforts to help me. Their intentions were good and pure, and I felt a responsibility to them, though not enough to wear it. I felt bad about that. Sometimes, as heavy as it was on my shoulder, it was heavier on the floor.

The arm was in the clothes closet because that's how I thought of it—as a part of my wardrobe, along with the pants and shirts and jackets I wore to school. It went on in the morning and came off the moment I walked through the front door at the end of the school day. The stump socks were folded in the sock drawer of the dresser. The elastic bands that operated the pincers but wore out so fast sat in a tangle on the bookshelf. "Where's your arm?" Mom would ask before breakfast. "Where's your arm?" Dad would demand as I gathered my lunchbox and homework. Some days I'd huff away, return to the closet, strip off my shirt, strap on my arm, and stomp off to school.

Others, I'd plead for a respite, just one day off, promising to wear it again the next day. Eventually, gloriously, there were no more tomorrows for my right arm, though twenty-five years later a man I didn't know contacted me, said he was in possession of my arm—guaranteed it—and asked if I would like to buy it back. I was mortified, though less so when he described what he had, and it turned out what he was hoping to sell could not have come from my closet. It was a left arm.

The back-and-forths with my parents petered out when I was maybe ten, when they'd recognized I was better off finding my way with what I had and, anyway, they had tired of the sulking arguments about it. I couldn't hold a bat with that thing, couldn't swing a hockey stick, and couldn't even run without it clattering against itself and whatever else was nearby. The technology that was supposed to be extending my physical boundaries was keeping me off the playground at recess and slowing me to a walk. The best it did for me was to grant the motivation to be rid of it, which meant working the right arm I had until it became more reliable. My true arm was thin and slightly short and lacked the mobility of my left arm, but it had some life in it. Not having fingers was problematic, but my wrist worked okay. With my right arm, I could push things around, wedge things between my forearm and body, trap things, hold things steady, carry things with some nimbleness, and that all seemed to be a reasonable place to start. I was forever staining the right side of my shirts, where I cradled oranges in order to peel them and bike parts in order to fix them and baseballs in order to pitch them. I dropped a lot of stuff. I was frustrated when the easiest tasks required two hands, and so were nearly impossible for me. But it was better than the alternative, better than being Captain Hook. I'd left that behind; where, I didn't know and didn't care.

Where it was not—cinched neither to my body nor my

consciousness—was good enough. Into a new world of the usual high school frailties and rather pointed tensions, enough of them drawn along racial lines, I arrived at Central a little gangly, a little intimidated, a lot self-conscious and with my right hand stuffed deep into my right pocket. This was a tough school, a burdened school, and a basketball school. It also was the neighborhood school, which meant a few warm faces and a somewhat soothing intimacy. I'd played pickup ball on the gym floor for years, so I'd crawled the grounds and hallways before. That's not to say it wasn't at times a dangerous place. Just like Flint itself, there were shadowy corners at Central where being young, alone, and unimposing drew unwanted interest. The rumor on campus—supported anecdotally by various bloody noses and black eyes—held that a black gang was recruiting new members. Gang leaders required their candidates to batter a predetermined number of white faces, which might have grown their membership but did little for the rest of the school's morale. This seemed a long way from the color blindness of Burroughs Park. I'd avoided those rites until a couple months into my freshman year when one morning I was climbing the stairs past the auto shop, heading for first period. The stairs amounted to a back entrance into school, the quickest route to my locker from Burroughs Park. Halfway up the first flight, I heard from around the corner what must have been a half-dozen boys coming from the other direction. They were talking loud, laughing, and at a quarter to eight in the morning quite obviously not coming to school but leaving. My stomach churned.

I paused, considered retreat, was caught in between, realized it was too late to run, and finally surrendered to the mobile gauntlet, thinking, "Aw, this isn't going to be good."

I reached the landing as they did and stood to the side as they passed. Single file, they looked me over coldly, one after the other, four of them, then five, and when I came to believe I'd been thankfully unworthy of their scorn, the last of them balled his fist and hit me square in the jaw, sending me staggering into the wall. They whooped and hollered, a celebration for the pledge who'd come a white kid closer to full membership. My mouth hurt, my books were scattered on the landing, and I felt like a dope for wandering into the ambush, but mostly I was relieved they kept going. It wasn't until I reached my locker that I began to shake. I brushed a few tears from my cheeks with the sleeve of my jacket. I'd assumed my turn was coming at some point, and I hoped that would be the worst of it. My buddy Mark Conover once made the mistake of allowing a stray basketball to roll into another game in gym class. The kid tripped by the ball waited for him in the locker room and beat him pretty good for it. Mark's attacker was expelled, but that hardly calmed a population of white kids who felt terrorized.

For a long time, at least the first couple years, that was life at Central. If you fit the victim profile, you kept your head down, minimized eye contact, and hoped it wasn't your day. The tough school in the tough town took its victims, and these were desperate kids who preyed on insecure ones. Fortunately, it was also a sports school in a sports town, which meant there were places where there were rules and pockets of etiquette and at least one way to rise above the random cold-cockings.

So started high school and the adolescent lessons. There were plenty of punches to be taken, ducked, and thrown. The next connected closer to the gut.

I regarded myself as a reasonably proficient basketball player, a certainty that blossomed on the asphalt courts around town and open-gym nights on the floor. Shortly after the flyers were posted announcing freshman basketball tryouts, I showed up on the first of two days in my shorts, T-shirt, and high-tops. Half the boys of the freshman class, it seemed, turned out. This was Flint; everyone could play basketball. Those who couldn't thought they could. Basketball was part of the culture of the city, like cars and unemployment.

The coach had a strategy that lacked nuance, but suited the crowd. He rolled out a few basketballs, blew his whistle and, from a distance with his arms crossed, sorted through the mayhem. On the hardwood of the Lavoie Field House, sides were chosen, games reared up, and the good players began separating themselves from the not-quite-good-enough players, and when the cuts came I was going to miss those not-so-good guys. I mixed in, made a very clever no-look touch pass with the coach—I was sure—staring straight at me, got a few rebounds, and a day later came to open-gym night for a pickup game when a few of us noticed the tryout results had been posted on the bulletin board. The names of the boys who'd made the team—fifteen of them—were listed in alphabetical order. It didn't take long, then, to realize Abbott was not going to be there. None of my friends' names were there, either.

Two months into high school, I'd been ambushed in a stairwell and lost the chance to play basketball.

Central basketball, as it turned out, was loaded. We—and by "we" I mean the guys who made the team—won three consecutive state championships beginning in 1981, drawing crowds from all over Michigan. As each banner was hung over the gym it became clearer to me why my name wasn't on that bulletin board. Flint was a hoops city, and Central was in those years its heartbeat. Stan Gooch, the varsity coach then, won 406 games at Central. The real glory years were in the early eighties, when he won with city legends Eric Turner, Mark Harris, Marty Embry, Darryl Johnson, and Terence Greene.

The Central basketball dynasty ended in 1984, when Flint Northwestern showed up with Glen Rice, Andre Rison, and Jeff Grayer.

Long before then, I'd turned to baseball.

The game had come to me, and I to it, at Pierce Elementary School, a low-slung building less than a mile from Burroughs Park. I entered in fifth grade, so another new classroom, thirty new classmates, and thirty more explanations for what happened to my hand. We'd covered that ground—"I was born this way." "No, it doesn't hurt." "I don't know why it looks like that." "No, nothing 'happened.'"—when in late winter the teacher passed around a signup sheet for Little League baseball, finally. My new friends, most of whom lived in the neighborhood and ran Burroughs Park with me, had played organized baseball together the year before. They talked about the hits they had and the teams they beat and who could pitch and who couldn't, and I was envious. I'd played T-ball and enough backyard Wiffle ball and, after being turned away a hundred times, I'd earned my way into some of the neighborhood games. Dad, of course, had played a large role in that, staring down at his sniveling firstborn in the kitchen and ordering him back to the park. If the older kids were going to ignore me and my hopeful gaze and my stunted arm, Dad wasn't going to hear it. This was the man, after all, who'd once convinced me I would do hard time for grand theft bubblegum.

I WAS MAYBE ten. Chad and I had accompanied Mom to the grocery store and on the way through the checkout line a pack of gum practically jumped into my pocket. On the way home, I'd dragged Chad into the crime, and we chomped away merrily in the backseat. Mom was on to me. Dad got home, drama ensued, and he and I left the house with him announcing, "Say good-bye to your mom and your brother." Chad, I think, eyed the big bedroom. We drove to Flint jail, the kindly officer played along, and it wasn't until the cell door was open and I was standing on the precipice of solitary confinement that Dad figured he'd taken the lesson far enough. Mom was kinder, but just as firm. Since the drive back to Flint from Grand Rapids and Mary Free Bed years before, the course was set: Jimmy was going to find his way, one way or the other. This was a boy, and that's what he'd be raised as. The world was unforgiving, and Jimmy might as well learn that now.

They weren't exactly right. At least I don't suspect so. There was a lot of forgiveness out there. For every five sneering kids on every sandlot field who couldn't imagine how I could possibly help their team, there was a man willing to teach me to tie my shoes. There was a coach who would be sure I got my at-bat and two innings in the field. There was Dad, who in his hard lessons ached to toughen me for whatever lay ahead, and Mom, whose soft heart could hardly bear to watch any of it, but did, and with uncommon compassion. Coaches, all those coaches, seemed to line up to help. Even as a child, I could barely summon the courage to complain, other than about the hook. That, I hated. When the frustration bubbled up, and one too many kids gawked at me for a little too long, and I didn't think I'd ever be free from what others must be thinking, I'd wonder how this thing had found me. Everybody else had been granted two hands and a life without complications. I was different, unfairly burdened, and always would be. How could I play ball like this? Meet a girl like this? Have a regular life? Immediately, I'd regret the thoughts, like I'd abandoned the fight for myself and my parents and all the people who were trying to believe in me. I'd burn it off by shooting hoops in the driveway, or lying on my back on the lawn and throwing a baseball into the air, counting its revolutions before it fell back into my hand.

Because, in the end, there was always baseball.

Mark Conover's father, Neil, coached that fifth-grade team. We played at Kearsley Park, a fifteen-minute bike ride from home, past the high school and the hospital and the community college, most of it following Gilkey Creek. For the first time, I had a team, and a game that wouldn't send me away, and a real uniform. In my mirror, a mesh shirt, matching cap, and jeans counted as much as a uniform as Al Kaline's whites and Olde English D. "Grant Hamady Realty," written across my chest, might as well have said "Tigers." I had a position: the left-handed third baseman. Mark's dad even put me in to pitch once in a while, innings that often would course through a walk or two, some reasonable velocity and, I'm guessing, a few parents concerned for the safety of their little batters.

But I belonged.

Kearsley Park was in a floodplain. The baseball field was mostly dirt, except for the times it was all mud. On game days, we'd hang our gloves from our handlebars, wedge our bats under our arms, and ride as fast and straight as we could without sending a bat bouncing wildly across the pavement. We had only a few that weren't already broken, after all. When it rained, we'd gather rakes and shovels from our garages, add those to our uneven loads, meet at the field, and push the puddles into foul territory. We couldn't bear the thought of not playing. We lived for it. That team made the city championship game, which we showed up for in sweatpants that actually matched our T-shirts. It was a magnificent moment fouled only by the fact that we didn't win.

By the time I left those alternately dusty and boggy fields and reached high school, my arm had hundreds of innings on it. Some were in the park league, the summer league, and the Connie Mack league, where I was gradually finding the strike zone. But most of those innings were thrown in my backyard, or up the road in Harold and Howard Croft's backyard, or in a corner of Burroughs Park, or against the side of the house. Again, my control was coming. By the end of the day, Chad generally was carrying fewer welts to the dinner table.

I played on the freshman team at Central, mostly as a pitcher and left fielder, occasionally as a first baseman. The season wasn't long, and when it was over I thought I'd hung in there pretty well, except baseball was becoming my sport even at a time before specialization, and I'd batted .ooo. It seemed low. In fact, teammates who weren't really ballplayers—as I was beginning to consider myself—got hits. But not me. I wish I could say it was bad luck.

Still, as I returned for my sophomore season, which presumably meant a promotion to junior varsity, two ideals were forming in me, one in my arm and another in my heart.

Baseball was the easy part. Not the game itself, but the mechanics of it and certainly my love for it. That spring came quickly, though the weather was wet and cold and so too was the field house at Central. On the first day of practice, the infielders spread out over the gym floor, the outfielders reported to the batting cages on the mezzanine level, and the pitchers went to the mounds—wooden risers topped with carpet—alongside the cages. The place was so alive with baseball I couldn't help but grin. Baseball talk, baseball sounds, baseball smells, baseball everything; it meant another Michigan winter would soon be over and another baseball season was coming. The year before, Bob Holec, the varsity coach, had gathered the pitchers and held up the front page from that day's paper. The photo was of Jack Morris, the Detroit Tigers' ace. Opening Day at Tiger

Stadium had been postponed because of snow, but Black Jack was on the mound anyway and about to deliver a pitch. In his right hand he held a snowball. Holec pointed at Morris's elbow, then his front shoulder, his hips, and his stride leg, all mechanically perfect. "This is what we're looking for," Holec announced. We nodded at Morris's supreme snowball-throwing form and headed to our stations. A year later, I thought of that photo again.

My heart was not so easy to manage. Something fierce and barely manageable was rising in me, manifesting itself in the game and on the mound.

I didn't *want* to play, I *had* to play.

And then I didn't just have to *play*, I had to *win*.

And I didn't want to win simply to prove that I fit in, but to prove I was better. Way better.

The notion of fitting in, once enough to push me onto the field, was becoming too passive. Sports—baseball mostly, but anything counted—were a way to fight back. Already, barely halfway through high school, I'd given so much of myself away by being the nice kid—laughing at jokes about me, pretending nothing hurt, hoping people would like me—simply to convince outsiders not to look too hard at my condition. Off the field, I'd ducked confrontation because I perceived myself an easy mark. I was so vulnerable I'd made myself compliantly invulnerable. Chad once got beat up trying to defend my honor when I wasn't around. I'd never thrown a punch at someone who spoke unkindly about my hand, but my brother, four years younger, had sucker-punched a much bigger kid for it. Unfortunately for Chad, the kid got up. For me, the fights came disguised as games. But I wouldn't fight for my dignity. That, I carried home with me. Rather, I'd found a place where I could stand up for myself, where the fight came disguised as a game. There, I wasn't ashamed of how I looked or how I felt about it. There, I'd fight anybody—batters, teammates, even myself. I'd lost control of it.

A couple summers before, during the annual CANUSA games between Flint and Hamilton, Ontario, I'd been selected for the Flint baseball team. The town turned out, the results would be in the newspaper, and I was excited to be the starting pitcher. The plan was for me to go four innings. We were way ahead when the coach came to me on the bench.

"Nice job, Jim," he said. "We're going to let somebody else pitch."

"But," I answered stubbornly, "I have a no-hitter."

He looked at me uneasily, nodded, and left me to the game, which I finished. When it was over, the one boy who hadn't gotten into the game, the one who was supposed to pitch the last few innings and gain his own CANUSA celebrity, was Mark Conover, my best friend on the team, the son of the first coach to give me a chance. While I was chasing my own achievement, he'd been denied a chance to play. During the game, it hadn't occurred to me. Afterward, I was crestfallen. Had it been that long since I was the one being left out? Achievement had a hold over me, no matter how it was gained.

The accommodations I made off the field were becoming my fire on the field. If people were going to search me for deficiencies, which I was sure they would, they wouldn't find them at the end of my fastball, or in my ability to field a bunt, or on the scoreboard. If they expected the kid who'd hide in his own right front pocket, well, baseball pants had no front pockets. And if they wondered if I'd shrink away, I was standing on the mound, ten inches taller than everyone else.

For those hours, I'd mostly forget how I was different, and forgive myself for the parts of me I'd already given away because of it. Those were the limitations and influences that were more inhibiting than any physical challenges, a greater handicap than missing four and three-quarter fingers. Once I'd begun to make peace with the physical creativity required to get through a day, the next challenge came in believing more was possible.

With a baseball in my hand and a cap pulled tight around my head, I could be different, but not in the way it might have seemed when I got off the bus. The second glances, the awkward handshakes, they were gone. I could push back as hard as I wanted. I could compete and fight and not care how I was perceived. More was possible. In fact, it was probable. That's what I carried off the bus.

BOB HOLEC WAS born at St. Joseph's Hospital in Flint, raised on the East Side, and graduated from Central in 1965, two years before my father graduated from St. Matt's. They played ball with and against each other and Holec knew my mother, the North Ender. Holec was a scholarship catcher and linebacker at Colorado State, returned to Flint as the junior varsity baseball coach in 1971, and took over the varsity five years later. He knew his baseball.

In Holec's program, sophomores played junior varsity baseball. After an early practice, however, Holec took me aside. He told me I'd be practicing from then on with the varsity. I thought about that.

"I think I'd rather be with the JV," I told him.

My friends were on the JV. I was so skinny. I wasn't ready. It was too fast. I wasn't good enough.

Holec shook his head.

"You'll adjust," he said. "It's best for you and us."

I seriously doubted that, but I nodded. The next day, carrying only a fastball and a floppy curveball, I reported to the varsity side.

I won six games as a sophomore. And I got a hit. We were co–City champions. The juniors and seniors on the team were supportive enough, generally seeing to me as they might a little brother. Of course, I had a little brother, and I knew how that went sometimes. The starting catcher, an older kid named Craig Stephens everyone called "Bubba," even had a nickname for me: One-Point-Five. I lacked the temerity to ask, but I assumed it had something to do with my disability. One and a half arms? One and a half hands? I didn't know. Maybe it represented the single, small, and generally useless bud of a finger on my right hand, followed by the decimal and the five fingers on my left hand. Anatomically inaccurate, but clever. Or, perhaps, Bubba had thought bigger and gone with the one full left arm and the half (give or take) right arm. I laughed along rather than demand an explanation, which was my nature, and quietly hoped the nickname wouldn't stick. I figured I was ahead of the game when they didn't issue me a uniform with number 15 on the back. Besides, it was slightly better than the usual backhanded nickname—Lefty—and infinitely better than Captain Hook.

The next spring, Holec again came to talk. I'd grown some. My dad had bought me a membership at the YMCA and all winter I'd walk from school to the gym and home, through the cold and slush and darkness. Along the road, Holec had passed me in his car a few times and waved. I did a lot of thinking on those walks about the game and how much I adored it. I wanted to be better. I had to be. Even then, trudging along the uneven sidewalks of East Flint months away from baseball season, the need to show people what I could be would rise inside me and settle in my jaw.

Holec looked me over, both of us now sure I was a varsity player.

"You're the ace," he said.

I won seven games and batted .367, even hit a home run. We were City champions.

By then, word had spread about the one-handed pitcher at Central. Considering how desperately I'd sought accomplishment, the attention made me uncomfortable. They'd come to see the kid with the fastball, to write about the player colleges, and scouts were beginning to recognize and chart, but mostly they'd come to see the one-handed kid who dangled his glove from his unborn hand and somehow pitched and fielded and hit. I wanted to play, to be good enough to win, and leave it at that. They wanted to see me slide the glove from one hand to the other and make a play. They wanted to cheer the effort. Screw the effort: I wanted to win.

They were nice, the people who came and applauded. Already, though, from the beginnings of a purely personal struggle to get on the field, there came to me a sense that I was being viewed through the prism of my condition. First I was one-handed and then I was a ballplayer. It felt flimsy, like the means to an excuse. Worse, it felt a little like pity. I was overthinking everything, projecting my own insecurities onto the people who'd come to the games and afterward shake my hand, but I couldn't help it. The joy of the game—of winning the game—was temporary, holding up just long enough to wonder who all these people were.

I'd look at my glove and consider what everyone believed was such a feat. When I was younger, when nobody was watching and it became obvious I'd need my left hand for both the ball and the glove, instinct had guided me. I hadn't set out to do any more than play catch with my dad. Then I wanted to be a little less clumsy so I could get into the neighborhood games. Only then did I have to be fast and sure, not to amaze but to catch a ball and to get an out at first so I'd be picked for a team the next day.

The glove switch was less ingenuity than survival, followed by repetition, and then a great hope that nothing too crazy would happen. It helped that I loved a baseball glove: the way it fit on my hand, how a new one smelled and looked, and what it felt like under my mattress, imagining its perfection come morning. Even the names—Wilson, Rawlings, Mizuno—sounded stout and trustworthy. It wasn't just me, either. When someone from the neighborhood showed up with a new glove, it was an event. Stiff and perfectly brown, the glove would move around the group, each kid giving it his blessing before passing it along to the next.

So I spent a lot of time with my glove, rubbing it up with Dad's shaving cream, working the pocket, making it just right, remembering to bring it inside at night. For its deficiencies, my right hand was a perfect breaking-in tool, pounding a perfect pocket. And I figured out a way to make my glove work for me. Popping the ball from the glove into the air, getting the glove off my hand, and then catching the ball with my left hand was inconsistent and time consuming. It wouldn't work. Trapping the glove and ball between my forearm and body, removing my hand from the glove and then gripping the ball was okay, but getting the glove back on was slow and unreliable. Sometimes, as the ball came shooting toward me, I looked less like a ballplayer than a guy wrestling with an angry throw pillow. But I had a rubber-coated ball and a brick wall and nothing but hours to kill. I kept throwing and the ball kept coming back, and so many times I'd just take it in the knee, or off my bare hand, or throw my glove at it, anything to avoid chasing another ball across the yard. Day by day, year by year, I drew closer to something reliable, so by the time I walked into Bob Holec's gym I'd hardly give it a thought anymore.

Like an unschooled jump shot born on a playground that nevertheless becomes trustworthy, the glove switch was unconventional. Of course, there was no convention to be had. I made it up as I went along, finding ways to get on the field and stay there. The glove exchange was going to be critical, I already knew. After a million tries and nearly as many clumsy failures, I discovered that by hooding the glove—pocket down—over my right hand, I could get my left hand back into it quickly. The exchange, from glove on left hand and ball in glove to my bare left hand, was the tricky part. So, I'd twirl the glove toward my chest by turning my left pinky toward my right arm, which allowed me to take my hand out of the glove. As I removed my hand, my right arm would cradle the glove and keep it rotating, so the glove would turn upside down and the ball would fall from the glove into my hand. By the time the glove was resting on my right hand, it had spun more than 360 degrees, as though turning on a spit that ran from the heel of the glove through the tops of the fingers. The opening of the glove—where I'd insert and remove my left hand—always faced to my left, toward my good hand. It mostly worked.

Then I had to find the proper glove.

If the glove's opening was too tight, which was often the case with the smaller gloves, I couldn't get my hand in and out smoothly.

A glove too big or floppy would lose its shape during the twirl stage and the ball wouldn't come out. That wasn't a huge issue between pitches on the mound, where, generally, there was little rush. At first base or in left field, however, the ball had to come out clean. I fumbled with it a lot. There were times when I'd sense a problem on a comebacker and in case of emergency start running toward first base, thinking some sort of movement would be better than standing around, and more than once in exasperation tossed the whole glove and ball to the first baseman. I'd let him sort it out.

In spite of all these requirements, I'd still buy gloves according to how they looked on the shelf or whose autograph was burned into the palm. I had my priorities. By late in high school, however, Raw-lings had identified a glove for me that was small in size but loose in the hand. My Connie Mack coach, Ted Mahan, was influential to me in larger ways—the game he taught and how he attacked it, for two—but he also was instrumental in locating a proper glove. As a catcher and captain at Michigan, Mahan had become friendly with Michigan alum Ted Sizemore, who played twelve seasons in the major leagues before going to work for Rawlings. Mahan introduced us and Sizemore delivered the perfect glove, which changed every-thing, until I went to college and discovered Michigan had a Wilson contract.

As gloves came and went, I forever worked on my fielding. I couldn't have that part of the game be a weakness. I practiced finish-ing my delivery so the follow-through nearly brought my left hand back to the glove waiting on the end of my right arm. Throwing against the brick wall, I'd sneak up as close as I could, challenging the speed of the exchange. Hitters bunted on me a lot, so I'd bare-hand what I could, or block balls on the third-base line with my glove still on my right hand, eliminating the glove switch. None of it was elegant, nor was it meant to be. I didn't care what it looked like, as long as it looked like an out.

As opposed to the ever-evolving glove adventures, I picked up a bat as a young boy, gripped it as best I could, swung it left-handed, and stuck with that for as long as I played. I wrapped my left hand around the handle and wedged my right hand—such as it was—slightly under that and then against the bat's knob. The knob was a big part of keeping a strong grip, so my right hand wouldn't come off and send the bat flying, which it occasionally did anyway. As a sophomore I'd unintentionally flung a bat into the opposing team's dugout, where everybody looked big, unhappy, and maybe unwilling to aid in the return of the bat. As I started uneasily toward the dugout, the bat came flying back and tumbled to a stop near my feet. Hitters let go of bats now and then. Still, I couldn't help but be embarrassed, like the very outcome everyone had expected had indeed been a helicoptering bat. And now in the middle of a ballgame, making my way back to the batter's box, I was one-handed again.

I could hit a fastball. The idea of my swing was to get the bat heading on a plane toward the ball, which was possible even without a sure grip or great front-side strength. When I started seeing better breaking balls as I got older, those adjustments were difficult. I couldn't manipulate the bat that way. But I believed I could hit and pestered every coach I ever had to give me the chance.

Besides, ballplayers pitched and had a position and hit. I wanted to be a ballplayer. I *was* a ballplayer. So, when Holec sat me down after my junior year for another talk, I figured it would be about developing another pitch during the Connie Mack season, or getting stronger, or taking care of my arm.

"Jim," he said, "any thoughts about playing football?"

Football?

"Your dad was a heckuva player," he said. "You're a good athlete. We need a backup quarterback."

Quarterback?

"I don't know," I said. "I've never played organized tackle."

"Think it over," he said. "Practice starts first week of August."

Connie Mack ball was about as cool as it comes. We had home and road uniforms, along with jackets that looked impressive at parties. Players came from all over the county, some headed to college programs. It was my first experience with and against such high-end competition. We won a lot of games and I made a lot of friends. The season went for most of the summer, so I was hardly thinking of anything else when the phone rang one morning.

"It's Coach Holec," the voice said.

"Hey, Coach," I said.

"It's the first day of football practice."

"Uh-huh."

"Get your butt out here."

So I became a backup quarterback and a punter, practicing every day and playing occasionally when the starting quarterback was hurt, holding secret desires to quit and never come back, but drawn to the romance of game night and a loud, passionate locker room that was so unlike baseball.

Again, the simplest tasks took time. The exchange from center required thought, as did a handoff to the left, when the back of my hand—not the ball—would face the running back. For the snap, my left hand was the top hand, placed deep—and rather intimately— under center. I'd lean right so my right forearm was low enough to guide the ball to my left hand. My center was extremely patient. For the backhanded handoff, I'd grip the ball close to a pointed end and offer it up like an ice-cream cone. I could throw, though. I could always throw.

These were the skills I took to the sidelines every Friday night, where I would appear quite prepared while watching my teammates win football games. I punted right-footed, an incongruity I tried not to give too much thought to.

That team led with its skill players, with Division I types at quarterback (Randy Levels) and both offensive ends (Terence Greene, the basketball player, and David Burks). The following fall, Greene would play basketball for Ray Meyer at DePaul University. Burks went to Wisconsin to play football. Levels became the quarterback at Central Michigan. I folded in, ran the coming opponent's plays in practice, took just enough first-team snaps in case calamity struck, and generally acted like the guy on loan from the baseball team.

We played our games at Atwood Stadium, an iconic brick-and-mortar structure in downtown Flint that lit up for football every Friday night. It reeked of six decades of football games and of history; in that U-shaped stadium, more than 20,000 people turned out for President Franklin D. Roosevelt in 1936 and, twenty-four years later, 13,000 attended Senator John F. Kennedy's presidential campaign stop. My dad played there. In Flint, everybody's dad played there.

We won often. And we followed the football routine of preparation, preparation, preparation, game. Football for me did not carry the personal consequences of baseball, beyond the usual comfort of inclusion. And winning, of course. My expectations were lower. I did not consider perfection, never mind demand it. The guys were fun, the games were fun, and I did what I could.

With the playoffs one regular-season game away, the practice routine began to change. I was getting more repetitions with the first team. There seemed a greater urgency to have me ready. As the team grew more curious, the head coach, Joe Eufinger, announced before a practice that Levels, our quarterback, would not play. He was academically ineligible. Like that, the season had found me. I was excited and reasonably optimistic. Even so, a stomachache developed Monday afternoon and hung around all week.

In my first start, a conservative game plan beat Flint Northern, our bitter rival, 43–14. Due to a quirk in the Flint school system, my math and science classes were on the Northern campus. I knew a few of the Northern players. In honor of my start at quarterback that night, some went to school wearing tube socks over their right hands and forearms. It bothered me, and the win tasted particularly good. I leaned on Greene and Burkes, along with tailback Ken Franklin and fullback Daryl Gilliam. I dutifully ran the plays that came in from the sidelines, mostly stayed behind our offensive line, and once rolled left and scored a two-point conversion. I needed time on the field to establish that I could stay out of the way of a win, and we needed an eighth win to continue the season.

It came, easily, and I'd begun to feel the rhythm of the game. The state playoffs opened the following week against perennially talented Midland, who had beaten us in the regular season with a stout defense and a relentless ground game, our only loss. And we'd be without our starting quarterback.

On a Saturday afternoon, Atwood Stadium was near full. Dad was up there, halfway to the press box, near the left-side 40-yard line. He sat with Mom and Chad amid a cluster of other parents. They huddled under ponchos and umbrellas, shivering against a cold rain.

As a boy Dad had sat in those stands for the biggest Friday night games. During halftimes he'd meet the other boys on the lawn outside the open end of the stadium. They'd choose sides for skeleton games of tackle, adopting the names of the players from Central or Northern or whoever was playing that night. Years later, St. Matt's won some big football games on that field. Dad knew the place well. In the minutes before game time, I could almost feel his anxiety for me. He knew I was nervous. The team had played well to get there and I didn't want to be the reason we lost. There was more: I hoped that whatever came Dad would be proud of me. Around Flint, carrying the name Abbott meant hearing a lot about Mike Abbott, the two-way football player and three-sport star. Though he'd say he identified first with basketball, which I'd washed out of three years before, I thought of him as a football player. He was tough like that. He talked more like a football player and related to the game in ways that he didn't to baseball.

Dad was barely in his mid-thirties. As I approached adulthood, not all that many years after he'd gotten there, our relationship was complex. He was effusive in his affection for Chad and me. He told us he loved us unconditionally and we believed him. He established rules and fundamental values, left us to our lives outside the house, enjoyed the victories and soothed the failures. When I disappointed him, I was filled with remorse. When I brought home a good report card or pitched well in front of him, I sought his praise. I looked forward to those moments and wanted him to be proud.

Dad seemed to be in a continuous search, however, for something. Sometimes it wouldn't be at home. He'd fight with Mom and leave. We figured he'd be back and he always did return eventually. But in the meantime we'd all be a little raw. Mom wasn't the same, the house was quieter, and my thoughts were never far from the drive-way, which I'd stare at, wondering when Dad's car would pull in. There were times I resented the way he treated Mom, and how his disappearances distressed her. I was protective of her, not him. By my senior year at Central, their relationship seemed to be in a tumultuous place, and I secretly wished my athletic achievements would somehow bring them together and then keep them together. I hoped our house would be more peaceful. My desire for them to be together was even stronger than my yearning for his approval. On a rainy fall night at Atwood Stadium, they were together. We were all together. It felt good.

The game was hyped all week. From the talk around school, stories in *The Flint Journal,* and the mood at practices, the buildup was unlike anything I'd seen. Coach Eufinger was a large, gravelly-voiced, well-regarded man who'd played offensive and defensive tackle at Central and then at Purdue. As that might suggest, he favored a running game. He'd adjusted to the speed and talent of our receivers, however, so our offense leaned toward the wide open, which had grown on him. He loved this team, as it was so rich in senior talent and character. He delivered an even speech about doing our jobs, trusting our teammates, and leaving it all out there, and then the senior captains began to shout. The locker room was as Spartan as they come, adorned with little more than hooks and benches. But it was filled with uncommon friendship and trust. For an afternoon and for this generation, these were the faces of Central, the black ones and the white ones, the true colors of Central. The fear of my early days there, and the scars of that stairwell whipping and others like it, had been replaced by admiration and a common cause. I wondered if everyone felt the same. I hoped they did. I joined in the chorus of camaraderie, and when our captains bolted for the door, we chased them onto the sodden artificial turf.

The following two and a half hours were surreal. Everything went right. Every play cut through the Midland defense. Every ball I threw found a receiver, and every receiver found a seam to the end zone. Accurate passes found their targets. Inaccurate passes found other friendly hands. Four went for touchdowns.

Near the end, we led, 26–20. The ball was deep in our territory. We needed only to punt the ball away to win. I stood twelve yards behind the snapper, wiping my hands on my pants against the rain. On the sideline, Coach Eufinger grinned and thought, *Here we are, a play from going to the state semifinals, it's pouring rain, the ball is soaking wet, and my punter has one hand. It's beautiful.* His faith in me was remarkable. I took the snap waist-high, swung my leg, and watched the ball fly away. We were going to the state semis.

From the field I watched my parents leave the stands. They'd go out to celebrate with the other parents. Tired and cold, I went home. The kitchen was dark. When I turned on the light, on the breakfast nook table was a page of notebook paper, and on that a few words of Dad's half-printed, half-cursive handwriting. I held the note to the light. It read:

Proud of you son.
          —Dad

He believed he'd seen me approach manhood that afternoon, when the playing field was something other than a diamond, and the game was something other than baseball, and the odds were long. He knew I was a little afraid. Those days he'd sent me back into the world weren't so easy on him, either. He was afraid, too. Now I'd gone out on my own, nodded, leaned in to take an uneasy snap, and helped win a game he knew everything about.

The following Saturday, we'd play Ann Arbor Pioneer in East Lansing. The winner would play in the Pontiac Superdome for the state title. Network television came to town to do a Thanksgiving Day story on the one-handed quarterback from Flint. It was a heady week, and then I threw six interceptions, all that had gone right against Midland went wrong against Pioneer, and we lost. And that was the end of football for me.

CHAPTER 8

In the dugout, I held the previous three outs in my hand. It might have looked like a paper cup half filled with water, but to me it was an inning gone by. I'd taken to marking my innings with cups, the first inning turned upside down on the shelf behind me, the second on top of that, the third soon to be stacked on those. My navy Yankees jacket zipped to my collarbone and a white towel draped around my neck, I studied the water in that cup, considered the dugout stairs covered in green outdoor carpeting, mulled the various liquids that pooled on the dugout floor.

Maldonado had been fooled on the last pitch in the top of the third inning, swinging over a curveball, trying not to at the last instant, flipping the bat away with disgust. In my head I held on to that release point, the feel of the ball rolling out of my hand, and waited for the fourth inning when all the runs I'd need arrived.

Bob Milacki, a big, thick right-hander, had started for the Indians and hadn't given up a hit through two innings. After spending most of the season pitching for the Indians' Triple-A team in Charlotte, Milacki was making his first big-league start in almost a year, when along came one of those innings that leaves a pitcher feeling terribly helpless.

To begin with, he walked Mike Gallego. Randy Velarde popped up a bunt that Milacki's catcher, Ortiz, made a terrific play on, diving down the third-base line for the out. Wade Boggs—being Wade Boggs—hooked a fastball and turned a good pitch away into a single to right field. It put runners at first and second, one out, for Dion James, a left-handed hitter who was having one of his better seasons but had one hit in his last eleven at-bats. He banged a 3-and-1 fastball through Milacki's legs and into center field, which should have scored Gallego and only Gallego, but instead scored everyone, including James.

The old Yankee Stadium's infield was crowned, presumably to promote drainage, and the grass was pretty long. From the dugout you couldn't see infielders' feet, ankles, or most of their shins. In moments like this, in order to see everything, everyone would slide off the bench, try not to slam their heads on the roof, and scale a step or two.

Gallego scored. Boggs dragged his sore back around second base and made for third, taking a chance on Kenny Lofton's arm. Lofton threw a two-hopper that skipped past third baseman Jim Thome while James trailed into second base, and Boggs scored while Thome fetched the ball in foul territory, over by the Indians' dugout. When Thome threw to the plate—a one-hopper through Ortiz's legs—James advanced to third. Then—when the ball rolled into the Yankees' dugout—he was awarded home. In the end: a three-run, two-error single that gave us a 3–0 lead.

Just to revisit, it's September, I've made twenty-six previous starts for the Yankees, and I've got nine wins. I'd won once since July. Now I'm ahead 3–0 going into the fourth inning, I haven't given up a hit, my stuff feels pretty good, and I'm trying to force thoughts of a win out of my head. My battle between innings was to quiet my mind, let go of what had already happened and the anxiety of what might happen. The time in between innings was used to reboot, clear my thoughts, rest my mind. Sometimes I'd listen to a song in my head, play it over and over, to escape the din and slow the game. To symbolize another fresh start, I'd gently swing my foot back and forth across the dugout floor, sweeping away the sunflower seeds and balled-up cups and gum wrappers. In Anaheim the floor was rubber matting, in New York it was that green carpet that reminded me of artificial turf, in Chicago—the old Comiskey Park—it was weathered wooden planks. I wiped away the past inning, watched the game, hoped for runs.

Scoring some runs—especially like we had—allowed me to believe that maybe things were going to go right today.

Man, I wanted to win a game. I won eighteen times in 1991, pitched better in 1992 and won only seven. It would be hard to exaggerate how hard it seemed to win a game by the end of 1993. After my first start that season—I pitched a complete game and beat David Cone and the Kansas City Royals in front of 57,000 people in the home opener—a writer asked if I wasn't a bit too happy about it, considering it was April 12 and there were five and a half months still to play. I was just damned happy to win a ballgame, and always was. I tried not to make it a focus during a game, but it wasn't ever far from my mind.

By the conclusion of that inning—Mattingly struck out, Danny Tartabull, the DH, popped to second base—I'd left those thoughts behind. I returned to the process of pitching, of tuning out the world and tuning in Nokes and the Indians, of trusting that I was good enough to do this, pitch by pitch.

Ten pitches later—Fermin grounded to Gallego, who made a great backhanded play on a well-hit ball, while Baerga also hit a grounder to Gallego and Belle pounded a cutter away to Boggs—I returned to the dugout, and went to add another cup to the stack. I was twelve outs in.

CHAPTER 9

The drive from Berrien Springs, near the southern tip of Lake Michigan, to Flint took almost three hours—longer, perhaps, in a worn Chrysler K car, which Don Welke preferred. The older baseball scouts told Welke he'd wreck his back running around the Midwest in that little thing, but he would laugh, say it suited him just fine, put another 200,000 miles on it, and go buy another. When Welke believed in something, there wasn't much talking him out of it.

In the summer of 1985, some two thousand miles on that odometer were dedicated to trips to Flint.

Among the first scouts hired by the expansion Toronto Blue Jays almost eight years before, Welke had been drawn east across the state by a phone call from Walt Head, a coach in Flint who had once scouted for the Baltimore Orioles and Blue Jays. Head told Welke there was a left-handed pitcher in town he might want to take a look at. The kid was in deep with the college guys down at Ann Arbor, Head said, but he threw hard and competed like few he'd ever coached, so it might be worth the drive. "Don," Head said before saying good-bye, "he doesn't have a right hand, but you'd never know it."

Intrigued, Welke pointed his K car toward Flint just as the high school baseball season was starting, when Michigan hadn't yet shaken winter. The baseball field at Central was only just thawing out. Welke came early and didn't say much. He wasn't one for announcing his presence, handing out cards, inflating the hopes of boys who'd probably be disappointed come draft day. There was, however, no mistaking what Welke was. His broad shoulders, barrel chest, close-cropped hair, steady stare, and binder outed him as a scout.

That first afternoon, Welke introduced himself to no one. During the game, he'd drift from the stands to the backstop to the edge of the dugout, watching and listening. This was how he'd measured Dave Stieb, how he'd one day look over Pat Hentgen and John Olerud—from the shadows. Few ever called him about a guy who couldn't play. They could all play, at least a little. What Welke wanted to see were facial expressions. He wanted to hear a prospect talk to his teammates. He wanted to see his eyes, then decide what was behind them.

Was this kid selfish? Was he a team guy? Did he know how to win? Minor-league ball was a meat grinder: Did he want it bad enough?

Head, Welke thought, was right about this left-hander. He had a good, loose arm that ran it up there from 88 to 90, sometimes 91. The velocity was effortless. He'd get more out of a body that was six foot three, too, as he had plenty of filling out to do. He commanded his pitches from a delivery that, in spite of his length, was rather compact. Welke couldn't take his eyes off him. He believed this lefty had nothing short of a golden arm, one that projected even more velocity as it matured.

Of the thousands of high school ballplayers Welke had seen, few jumped off a baseball diamond because of their competitiveness. The sport didn't always allow it. In a team game wrapped in individual moments, sometimes the game just never gets around to one player. But a pitcher could drag a game along with him through will alone, and Welke looked out at this lefty and thought how easy he made it look.

If there were two things Welke had learned scouting over the years—and, really, there were more like a million—they were: Anytime you see a guy do something easy, you better pay attention; and, there are no absolutes in baseball.

This lefty, Welke believed, carried desire that was bigger than his talent. He carried himself genuinely. He liked his teammates. They liked him. And, dang, if he couldn't hit, too.

Welke often took special interest in the young men other scouts left behind. He was curious about the troublemakers, the attitude problems, the boys with the tainted backgrounds. He took longer looks at players who clearly were injured but playing through the pain for the good of the team. He scouted deaf kids and fat kids and kids whose growth spurts had temporarily rendered them clumsy. He watched their hands and their feet, wondering if they were windows to their baseball futures, their baseball souls.

The only absolute, Welke thought again as he leaned against the backstop and watched the lefty, is there are no absolutes.

When the game ended, Welke walked to the K car waiting in the parking lot. He had three hours to cover on the ride home. He had spoken to no one and hadn't ever broken his poker face, hadn't even raised an eyebrow as the lefty overwhelmed an overmatched lineup. He had, however, filled a few pages in a notebook, some of it from memory while the car idled in the parking lot. In a life filled with highway rest-stop food and fool's gold, Welke mused that days like this were the reward. In a gritty neighborhood on Flint's East Side, he'd witnessed a can't-miss arm attached to a can't-miss fighter. He was sure of it.

He closed his notebook, laid it on the passenger side of the front bench seat, and put the K car in drive. He would not return, he decided, for many weeks. In a matter of two hours, he'd come to believe this lefty was special. Hanging around through the season, getting friendly with the kid and his family, would only signal to other area scouts and their big-league teams that the Blue Jays were on him. Welke wouldn't draw their attention. He wasn't in the business of doing other people's work for them. The other scouts, those who maybe believed in absolutes, would have to make up their own minds.

Back in Berrien Springs, Welke started his report for the Blue Jays and their scouting director, Bob Engle. The draft was more than two months away, but he did the paperwork before his thoughts drifted into the next long stretch of road, the next kid.

Under the heading ABBOTT, JIM, he wrote: "Left-handed pitcher. 6-3, 180. Great arm. Good changeup. Makings of a breaking ball. Natural cutter. Big competitor. Good athlete. Plays football. Good hitter."

Over the final line, his pen hung over the paper for a moment before adding four words: "Has no right hand."

Then he walked across the room and powered up the fax machine.

SOME COLLEGE COACHES had their assistants handle much of the recruiting, and that meant covering most of the miles. Some employed pitching coaches.

Bud Middaugh traveled, and Bud Middaugh was his own pitching coach.

When he drove up to Flint from Ann Arbor in the summer of
1984, he'd been the head coach at Michigan for five years. He was in
his mid-forties then, and you knew by the way he held his eyes on
you that he expected ballplayers to be ballplayers. For Middaugh,
you could play or you couldn't, you did things right or you didn't,
and there wasn't much in between.

In Michigan and the surrounding Midwest, a college coach could
drive for weeks and not find exactly what he was looking for, not like
in California and Florida where the ground never froze, the gloves
never toughened in the cold, and the kids played year round. Middaugh, like a pro scout, had to look across a field and calculate what
a boy might look like in a twelve-month program such as Michigan's. He called it "projecting," which is what pro area scouts and
cross-checkers did all the time, except Middaugh forecast a boy of
seventeen into a young man of nineteen and twenty, which wasn't a
lot of time.

Middaugh was in Flint on a tip from a Michigan booster who
lived in town, who'd called to rave about this lefty on a local Connie
Mack team. Sometimes you can trust a booster, and sometimes he's
somebody's overzealous uncle. Mid-morning, Middaugh had put everything aside to haul that straight shot up US 23 to watch a game
of summer ball. He'd first called Central's counseling office to check
on the lefty's grades; there'd be no sense making even an hour's drive
if the boy couldn't hack it in school. The lady there told him the
lefty was a fine student and that she heard he'd be on the football
team this fall. *Football, too,* Middaugh thought, and then he just had
to see what this kid was all about. He'd never seen a ballplayer like

the one the booster had described. Heck, he'd never even *heard* of one.

Middaugh sat in the bleachers and watched the lefty pitch. He was a big, tall kid with solid arm action, Middaugh thought. He wandered along the chain-link fence on the first-base line when there was a runner on first, to see how the lefty looked out of the stretch. Could he hold a runner? He wandered up the third-base line for another angle on his mechanics. The lefty was throwing hard, he could see, but his stride took him across his body. Middaugh decided he'd get another three or four miles per hour on that fastball if he'd come cleaner to the plate. He wondered how coachable he'd be. As he watched, one thought did nag at him: Could I protect him? Those were big kids in the Big Ten and they swung aluminum bats. Then: Would they bunt him all day? Could he *compete* there?

Middaugh didn't take a note. He didn't even carry a pencil. There was no sense letting on to other programs, to the pro scouts, that he was around. It was the game they all played and nobody had to know anybody else's notions, least of all his. On a veteran Michigan team, he needed a freshman to walk onto campus and give him innings. A left-hander—a big, rangy left-hander with a hard fastball—well, that would be even better.

On the hour back to Ann Arbor, Middaugh stirred in his mind what he'd seen. The big fastball, so overpowering Middaugh had not had a chance to analyze any of the breaking stuff. The kid hadn't needed it. The slightly skewed mechanics. The composure. As he drove, he realized the lefty hadn't even thrown an inning before he'd made up his mind. He knew he wanted him at Michigan. And he'd all but forgotten the kid didn't have a right hand.

BY THE SPRING of my senior year, the experiences of the previous four years—the spring and summer baseball seasons, the one season I'd spent on a football field, and then the interest from college coaches and professional scouts—had made me stronger and more confident.

In early April, Middaugh had called on signing day and I'd committed to Michigan, my dream school, simple as that. Other programs had called—Central Michigan, Western Michigan, and Michigan State—but Michigan's reputation, its aura, its uniforms, and its success were persuasive, particularly for a boy from Flint. I'd fold into a good team headlined by Casey Close, Scott Kamieniecki, and Hal Morris. And while Middaugh could not offer a full scholarship, the school would pay room, board, and books. My parents, who'd always preached education, would handle the tuition.

In my senior season at Central, I won 10 games, three of them no-hitters. My ERA was 0.76. I struck out two batters an inning. I played first base, batted cleanup, and hit .427 with seven home runs and 36 RBIs. We were conference champions. In case I'd forgotten, the newspaper reporters and television crews were eager to remind me I was first a one-handed pitcher and then a ballplayer.

It wasn't just them, either. I'd pitched for going on six years in ballparks all over Flint, so the novelty of my condition had faded for some. Not for all. In a game against Bay City, a team we'd beaten easily, its bench had found a place to soothe itself in defeat—at the end of my right arm. I'd heard it before, tuned it out before. Still, I heard the insults, the familiar taunts. When Coach Holec came for the ball in the sixth inning, hoping to save some pitches for another day, I looked at him blankly. He held out his hand and I refused to place the ball in it.

"Nope," I said. "I want to stay in and pitch."

He peered over at the Bay City players. It wasn't anything he hadn't heard before, either. He understood this wasn't his fight. It was mine.

He nodded, patted me on the back, and returned to the dugout. I finished the game and left satisfied.

LATE IN THE season, Don Welke fired up the K car and headed east. He drove past Flint, through Detroit and to Dearborn, where Engle, the Blue Jays' scouting director, waited at the airport. The draft was near. They drove together to Flint. The lefty Welke had written up was pitching in a playoff game. Maybe a thousand people would be there and Welke wanted to make one more argument for the lefty, this time with his boss. Engle, in turn, would report to the Blue Jays' general manager, Pat Gillick.

Against all convention, the lefty was number one on Welke's list of area prospects. That meant he rated him ahead of, among others, Barry Larkin, the slick All-American shortstop at Michigan. He'd introduced himself to the lefty on a previous visit, asked him his feelings about signing a pro contract, and been told the lefty's heart was in Ann Arbor, at Michigan. They exchanged phone numbers, and Welke told him to call anytime.

Welke arrived at Whaley Park with Engle, cased the stands, and spotted one other scout—a part-timer for the Kansas City Royals. In the din of the playoff game, the lefty struck out fifteen. Over the ninety minutes back to the airport, Welke and Engle drove in silence.

Finally, as Welke steered to the curb in front of the terminal, Engle turned to him and said, "You're telling Gillick about this one."

Welke smiled. There are no absolutes.

In his final report, he advised Gillick to sign the lefty. His worth in the draft, Welke advised, was $200,000. The first overall pick, a shortstop and catcher out of North Carolina named B. J. Surhoff, would later sign with the Milwaukee Brewers for $150,000.

The night before the 1985 draft, Gillick called Welke. "Don't change your mind on the guy," he told him. "We're going to take him."

Welke hung up and called the lefty.

"Any other scouts talk to you?" he asked.

"No."

"How about Detroit?"

"No."

Welke called Gillick back.

"Nobody else is on him," he said. "We can take him anywhere."

The Blue Jays selected me in the 36th round, 826th overall—and 822 players behind Larkin, who went fourth to the Cincinnati Reds. And they didn't agree with Welke's assessment. They offered $50,000 plus a college scholarship plan in case baseball didn't work out. The offer was more than decent. They flew me to Toronto to see Exhibition Stadium, pitch batting practice before a game, and meet manager Bobby Cox, along with some of the players. I was awed. I threw batting practice to the big leaguers, then shook their hands with the crossover, backhanded grip I'd practiced for years.

On the short flight home, I told Welke what a wonderful time I'd had.

"Jim," he said, "I didn't take you here to have a great time. I took you here to sign a professional baseball contract."

At the airport I called home. Mom picked up.

"I want to sign," I said.

"Come home," she said.

I enrolled at Michigan in the fall. Before I did, Welke sat at our kitchen table. He talked about pitching in college, about protecting my arm. Don't throw too often, he said. Get your rest. Avoid too many breaking balls. He shook my hand, and my mom's, and my dad's.

The first time they'd met, Dad asked Welke what he should make of the interest from the Blue Jays. Welke thought about that, about what Dad was asking. He could see how deeply Mike cared for his son and that this was his way of being protective. Mike didn't want his boy to be a publicity stunt. This was a delicate subject for Mike, Welke knew. It was delicate for him, too.

"Mike," Welke had said, "that's the farthest thing from my mind. I think the guy's going to be a top-flight major-league pitcher. That other stuff doesn't mean a thing to me. Nothing."

Two months later, Dad said good-bye to Welke on the front walk.

"Hey, Don," he said, a smile coming slowly. "We might have taken a hundred thousand."

Welke laughed at the joke, waved, and drove off in his K car.

As I prepared to leave for Michigan, it seemed that every banquet in the state had a Most Inspirational award. Dutifully, I attended. Everyone was very thoughtful. Even some of the Central coaches would attend, sometimes renting a van for the trips around the state, having a good time with it. Their support was meaningful then, just as it was in the daily practices. I'd find them in the audiences, still amazed at their capacities to believe in me, and the patience and faith it must have required. I sat beside the golfer Ken Venturi on a dais at a Detroit country club. He told me golf had helped ease a childhood stuttering problem and that he'd eventually overcome it. He looked at me like I'd understand.

Near the end of summer, there was one more banquet, a charity event in downtown Detroit at the massive Renaissance Center. Lou Holtz and Sugar Ray Leonard were going to be there. My parents came with me. I even had my own room and a rented tuxedo. It was a big deal. Somewhere in that summer, however, my view of the banquets and the awards they handed me had changed.

.   I didn't want to be there and, once I was, I didn't want to go downstairs. I didn't want to be known for this, for something I was born with rather than something I'd worked for. I hadn't done anything yet, hadn't even thrown a pitch in college. And everybody was treating me—looking at me—as if I was something more than a high school pitcher. I wasn't. The people were all very kind and well intentioned. Honestly, sometimes I wished they hadn't been.

Early that evening I went to my room to change into my tux and look over my public thank-yous, which I'd written on a note card. As I sat on the bed, thinking about the evening and the suit hanging in the closet, I thought I knew exactly what this award was for. But I wanted to win a college baseball game. I wanted to pitch in the big leagues. I wanted to win a Cy Young Award. I wanted to be more than a human-interest story.

Something felt wrong about taking those awards. I began to believe that every story about courage over adversity exhausted a little of the momentum I had. I wondered why I could not accept the praise as it was intended. Instead, what I felt was not pride, but unease; they were not only dragging me into recognition of a birth defect, but I was allowing it.

They called me courageous. I was a ballplayer. People called it more. I didn't see it. They said what I did was heroic. No way.

I searched for a defining sentiment. Was I mad? Was I bored? Was I impatient?

I settled on sad. What I wanted on a Saturday night in summer was to be with my friends, far away from this. And I wanted to know why a ceremony, an award, and a round of applause felt wrong.

And I began to cry. I wasn't even sure why.

Where was I headed? What was I becoming? I wondered.

About the same time, Donn Clarkson, the teacher who'd taught me to tie my shoes so many years before, stopped for a hot dog at Angelo's Coney Island on Davison Road in Flint. It was a place that fed assembly-line workers, judges, and everyone in between. While Clarkson waited on his dog, his eyes wandered to a photo hanging over a food case. Imagine that, he said to himself. It was that little boy with the prosthetic arm, but grown up, wearing a ball cap and a uniform. Near the photo, he read down a list of accomplishments, all that little boy had done on ball fields since he left third grade. He smiled broadly. Jimmy must be doing pretty well, he thought. Good for him. And he must come in here a lot.

What I wouldn't have given to have been at Angelo's that night.

Jim Schneider, the long-time media relations man at Michigan, used to tell me that my story was about outstanding timing.

I hadn't been on campus more than a few days before I met Schneider, a man of unusual enthusiasm for the institution and its teams, even by Ann Arbor standards. He'd seemingly keep a pile of media guides in his head. Anything about baseball that wasn't in those guides, well, that also was in his head. He also filtered the many media requests—the job Holec and my parents shared in high school—which for the first time I found daunting. I trusted Schneids to make sound decisions, and he was good at it. We connected over Michigan baseball, but there was more to it than that. He cared for me.

Three years later, as I prepared to leave Michigan, he reminded me again of my tendency to land on the happy side of chance. I laughed with Schneids, who had a funny way of looking at things, and did not disagree.

Those three years, beginning with my first day in the program and ending in the Seoul Olympics in 1988, were exceptionally gratifying. My mother's words from years before—every step is a gift, she'd said—echoed in my head many nights. I never assumed another inch, not until it was directly under my feet.

Maybe that's what Schneider was getting at, too. My baseball was part desperation, part gift, and part providence. Maybe everybody's is. Only I was the guy without a right hand, and great efforts were made to attach significance to anything that might have followed. I guess I thought making the high school team would change that. When it didn't, the varsity letter certainly would. But then, none of the wins or the conference championships or the All-Whatever teams dulled a perception that something special was happening. The awards, the cameras, and the long stares from the other dugout didn't make me feel special, they made me feel different.

But, wouldn't you know, stuff just kept coming. And, turned out, the harder I worked, the more people wanted to believe in me, and the more I believed in myself, the more often it came. That's not to say the journey was without its crashes. It wasn't.

By the time he, Mom, Chad, and I packed the Chevy Suburban and made toward Ann Arbor for my freshman year, Dad was having thoughts that preceded Schneider's right-place, right-time theories. Like there was some kind of plan for his firstborn. Already, parents of children with birth defects or amputations sought in me comfort for their personal challenges. I knew their burden. I sensed their fear, that their little boy or girl was headed toward a life that was less than satisfying, certainly less than they deserved. At seventeen, I hardly knew what to say, other than to smile and praise my own parents for their strength. They'd allowed me to fail. When I teetered, they let me fall, but strung the net. Those boys and girls were so sweet, their parents so scared, and I felt so helpless. How was I to articulate to them what I didn't understand myself?

If there was some plan, it was well beyond my reach. Instead, as the Suburban wound through the Michigan campus and arrived in front of Rumsey Hall, where the freshman ballplayers were housed, I was far more concerned with my left elbow. A long summer playing Connie Mack ball had left it sore. The season ended bitterly, both because I could barely comb my hair for the innings I'd pitched and because we'd lost at the end, costing the team—Grossi Baseball Club—a chance at the Connie Mack World Series in New Mexico. I was on the mound and suffered from a little wildness, a few hits, and a failed attempt to defend a double steal with runners on first and third. The defeat stung, and I bore the blame. My arm was killing me and I wasn't sure what I would have going into fall ball. So, after dragging a trunk to the dorm room, claiming the bottom bunk, and considering my new home, with some trepidation I said good-bye to my parents. They were tearful, but I was so thrilled to be there, on that campus, part of that history and legacy, a Michigan man at last.

Mom lingered in her hug and tears. Proud of me but anguished over letting me go, she was hardest to part with. In the years that followed, I'd conjure that image of her many times. I wanted to please and protect her, especially after I left home. Dad could be more difficult to satisfy, but, often, Mom's expectations drove me harder.

The University of Michigan was a huge place, all bricks and people, promise and nerves. In the courtyard outside the dorm, I met my roommate, a freshman infielder from Toledo, Jim Durham. Freshman girls mingled nearby. I hadn't much experience in that area, where I assumed a girl who liked me would have to be somewhat forgiving. Generally, my strategy was to let them come to me, which wasn't going all that great, but I thought probably saved me from a lot of humiliation.

As I ventured away from West Quad, a large square building with four halls—one of them Rumsey, built nearly fifty years before—on the perimeter, the size of the job ahead grew. The other freshmen—both in the classrooms and on the ball field—seemed so accomplished. The notion of competing with them in either arena was daunting, but inspiring. For a kid from Central, it was cool, like stepping into a world where just enough wasn't going to be near enough. I assumed I'd gotten a good education in Flint, then sat in the classrooms, listened to the conversations, tried to process the words, and thought, "Man, where the heck did you people learn all this stuff?"

My arm began to feel better. Maybe it was the excitement or the new jersey and cleats, but I was healthy, and then started to become the pitcher I would be. I had a cut fastball, though I didn't know it at the time and never called it that. It was just my fastball and naturally it would run toward right-handed hitters, though sometimes—and unpredictably—it wouldn't. I had a pitch that would sink on the left side of the plate. A slow curveball came and went. Following an afternoon practice during which the curveball was rather good, Middaugh and I studied videotape of the throwing session, trying to reconstruct the mechanics that had made it effective. In spite of numerous rewatchings, the curveball remained something of a mystery, and then blended into a slider, developed after reading in a book how Tom Seaver threw his. I began lowering my arm angle—somewhere around three-quarters—against lefties and righties, which became effective.

Practices were held at Ray Fisher Stadium, which hosted its first collegiate baseball game in 1923. Michigan beat Ohio State, 3–2, in a game that, appropriately enough, was called after five innings because of rain. Occasionally we'd throw from the main mound of the ballpark. The surrounding stands were old, tall, and made of steel, extending from first to third base. When they were empty, the sound of the ball hitting the catcher's mitt was loud, authoritative, bringing a sense of great velocity. Middaugh was changing my mechanics, which I'd shadow practice in my dorm room, in the hallway outside his office, eventually even in airport gate areas. I was throwing harder, beginning to command my pitches and starting to believe I could pitch well enough to help the team.

I was also having a pretty good time. The incoming freshmen ballplayers were talented and, well, free-spirited. I became close with most of them, guys such as Chris Lutz, Doug Kaiser, Billy St. Peter, Darren Campbell, Mike Gillette, and Durham. Coming from Flint, I was no angel myself. But these guys were especially adept at making a good time where there wasn't one. If there wasn't trouble to be had, they'd often enough make their own. St. Peter, who'd go on to spend four years in the Chicago Cubs organization before making his name as a pro walleye fisherman, was especially gifted in that area. We'd had a couple beers one night when we discovered a duck pond behind a fraternity. St. Peter captured a duck and with great pride carried it from party to party like it was a living, breathing, irritated man purse. When the duck smelled freedom back at the dorm, it made a dash for it, just ahead of six of us who hounded it through the hallways. This is where our senses of humor tended to run, and they ran a lot.

A few weeks into the semester, I was having the time of my life. I kept thinking about the movie *The Big Chill,* and understanding why the characters thought so highly of their years at Michigan. The football team opened with a win against Notre Dame and lost once all season. There seemed to be a party on every corner. Bruce Springsteen and Pink Floyd were on my headphones, providing escape when I needed it. I didn't even mind the dorm food. And by spring, I was learning how to pitch.

We won 47 games my freshman season, of which I was the winning pitcher in six, and during which Schneids began developing his right-place, right-time principle. My first collegiate win was against North Carolina. After a couple rocky early starts, I came in in relief against the Tar Heels in a tie game. Two were out and a runner was at third. On a return throw from the catcher, I heard something from my right, glimpsed a commotion near third base. The coach was urging the runner to "go, go, go." And he was gesturing. The runner made for the plate.

Later, my coaches and teammates would agree that the tactic was unseemly and bush league. To me, it was baseball. *My* baseball. Trying to steal a run on my glove switch was no different from having the first eight batters in a lineup lay down bunts, which happened once in Little League. (The first batter reached base, the next seven didn't.) It was no different from taunting me from the dugout, which was routine. The game and my hand's place in it were metaphoric like that. Like life, baseball would go along as usual, me riding along, and then with the slightest tilt there'd be seventeen players on one side of the field and me on the other. I was different, and always was.

Yet, to have it happen here, in college, in a game of Division I powers, and with everyone watching and judging, was unsettling.

Middaugh had called upon me for a big out and I stood on the mound calming my nerves and thinking of my mechanics, barely aware that I might be vulnerable. It was the perfect play.

As the players on our bench shouted an alarm, I caught the ball, made the switch, and threw out the runner by ten feet. In Michigan's half of the inning, Casey Close singled and Hal Morris hit a home run to right field that landed in the parking lot of a car dealership. Then Close, a senior who'd given up pitching in order to specialize as an outfielder—and batted .440 with 19 home runs as a result, and was named Baseball America's national player of the year—was summoned to pitch for one of only two times that season. He got the last nine Tar Heels in order. By the end, it seemed the coaching staff and my teammates were determined to punish North Carolina for its temerity.

I appreciated the support. It was kind of them. I'd been ecstatic to get the out, to get us off the field still tied. But sitting in the dugout afterward, I was embarrassed. What must my teammates be thinking of me? Would this be a constant ploy over the season? Surely, one guy thrown out at the plate hadn't answered all the questions for them or for me. Was this what it was going to be like from now on? Already, Middaugh and I had spent dozens of hours drilling on bunt plays. And still he'd have the first and third basemen play closer when I pitched, which meant hard-hit balls down the lines had less chance of being caught and middle infielders had to cover more ground.

Now this.

I scraped at the dugout floor with my cleat. I was different. There was no getting around it, and there wasn't much use pretending otherwise.

Middaugh tapped me on the shoulder.

"Nice job," he said.

I wondered.

The experience at Michigan went that way: Personal and athletic growth followed subtle indignities that I tried to keep to myself. Probably no one noticed, but I couldn't be sure.

The season ended for me with a long relief appearance against Minnesota in the Big Ten tournament, a live fastball, a lot of strikeouts, and a team win. After trying to find my way, reworking my delivery, adapting to the best baseball I'd ever competed against, I was getting more comfortable. Through the usual internal bouts with confidence, and as games and time passed, I was becoming pretty sure I belonged.

The feeling grew over the summer, which I split between arranging Anheuser-Busch products in markets for Dad's beer distributorship and pitching for an Ann Arbor summer league team with some of my Michigan teammates. In my final start before my sophomore year, in front of a sellout crowd in a wonderful old ballpark—Point Stadium in Johnstown, Pennsylvania—I pitched one of the better games of my life. So, into fall ball and then into spring, the anxiety that chased me onto campus a year before had mostly dissolved. I was in the right place, and at the right time, like Schneider said.

The 1987 team won 52 games and lost 12. We won another Big Ten championship. We lost again in the NCAA regional. And I won 11 games. The Golden Spikes Award, the first given to a pitcher, followed from that season, as did a place on the USA Baseball team, which traveled most of the summer, including to Cuba.

The game already had taken me to many places, but there was nothing quite like the Cuban experience.

Fidel Castro was larger than I expected him to be. His eyes were gray. He wore military fatigues made, I think, of silk.

He had emerged from the visitors' dugout at Havana's Estadio Latinoamericano surrounded by security personnel, their shirttails laid over bulges on their belts. The crowd, 50,000 or more that summer day in 1987, cheered him wildly. The Cuban National Team had rushed to greet him when he'd waved from the stands behind home plate, but not us, Team USA. We'd looked over to Ron Fraser, our coach and the long-time, well-regarded coach at the University of Miami. He shook his head, as if to say, *Nobody moves.* He'd lived in Miami for three decades, had a lot of Cuban friends, and I assumed then he had his opinions about el Presidente.

Castro disappeared under the stands and reached the field through the visitors' clubhouse, the crowd roaring again when he stepped onto the field for the start of a seven-game exhibition series. We stared blankly, unsure of our obligations to our host. His aide asked that we line up so that Castro could greet us.

For more than a week we'd had the impression we were being watched every moment, from our workouts to our afternoon strolls searching for edible sustenance after being served pork—with the skin and hair still on it—and fried cow brains. The suspicion was confirmed one afternoon at the Hotel Habana Libre. A handful of us were horsing around in our rooms when we spilled into the hallway, and in the commotion a baseball bounced through an open window. We were on the twelfth floor. Alarmed, and somewhat fearful of the consequences, we frantically dashed to our rooms, slammed the doors shut, and hoped that was the end of it. A knock on the door came only a few minutes later. A middle-aged man stood with his shoes on the threshold. He wore an oversized button-down shirt with pockets on the front and a sober expression, like most of the security men on the island. He was neither amused nor angry. He held the baseball.

Without a word, he handed back the baseball, turned, and disappeared down the hall.

Now Castro stood before us. He approached me with his translator just off his shoulder, extended his left hand and in Spanish complimented me on my play. He grinned and playfully—I assumed—cuffed my head with his right hand. At that moment I'd wished I knew more about Castro, about Cuba, about the revolution and all that had gone on here. In the cities and the countryside there had been billboards extolling communism and Castro, and promising great rewards for the people's sacrifices, but I'd been taken more by their love for baseball. So, as I smiled and nodded at Castro I wondered if I should have been so gracious, and after what seemed a long time was relieved when he moved away from me and toward my teammates.

Before Castro left he addressed us as a group, his translator filling in the pauses for our benefit. He said that while our countries did not share political ideology, the people did share a belief in culture and arts and, of course, baseball. He said that if there was anything we needed, we should ask "my people." And he said he hoped we enjoyed the island and who "we are as people." I thought he sounded genuine. And then he left.

We all looked at one another, smiling slightly, retaking our bearings. Then we lost the first two games of the series.

I was to start game three. A U.S. team hadn't won on Cuban soil in a quarter century. The big stadium was packed and loud and the sun seemed to be burning holes into our caps. The local paper had announced that the one-handed pitcher would start that afternoon, and as I warmed up Cubans crowded to the railings, yelled my name, and pointed to my hand. Their voices were nearly lost in the shrill of horns and bongos and sirens from higher in the stands, but their passion for their game—and this game—would not be obscured.

I'd never witnessed such a scene, much less pitched in one.

Ron Fraser, pitching coach Jim Morris, and I had thought a lot about this game, about how to beat the mighty Cubans of Victor Mesa, Lourdes Gourriel, Omar Linares, Orestes Kindelan, and others. Every time we played, Linares, the third baseman, was the best player on the field. Their reputation was as perhaps the best fastball-hitting team in the world and yet they'd hammered breaking balls in the first two games of the series. I'd pitch off my fastball, try not to miss in, and hope that worked.

The first batter in the first inning was Mesa, the most flamboyant of the Cubans on a roster that played with style. A center fielder with amazing skills, speed, and personality, Mesa was known as El Loco, or "The Orange Explosion," and the people loved him. At the sight of him in the batter's box, jumping around, twirling his bat, readying himself against this pitcher, the crowd stood and hollered and stomped its feet. The old stadium shook in anticipation.

I threw a fastball near the middle of the plate. And Mesa bunted. Of course he did. The ball rolled near the third-base line as Mesa flew from the box. I dashed from the mound, barehanded the ball, turned and threw as hard as I could toward first.

On a bang-bang play, Mesa was out.

The place went nuts. The Cubans stood on their seats, threw their arms in the air, and cheered the play, the call, and the pluck of this pitcher they'd read about in the paper that morning. Mesa had thrown his helmet in disgust and was arguing with the first-base umpire.

Despite the heat and a weak stomach brought about by unfamiliar food, I pitched deep into the game and we won. We'd played well and we'd won. For a couple dozen young ballplayers, most of us experiencing international baseball for the first time and the core of a team that would go on to play in the Pan American Games later that summer and the Olympics the following year, the victory was not insignificant. We'd stood in the heart of the Cuban capital against some of the best players we'd ever seen, we'd hung together, and we'd won. We'd win two more times in the series, too.

The locals had taken to calling my name in broken English on the streets, and it was strange to be recognized so far from home. I'd had difficulty getting back to the hotel after pitching. The sidewalk outside our clubhouse and narrow street that led away from the old stadium were nearly impassable because of the people who'd massed there. They shouted and grabbed hold of my jersey, and the security guards pushed back, and eventually a small path cleared for Fraser and me to squeeze through. The bus then led a slow parade of Cubans through the streets toward the team hotel.

Life and baseball, for all of us, had taken a dramatic turn.

A FEW WEEKS earlier we'd walked into a large room with high ceilings and several rows of bunk beds, the bachelors officers' quarters at Naval Air Station Memphis. The 3,800-acre base was actually in Millington, Tennessee, about forty miles north of Memphis, and a long way from Cape Cod, where I'd planned on pitching for the summer. For a Northern boy, the South's sweetened tea, fried food, and slower pace were a charming diversion.

The facilities there included a baseball diamond and room enough to board about forty of us invited by USA Baseball. Those of us who made it through the cuts would form the core of a team that would represent the country in the 1987 Pan American Games in Indianapolis, the 1988 Olympic Games in Seoul, Korea, and, soon, before any of that, the seven-game exhibition series in Cuba.

I'd just finished my sophomore season at Michigan. One of the benefits of staying in one place for a decent period of time—the east end of Flint, Central High, then Michigan—was the routine. New environments meant old questions, old awkwardness, old reminders. I knew everyone was watching. I knew their curiosity. Eventually, if I stayed around long enough, my disability would be forgotten, or at least become familiar enough to have lost its appeal as a conversation subject.

But that would take time.

Pretty soon I'd be Jim or Jimmy or Abby. But, first, I knew, I had to be the one-handed pitcher, play that for a while. They'd stick out their right hands and I'd grab on with my left, establish that. Then we'd go play ball, establish that. I'd laugh at the jokes, make a few myself, be one of the guys, establish that. Usually it was enough. But that doesn't mean that it happened quickly enough for me.

Tino Martinez was there from the University of Tampa; Ty Griffin from Georgia Tech; Dave Silvestri from the University of Missouri; Gregg Olson from Auburn; Mike Fiore from Miami; Pat Combs from Baylor; Ted Wood from the University of New Orleans; Scott Servais from Creighton; Ed Sprague from Stanford; Scott Livingstone from Texas A&M; Frank Thomas from Clemson; the one-handed guy from Michigan.

That summer in southwest Tennessee was hot, presumably like all summers in southwest Tennessee. We were holed up on the Navy base, practicing twice a day, sleeping on bunks, and getting vanned into town for meals. We ate at a restaurant called Old Timers, over and over. The theme was railroads; a miniature train buzzed around on an overhead track in the main dining room. Old Millington was in black-and-white photos on the walls.

The few working fans seemed only to force more hot air into our barracks. We shared one pay phone. The television received only local channels through a rabbit-ears antenna, so during our breaks we watched the only thing that was on: Oliver North testifying before a joint congressional committee investigating the Iran-Contra scandal.

It might not sound like much, but I loved it.

I was meeting and playing against some of the best college players in the country, players I'd only read and heard about. I was fitting in. I was pitching well. For the first time, I thought maybe I could compete against anyone and have the same chance to play professionally.

And while we were all griping about the humidity, and the food, and the conditions, and the tedium of the workouts, we also were drawing together, maybe what USA Baseball and Coach Fraser had in mind. In only a few weeks, we would be sent to Havana, Cuba, to play a team widely believed to be among the best on earth—even considering the U.S. major leagues. We had a long way to go in a short time, because there was potential for intimidation and embarrassment in Cuba, where Castro demanded hardball superiority and generally got it.

"Guys, they're not that good," Fraser would growl through a curled lip. "They'd probably only finish fourth in the AL East this year."

Fraser was a character like Tommy Lasorda was a character, equal parts baseball man, pitchman, and grandfather.

Team USA left for Havana in mid-July. We flew into Miami, where in a special area of the Miami airport we boarded a government-sponsored charter. We were greeted on the plane by officials from state departments of the United States and Cuba. It was all very formal, more so than we'd expected, and the short flight through the darkness to the communist nation didn't foster the usual levels of goofing around. We were all a little nervous.

The great Cuban players awaited, along with a team that many compared to the near unbeatable Russian hockey teams of earlier generations. Beyond the baseball, we wondered what the hotel would be like, the food, the water, the people. It would be daunting enough to play the Cubans on a neutral field, but this would be on their turf, before their countrymen, and their president. For some among them, there would be not just the baseball result, but a commentary on the two governments and their people. We were a bunch of college kids, so it seemed a lot to carry. We arrived at night to a tedious customs process. Cuban officers kept us at the airport for what seemed to be three or four hours. They checked every pocket of every person, every compartment of every suitcase. There were, I'd say, forty of us in the traveling party. And one by one we'd gather up our clothes and gear, repack them, and drag it all across the tarmac to the bus, where we'd watch the next guy go through the same laborious pat-down, all while press photographers rushed us, lighting the tarmac with their flashbulbs. They took a keen interest in me, too keen for it to have been about baseball. I slid my right hand into my jacket pocket and tried to seem friendly.

The Cubans had invited us down, but clearly weren't ready to trust us. A few days later, when Castro came to greet us, they'd even secured the bats.

Years later, when I was pitching for the California Angels, I'd hear from Castro again. He wanted an autographed baseball.

CHAPTER 10

Most of my life when I wound up and threw a baseball it started out straight, but as it neared its destination it would move—sometimes hard, sometimes slightly—from left to right, as if drawn by a magnet. For all I knew the first ball I ever tossed to my dad did the same thing, as did the first ball I threw at the brick wall outside my house, as did the ball that counted for my first strikeout in Little League.

Baseball people called it a cut fastball, or a cutter. Through high school the ball would drift right, almost imperceptibly. At Michigan, purely by accident, I came upon a grip that felt good in my hand and would be considered quite unorthodox. The ball cut even more. I'd never seen anyone pitch with that particular grip. As a matter of fact, I never would. Occasionally I would show a fellow pitcher how I held the ball. Almost without fail he would stare for a while, mimic the grip, and hand the ball back, as if I were crazy.

It worked for me. And on good, warm days I could crank it up into the mid-90s. Another element: because I had to hood my glove over my right hand, I could not hide the ball or my grip. Even if the hitter couldn't necessarily see my hand on the ball, he was about the only one in the ballpark who couldn't, and it would have been simple enough for him to find out. Ballplayers find their ways. For one, that's what teammates are for.

So, rather than grope at the ball, changing grips, going to different pitches, sometimes it was easier—and more effective—to simply locate the cutter. For me, it was the most natural thing. I'd throw it as hard as I could, keep my front shoulder closed and finish as far out in front as I could, and watch it go. It was a good pitch in college, and an even better pitch in the big leagues, where the bats were wooden and prone to splintering.

I'd learned and developed other pitches along the way—the curveball, the changeup, the slider—but nothing was quite so comfortable as the cutter, and as I pitched into the fifth inning against the Indians, their hitters were still looking for it. The righties, especially, were opening up early, trying to get the thick part of the bat to the ball before the ball got to the thin part of the bat. So, they pulled my off-speed pitches foul, or hit them off the ends of their bats, generally toward my guys.

We'd drawn to within two games of the AL East–leading Blue Jays, the rain was holding off, and we were beating the Indians, so the crowd was happy and lively. The people in the stands were as pleased that we were winning as I was. Well, maybe.

Of course, I wasn't perfect. I'd walked Lofton in the first inning, Milligan in the second and, now, leading off the fifth inning, Milligan again, on four pitches. There are few things more annoying than holding a lead and walking the leadoff hitter, particularly one who'd bat .190 against me in his career. But I missed away a couple times, threw the 2-and-0 pitch too far inside and to the backstop, then missed inside again.

That brought Manny Ramirez, who—wisely, given the events of the first hitter of the inning—took the first pitch. It was a curveball and it nicked the outside corner for a strike. He then swung through a cutter up in the zone, so I'm ahead, o and 2. After I bounced a curveball for ball one, I think Ramirez saw another curveball coming, because he crushed it.

Randy Velarde, at shortstop, had just enough time to lean a little left and get his glove in front of his belt buckle. The ball was hit so hard Milligan couldn't tell if Velarde caught it in the air or it had bounced. So, while Milligan's instincts carried him a little toward second, then a little toward first, then back to second again, his legs checked out. While Velarde flipped to Gallego, who made the relay to first, Milligan finally gathered himself and took a few steps backward toward right field, surrendering the double play.

Fifteen years later, asked about the Saturday afternoon game against the Yankees with so many of his friends and relatives in the stands, Ramirez would shrug and say, "We hit some balls hard."

That might have been the ball he remembered.

Maldonado, who so concerned Nokes, ended the inning by flying to Dion James in left field on the eighth pitch of the at-bat.

I was five innings in. Into what, I didn't know. But, we were ahead. I'd gotten fifteen outs without any major crises. The stack of cups was growing.

CHAPTER 11

The dark and dusty tunnel beneath the Indianapolis Motor Speedway led to a short flight of stairs, which led to light. Behind me, 676 men and women shuffled through the darkness.

I held their flag.

Ours was the last nation to be announced, and after a long wait we were summoned by a gentleman's nod and wave. As we began to advance on the light, the volunteer workers among us at the 10th Pan American Games began a chant of "USA! USA!," urging us forward, when finally a great voice announced our arrival to the 70,000 whose eyes were on the mouth of the tunnel.

"Los Estados Unidos," the man bellowed across the racetrack.

The people stood with a roar, honoring the flag. In the late-summer heat, goose bumps rose against my white suit, which long before had become soaked with sweat.

I turned to wave to the crowd. My parents were up there somewhere. So were George H. W. Bush, the vice president, and Juan Antonio Samaranch, the International Olympic Committee President. I searched for Mom and Dad, in vain.

Days before, to my astonishment, I'd been chosen to lead the American contingent down the straightaway, along the banked turns, and into the field with the other competing nations. As the host country, we'd appeared thirty-eighth and last, and to great anticipation. The Cubans, whom we were getting to know quite well, stood not far away.

The flag felt heavy in my left hand and in the curl of my right wrist. I couldn't quite get over the notion that Greg Louganis, the Olympic gold medalist in diving, or David Robinson, the All-American basketball player from Navy, should be out in front, or so many others. And I continued to be nagged by thoughts that the recognition went beyond what I'd done on baseball fields. Really, I assumed when I'd arrived in Indianapolis I'd be somewhere amid the swarm of white fedoras with my friends and teammates.

Still, of course, I was touched. And proud.

In the hours leading to the opening ceremony, I'd been led into a press conference, where I was asked about the personal significance of carrying the flag, and about our growing rivalry with Cuba (mostly in our heads, I speculated, not theirs), about our chances for gold, and, of course, about my physical situation. From the back of the room, a reporter had posed a lighthearted question, given I'd met Castro only weeks before: What would Michigan's iconic and old-school football coach Bo Schembechler think about me consorting with the communist leader?

"Actually," I answered, not really thinking but willing to go along, "they have a very similar presence, except that Castro is bigger and wider. They both have a dictatorial presence."

It got a laugh.

I surmised, playing to the crowd, "It's about even."

At ivy-walled Bush Stadium, we won eight games in the tournament, and lost once. The loss was in the gold medal game to the Cubans, whom we'd beaten earlier in the week. While disappointing, the silver medal assured Team USA a place in the 1988 Summer Olympics, where baseball would be a demonstration sport. In two starts I hadn't allowed a run (the first batter of my first start, a Nicaraguan, bunted, of course), a pleasant conclusion to a summer of USA Baseball in which I'd won eight games in ten starts. More important, we had rewarded USA Baseball's courage in assembling a team of mostly sophomores in college. The organization's intent was to build toward the Olympics, where it would field a team that had grown together, through the trials of the Cuban series and the Pan Am Games. A more veteran team perhaps would have qualified with greater ease, but also would have been stripped down by the next major-league draft. In spite of our youth, we'd left the summer convinced we could compete with the most talented amateur teams in the world, including Cuba, no matter the venue.

From mid-June to late August, we'd played forty-three games, from Millington, Tennessee, to Havana, Cuba, to Indianapolis, Indiana. We won thirty-four of them. Mike Fiore had hit .398 and now he was returning to Miami. Tino Martinez, who had hit nine home runs, was going back to the University of Tampa. Cris Carpenter and his 1.39 ERA were headed to Georgia, Ed Sprague to Stanford, Ty Griffin to Georgia Tech, Scott Servais to Creighton, and Dave Silvestri to Missouri.

We'd grinded through a lot of innings, filled up on a lot of buffets, and logged a lot of miles in yellow school buses, so much so that our arrival in Indianapolis was a relief, and in itself was a victory, like we'd survived so much. When we pulled into the athletes' village and then our dorm parking lot, a synchronized swimming team practiced its moves on dry land. The women were dressed for summer, in Dolphin shorts and T-shirts. We gazed from the bus windows, happy to be there. Ed Sprague married one of those girls.

And I returned for my junior year at Michigan, which, due to the June Major League Baseball draft, I knew could be my last. Most of us would meet again the following summer in preparation for the Olympics. I'd miss them. The experience had been roundly rewarding. We parted with the knowledge that we'd grown as ballplayers and with the confidence that, together, we could not be intimidated.

Feeling pretty good about myself back in Ann Arbor, I began the fall semester. I returned to my routine, beginning with classes and then afternoon workouts in the weight room, the path to which led me directly through the athletic department. A voice boomed from behind me.

"What the *hell*?"

I turned. It was John Falk, trainer for the football team.

"Bo is *pissed*," he spat.

"What? Why?"

"Compared him to *Castro*?" he said, his eyes wide. "You *gotta* be *kidding* me. He's looking for you."

I flushed, thanked Falk for the warning, and avoided the athletic department for a month. When I figured the smoke had cleared, I took my chances and returned to my regular route, through the athletic offices.

"Abbott!"

Like he'd been lying in wait for a month.

"Abbott!"

He stomped down a flight of stairs, walked straight up to me and thrust his face to within inches of mine.

"What is this Castro stuff?" he demanded.

"Coach, I dunno. I didn't mean it."

Schembechler had always been so nice to me. Once, in a newspaper story, he'd said I could probably play quarterback for him had I wanted to. It wasn't true, but I'd appreciated the sentiment. Now . . . *this*.

For ten seconds—it seemed like a month—he didn't move. Just stared at me, his face taut and his eyes hard, and had he risen up and bitten my head off at that very moment, leaving my headless corpse on the floor of the athletic department for the cleaning crew to bag and discard, I would not have been surprised.

Finally, he blinked.

"Are you getting to class?" he ordered.

"Yessir." Meekly.

"Then get out of here," he commanded, and flung his hand in the direction of one exit or another.

Dismissed, I weaved toward the door.

The coming months seemed a buildup to amateur draft day, June 1. Even through the summer, idle chatter on the buses and in the hotel rooms was filled with speculation on who would go where. We dreamed of big signing bonuses, the towns we'd play in, and someday making it to the big leagues. We'd never been closer, yet it all seemed still so far away, as if one of those clunky yellow buses were carrying us there. Up a long hill. In first gear. With a balky clutch.

Before long, I was back in Indianapolis for another banquet. It was early March, when the Sullivan Award was announced. The award honored the top amateur athlete in the nation. Properly, I thought, my seat was at the farthest end of the dais. A baseball player had never won. This was for elite athletes, most often individual athletes, and while I appreciated the gesture of the nomination—which came with the Golden Spikes Award—I figured I was there to fill out the front table. Between the trophy and me sat the likes of boxer Kelcie

Banks, hurdler Greg Foster, David Robinson again, swimmer Janet Evans, volleyball player Karch Kiraly—all deserving. Me, I was just hoping the food was good.

The gentleman from my host family who had picked me up from the airport mentioned that the last time he'd hosted, it was for the eventual winner. I apologized ahead of time for breaking his streak.

So I was astonished when the previous year's winner, the heptathlete Jackie Joyner-Kersee, read the name of the honoree: Jim Abbott.

Honestly, I was so far away I could barely hear her. Then I didn't really believe her. The Sullivan honors athletic achievement, along with "those who have shown strong moral character." I assumed they hadn't known about the duck.

When I arrived at the microphone, other than thanking my parents, who were in the audience, along with my teammates and coaches, I could think of only an old joke, one that always got a laugh: "I'm not an athlete. I'm a baseball player."

I won nine games my junior season, bringing my three-year record at Michigan to 26-8. The team won forty-eight games in 1988, won the regular-season Big Ten title, and lost—again—in the NCAA regional. With the draft coming, and with another long summer of baseball ahead, this time in preparation for the Olympics, I believed I was done pitching at Michigan. Part of me wished it could go on forever, but the time had come for another fateful step.

I knew Scott Boras a little. At Coach Middaugh's request, he'd spoken to the team during the season, educating us on an agent's responsibilities, what to look for in an agent, and how to protect one's amateur standing through the draft process. He represented Cris Carpenter, as well as a number of players on the USA Baseball team, guys whose opinions I respected, and he was impressively informed. Before the draft, Boras traveled to Flint to meet with my parents and me. He was young, polished, smart, and sure of himself, and very sure of me.

"You could pitch in the major leagues tomorrow," he said.

"Oh, I don't think so," I said.

We went back and forth like that.

"Jim," he said, somewhere between impatient and amused, "I'm not just being nice. You have an out pitch, the cutter. You have big-league velocity. Not only could you pitch in the big leagues, you could win there."

"Oh," I said, "I don't think so."

Mom, a lawyer herself, liked that Boras, in 1988 relatively new to the field of sports agents, had a law degree. And Mom and Dad liked that Boras explained precisely how he could advise us while not risking my final year of eligibility at Michigan, were it to come to that.

He was thirty-five, but already had begun to challenge baseball's long-standing draft paradigm, in which the professional franchise told the player what he was worth, and the player, after some half-hearted negotiating, reported to work. The idea was the player was supposed to be thrilled and flattered to be offered the job. Boras, who'd played four seasons in the minor leagues with the St. Louis Cardinals and Chicago Cubs, had other thoughts and already had rankled some big-league brass with his own ideas. He was aggressive and tough in ways I was not, kept the conversation on baseball and away from marketing my "story," such as it was, and would be deft at filtering out the distractions peripheral to the baseball side of things.

"I don't know Jim," he told us. "But I know the ability."

While I was naive about the draft and what came after it, Boras was persuasive on the topics of a young player and his leverage. In that way, and given that the major leagues still seemed a distant reality, a signing bonus represented the only guaranteed money I'd make in baseball. And that was Boras's specialty.

On that perhaps thin requirement, I hired Boras, beginning a relationship that was not unlike a marriage, and that ultimately would disappoint both of us.

ON JUNE 1, 1988, the day of baseball's amateur draft, Bobby Fontaine, the scouting director for the California Angels, stood in a doorway in the executive offices at Anaheim Stadium and told Tim Mead, the Angels' PR man, "We did it," just like that.

Mead knew immediately what Fontaine was saying. He'd overheard enough of the deliberations prior to the draft. After weeks of debate, analysis, debate, general agreement, and more debate, the club had taken the left-hander from Michigan, the Olympic hopeful, the Sullivan Award winner, the one-handed guy.

Not in the second or third round, as many had projected, but in the first round, eighth overall.

The phone rang in the living room on Maxine Street in Flint. A reporter wanted to know what it felt like to be a pro ballplayer and an Angel, the first I'd heard. I didn't really know, actually. The Tigers, where my heart was and who carried the unimaginable dream of playing at Tiger Stadium, had the twenty-sixth pick, and speculation held that they might select me. In my neighborhood, they were professional baseball. The Angels weren't one of those teams people in Michigan thought much about, but I was thrilled to go so high. Eventually the Angels' general manager, Mike Port, called. It was true, I was going to get paid for playing baseball, which I'd only recently begun to consider. I'd been 26-8 with a 3.03 ERA in three seasons at Michigan, but the big leagues, any pro ball, seemed a long way off, until the phone rang, and then I was never so happy that the battery held up on that old remote receiver.

George Bradley, one of the team's scouting coordinators, had been around the Michigan team earlier that spring. In Austin, Texas, for one of my earlier starts, he'd run into Don Welke. He shook Welke's hand, nodded toward the lefty on the mound, and said, "You knew what you were looking at three years ago, didn't you?"—more a statement than a question, really. On draft day, Bradley told the newspapers that the club was not concerned with my condition.

"We didn't even look at it that way," he said. "Over the years he has overcome that handicap. It's like a guy with glasses. He uses glasses to correct his vision. Jim has overcome his problem. He won't have a problem fielding. He's mastered fielding.

"Take a look around the big leagues and see where the left-handed pitching is. Our club needed left-handed pitching and there were only a few in the draft."

The Angels set up a conference call and the questions were predictable.

"I always grew up playing baseball and liking it," I told reporters. "I never thought about anything holding me back. I was going to play until someone grabbed my spikes away from me and told me to sit down, you're not good enough anymore. As I look back on it, I guess it was a different situation and if I had any common sense, I probably would've stopped. But growing up, playing with one hand never entered my mind as holding me back."

It was mostly true.

While Andy Benes, another Boras client and eventually an Olympic teammate, was chosen first overall by the San Diego Padres, the headlines the following day generally focused on the eighth pick.

The New York Times was representative enough: ANGELS GET AB-
BOTT, ONE-HAND PITCHER.

The rest would be left to Boras and the Angels, for two weeks later
I was back in Millington, Tennessee, with USA Baseball, back in the
same bunk with the same thin mattress, back for fifty-one more
games that would lead to a medal stand on the first-base line at Jamsil Baseball Stadium in Seoul, South Korea. The summer of '88 saw
us tour from Tennessee to Japan to Boise, Idaho, to Tulsa, Oklahoma,
to Battle Creek, Michigan, and many other U.S. stops, to seven cities
in Italy, back to Japan, and then to Korea, with dozens of ballparks
in between. Along the way, Cuba was lost as an Olympic antagonist
because of its boycott for political purposes, but we played the Cubans nine times between a U.S. barnstorming series and the World
Cup in Italy. We lost six of them, five by one run.

By the time we reached South Korea, there were twenty of us. For
most, the Olympics were the conclusion of a sixteen-month hardball
odyssey. We'd done our college time, set ourselves up for the draft,
been drafted, and, in many cases, signed. These last days of September and first of October, then, were our final hours of amateur baseball. Most of us would never again wear USA across our chests, or fall
in with a team so singular in its objective. We'd won mostly, lost
sometimes heartbreakingly, and kept showing up at the bus the next
day, without regard for personal glory. We'd steeled ourselves on
diamonds across the world, and under Fidel Castro's gaze, and amid
speculation we were built too young to stand against the Cubans or
the Asians, and through political turmoil we had no time for.

We wanted to play baseball and we were pretty good at it. When
we'd bused to the outskirts of the Olympic Village in Seoul, then
boarded the tram for our apartment and dragged our gear to our
rooms, we believed in who we'd become. The grueling travel, un-

identifiable food, and months of pressurized baseball had brought us to something like a crescendo, except at a time in our lives when everything seemed ahead of us. This was not to say we were entirely focused on baseball.

We wandered the streets of the village, a bunch of jamokes gaping at the people who did this sort of thing for a living—swimmer Matt Biondi, diver Greg Louganis, sprinter Ben Johnson, tennis players Steffi Graf and Gabriela Sabatini, basketball player David Robinson. At the center of the sporting universe, we walked their hallways, shopped their shops, and ate in their cafeterias, and were amazed to be so close to them. There was a tartan track in the village, and we'd spend some of our early evenings along the straightaways watching the sprinters train. We wondered aloud if this could be real, if we really were intended to mix with such royalty.

Most of us were just arriving into adulthood. The occasional lapses into mid-adolescence were unavoidable and, we were convinced, as humorous as they were harmless.

There was the piece of lunch meat flung from a bus in Tokyo that landed randomly and indecorously on the lap of a woman in a passing car. Sadly, the woman wore a silk dress and was on her way to a wedding. Worse, her escort—a stern gentleman intent on avenging the bologna strafing—stopped the bus and demanded answers.

There was the beautiful and expensive floor-to-ceiling glass partition that lost its life in a hotel tussle, also in Tokyo, leaving this world in shards and bleeding USA Baseball's budget by another four thousand dollars.

And there were the dozens of baseballs that would be found floating in the moat surrounding the Olympic Village, each ball having fallen woefully short of its intended target—that being a security tower manned with guards waving machine guns. On the field the following day, we had exactly seven baseballs left for batting practice.

Each event—and there were plenty others like them—would conclude similarly, with head coach Mark Marquess standing over us, arms crossed, demanding the identity of the culprits. No one ever broke ranks. We'd lower our eyes and Marquess, a good man with the impossible job of maintaining order, would stare holes into the tops of our heads until the moment became uncomfortable for everyone, him included.

We weren't trying to be idiots. Sometimes we simply tired of the late-night raids on one another—pitchers attacking position players with soap bars, position players exacting their revenge with buckets of ice, grudges that extended to locales all over the globe.

What it fostered was extreme trust on a team that didn't feel thrown together for a single baseball tournament or even one extended summer. Just because you would return to your hotel room and find the hotel ice machine had been emptied onto your bed didn't mean you'd been bullied. It meant you'd been initiated. Or called to action. And it meant it was your turn for payback. Maybe it wouldn't come in Tidewater, Virginia, or Quakertown, Pennsylvania, or Verona, Italy, or even Kobe, Japan, but it would come. I think, more than two decades later, there might still be contracts out.

And what it furthered was a winning culture. There wasn't a guy on that team who knew his statistics for the summer and then the Olympics. But each of us could tell you whom we beat, how often we beat them, and who was next. We could also tell you where the ice machine was in every hotel from here to Seoul. And that flying lunch meat in Japan is more likely than not to cause an international incident.

As we reached mid-September, Marquess was mostly adhering to a lineup of Tom Goodwin in center field, Mike Fiore in left, Robin Ventura at third base, Tino Martinez at first, Ed Sprague as the designated hitter, Ted Wood in right, Ty Griffin at second, Doug Robbins at catcher, and Dave Silvestri at shortstop. The pitching staff was deep: Of Andy Benes, Ben McDonald, Charles Nagy, Joe Slusarski, and me, three were selected in the top seventeen picks of the amateur draft in 1988 (Slusarski went in the second round), and McDonald was taken first overall in 1989.

Three games into the Olympics, Marquess chose to pitch McDonald in the semifinals against Puerto Rico and to pitch me in whatever followed—the consolation game or the gold medal game. Twenty-two years later, Marquess explained to Fiore over dinner, "The bigger the game, the more confidence I had in Jim."

McDonald beat Puerto Rico, which put me in line for Japan, who, without the Cubans around, was the team most likely to send us home without the gold medal. We had two days to prepare, one day to practice, and while waiting for the tram we came upon the U.S. boxing team training in a courtyard outside the apartments. A boom box accompanied their workout. Roy Jones was on that team, as were Michael Carbajal, Ray Mercer, Kelcie Banks, and Andrew Maynard. They were in a circle, working up a sweat under the constant banter of their trainer, who seemed most interested in the heavyweight, Riddick Bowe.

"C'mon, Riddick, let's go," he shouted. "Or you're gonna get yer ass kicked."

Bowe looked up, bemused. He was due to fight some big kid from Canada.

"Aw," he said, "I'm gonna give him a left cross, then a right cross, and he's gonna need the Red Cross."

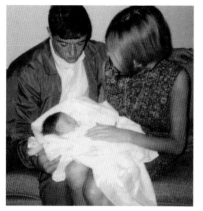

Grandma Abbott had told Dad,
"God takes away once, he gives
back twice." *Family photo*

May, 1969: Me and Mom's parents—Grandma
and Grandpa Adams, with whom I spent much
of my childhood. *Kathy Abbott*

Mom and Dad outside St. Agnes church on
their wedding day. That afternoon, she
would go home to me and he would report
for work. *Family photo*

Along the way, Dad and I figured out how to do
most things. Once in a while, I'd need a little
push. *Family photo*

Dad taught me how to fish with a Zebco reel, which led to the first and last big fish I ever caught. *Mike Abbott*

I didn't want to be different.
Family photo

New shirt, check. Toughskins, check. Right arm, check. My first day of kindergarten.
Family photo

Dad, as a promising freshman for St. Matthew's football team. *The Flint Journal*

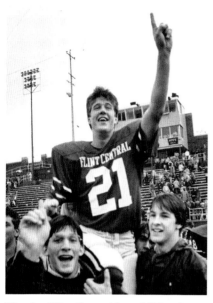

The day Flint Central beat Midland in the state playoffs. That's Danny Nathan on the left, Andy Turpen hoisting me on his shoulder, and Stuart Kale on the right. *The Flint Journal*

My Connie Mack coach, Ted Mahan, wore number 5 at Michigan. My number 5 was a tribute to him. *Family photo*

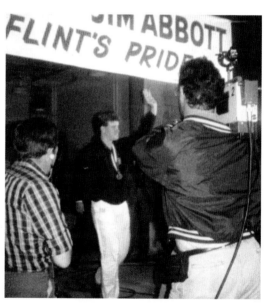

Wearing the Olympic-issued warm-ups and gold medal, and I more proud of my city than it was of me. *Family photo*

I loved everything about the University of Michigan, including Ray Fisher Stadium. *University of Michigan*

My brother, Chad, takes in my big-league debut at Anaheim Stadium. I'm glad he was okay. I was a little nervous. *Mike Abbott*

Tiger Stadium, my rookie year. I'd grown up dreaming about playing on that field. *Still Perfection © 1990 D. Sell*

Dana and I at the White House to receive a 1991 Victory Award. *Family photo*

Gene Autry, as kind a gentleman as I ever met, never said a harsh word about anyone. *Getty Images*

Hiding my grip on the baseball was a challenge. This is a fastball, which the first-base coach and everyone in the first-base dugout could have told you. *Getty Images*

The Freeway Series at Dodger Stadium, 1990. Sometimes, swinging the bat was the easy part. *Getty Images*

They came with baseball cards, balls, and photos. Some came with stories a lot like mine. *Getty Images*

While the rhythms of the big leagues were becoming familiar at the start of my second season, the attention could still be overwhelming. I'm glad the mullet didn't scare off the younger fans.
Mike Proebsting

First spring training with Marcel Lachemann, my first professional pitching coach. I made the team.
Courtesy of the Los Angeles Angels of Anaheim

Lach once told Angels management, "You send this kid out, you send me with him."
Courtesy of the Los Angeles Angels of Anaheim

About the only thing Doug Rader enjoyed more than a good ballgame was a good laugh, and he had plenty of both. *Courtesy of the Los Angeles Angels of Anaheim*

Rader used to say that Jimmie Reese and I were put on the earth to meet each other. *Courtesy of the Los Angeles Angels of Anaheim*

Groundskeeper Frank Albohn, in the white shirt, and his crew the morning after the no-hitter. They must have worked all night getting that pitching rubber out of the ground. *Courtesy of the New York Yankees*

A no-hitter is not a solitary effort, as Mike Gallego (top), WadeBoggs (left), and Matt Nokes would attest. *Getty Images*

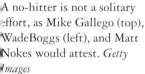

On June 30, 1999, at Wrigley Field, this is how a career .095 hitter handles the bat. An inning later, I singled home two runs, accounting for two of the three RBIs in my career. *Getty Images*

On my way back to the big leagues in 1998. First I'd have to be a (Winston-Salem) Warthog, among other things. *Bill Setliff Photography*

My first Old-Timer's Day at Yankee Stadium, with Don Larsen and Robin Ventura, in 2003. I was thirty-five, feeling a bit young to be an old-timer. *Courtesy of the New York Yankees*

Maddy and Ella on the day Michigan retired my number. They made a wonderful day better. *Dana Abbott*

We thought that was hysterical.

I remember reading a couple days later that Lennox Lewis beat Bowe in the second round by technical knockout for the gold medal. The line was still funny.

The four other pitchers and I talked all summer about the Olympics, about getting to the gold medal game, who among us would start it, who would finish it, and how it would feel to pitch for our country, do or die. When it became real, when Marquess said I'd be the one, I was profoundly honored. The five of us were housed in the same apartment, which had a balcony that overlooked the Olympic Village. We sat on the balcony the night before the game, listening to Springsteen, talking about everything, but always returning to Japan, the game the next afternoon, and what it would bring.

When everyone went to bed, I lay for hours with my eyes open. I imagined the stadium, the grass, the Japanese hitters—with whom, by now, I was pretty familiar. When doubt crept into my mind, I'd blink hard to chase it away. We had worked too hard to get there, having played the longest pre-Olympic schedule in Team USA history. Hadn't we come too far to lose? I blinked hard again.

Seoul felt so far from home. There were phone booths in the lobby of the apartments, but I hadn't been able to reach anyone back in Michigan to tell them I'd be starting.

Jamsil Stadium was about three-quarters full that afternoon. A large contingent of American servicemen was in the stands, many in the outfield corners. I guess you could say they were supportive.

"Don't dishonor the Stars and Stripes!" one yelled.

"Tell your boy, throw strikes!" said another—meaning me, I supposed.

I was not dominant in the early innings. But Tino Martinez hit a long home run, and then another. As the game went on, Japan was getting fewer runners on base. My cutter was finding the corners. Guys were making plays. We'd go a couple innings, Tino would hit a home run, and then we'd hold on for a couple more innings until he did it again.

Then, sooner than I expected, it was the ninth inning. We led, 5–3. I walked to the mound needing three more outs. Tom Goodwin jogged toward the outfield alongside Mike Fiore. He turned to Fiore and said, "I'm too nervous." We all were. We were on the brink of something so special.

The first batter of the ninth inning hit a ground ball to Robin Ventura at third base.

Ventura was an excellent fielder. He'd go on to win six Gold Gloves in the major leagues. In a ninth inning three weeks before, however, he'd thrown a ball slightly up the line against the Cubans in the gold medal game of the World Championships. Martinez had made a deft play and tagged the man before he crossed the bag. The umpire didn't see it that way. The next batter homered (off me) to tie the score, and eventually we lost the game and the gold medal. I blamed myself. Ventura wasn't happy, either.

So it was with a sense of closure that the first ball of the ninth found Ventura. He threw high. Martinez leaped, snared the soaring throw, and came down on the bag for the first out.

I took a breath, turned the ball in my hand, and went after the second out. On the first pitch, the ball bounced again toward Ventura.

"Hit him in the chest!" the shortstop, Dave Silvestri, screamed. "Hit him in the chest!"

Martinez jumped again and, on his way down, tagged the runner before he reached the base. We were an out from all we'd worked for. And Ventura's throws were getting slightly better.

I threw one last cutter. It produced one last grounder. To Ventura.

Silvestri was screaming again. The crowd rose, expecting the final moment of the game, of the tournament. We stood with our mouths open, stared, and prepared to follow the ball across the infield.

Ventura threw and hit Martinez in the chest.

We'd won.

If I hadn't yet felt the weight of all those months, and bus trips, and bad food, and great baseball, and greater expectations, I felt it at that moment. That's because nineteen guys were lying on top of me. We shouted things that made no sense. We laughed a lot and tried not to cry. We used up the last few ounces of our child-hoods, whatever was left after pushing so hard for so long. I'd never been around a more cohesive group. There was not a single man in that pile who didn't believe he deserved that victory, that *we* didn't deserve it.

Jim Schneider was correct and so was my dad. I'd come along dur-ing a fascinating and exceptional era in American baseball. With some of the most talented and decorated amateur players ever, we survived Cuba, won a silver medal in the 1987 Pan Am Games, and became the first U.S. baseball team to win Olympic gold. We'd had a great time doing it.

While we caught our breaths and the Marines in the stands granted we'd done nothing to dishonor the flag and the coaching staff—Marquess, Skip Bertman from Louisiana State, Ron Polk from Mississippi State, Rich Alday from New Mexico, and Dave Bingham from Kansas—looked on proudly, I again was struck by my timing. There was nowhere else I'd rather be than with these guys, winning and losing with them, sharing their laughter and hardships. Over those two summers and then some, we'd become as close as people could be without sharing a bloodline. I wondered what I'd done to deserve this time and this place, 6,500 miles from home and a life-time away.

A dozen volunteers assembled risers on the first-base side. We stood to the side, smiling dumbly.

Sometimes I felt Dad believed there was a plan to the arc of my life through baseball, beginning even before high school, then at Michigan, and in an opening ceremony in Indianapolis, and through a ballpark on the east side of Seoul, as though it were fate that so many people would see me play. The journey would continue, of course, to other ballparks in other cities far beyond this. As it did, he'd see and hear of the mothers and fathers, their stricken children and their hope, and decide there was a plan for all of us. He had great faith—greater than mine—and searched for connections and mean-ings. I wasn't sure of his conclusions, but I had questions that came with no clear answers. How did this all happen to me? How did I find myself in these amazing places, with these amazing people? Didn't there have to be a reason?

There would be times when I was critical of—or, perhaps, realistic about—my abilities, and it was then I'd come to understand what Dad was feeling. Not in a mystical sense, so much, but in the place where dumb luck meets opportunity and collides with the hopes of those who held some affection for me. I guess I was fortunate in that way. Further, perhaps, it went to the early teachings from my par-ents, who told me I was special for being born this way, and not cursed. When you are told all your life that something meaningful is waiting, maybe you start to believe it.

We took our place on the podium, on the highest platform, Japan to our right and Puerto Rico to our left. The announcements were made first in Korean, then in English. They called our names, we stepped forward, received a bouquet of flowers, and then felt the weight of gold around our necks. I'd heard people say that the Olympic movement resides in the hearts of the athletes, and at that moment I understood. We held our caps to our chests, and then our anthem mingled with our admiration for one another and what we'd done together. I wished that song would never end.

When the bus pulled away from the stadium, and we were still burning nervous energy, Ed Sprague stepped into the aisle and asked for everyone's attention. We were in our uniforms still, caked with dirt and sweat and eye black. Duffel bags lined the aisle. Like all of us, Sprague wore his gold medal. He had been the team's emotional glue since early the summer before. He also was the guy who instigated many of the late-night wars, early-morning pranks, and random acts of madness.

"Coach Marquess," he announced, "we have something to say to you."

Marquess turned, his stoic expression softening slightly after four months.

Sprague grinned and continued: "Ted Wood threw the meat, Joe Slusarski broke the glass partition, and Mike Fiore threw all the balls in the moat."

The bus exploded in laughter. And Marquess, in spite of himself, joined in. He'd been waiting to exhale as much as we had been. Maybe more. We'd been a handful.

Hours later, when night had fallen in Seoul, we'd taken the party outside the Olympic Village and to some of the finer establishments of the city. There would be no more games, no more practices, no more scouting reports. For months, in order to sample the local ales, we'd slipped away from the coaches. In taverns and cafés, amid the ruins of Rome and sculptures of Florence, from the joints of Charlotte and Jackson and Colorado Springs, we'd found time for boys to be boys. There, we'd release the tensions and fatigue of barnstorming baseball, and observe the rituals of the road, and mostly adhere to Coach Marquess's rules. We figured we'd done a reasonable job having our fun and playing winning baseball. After all, for a couple dozen college kids tethered to a rigid schedule of travel-play-travel-play, this wasn't supposed to be a death march. We'd grown together during some of those escapades, and they helped make us the young team that belonged on a field with the world's best, and in ballparks where we were the enemy. Besides, what Marquess didn't know, couldn't possibly hurt him.

So it was with some discomfort and plenty of amusement that on the team's final evening together Charles Nagy and I found ourselves in a casino and at a blackjack table directly across from Coach Marquess. Through several hands we noted that—through blind luck, neither of us had played before—our good fortune apparently would extend beyond the events at Jamsil Stadium that afternoon. Marquess bore the look of contentment, having shepherded us across the world and delivered to USA Baseball a gold medal, with no major incidents beyond soaring mystery meat and an empty ball bag and a lot of near misses. Nagy and I couldn't quite figure what to make of the grinning, tolerant man who shared our table, who for months had refused to break from his character as the gruff, buttoned-down leader.

After we shared a few winning hands, a waitress appeared at the table. Marquess stopped her and deliberately ordered himself a Diet Coke. He glanced at us, then back to the waitress. A smile crossed his face and he raised two fingers. "Beers for them," he said in English. The waitress nodded.

Nagy and I looked at each other in disbelief, then back to Marquess, and the three of us laughed. This, apparently, was his thank-you for the hard work and dedication to the cause. And his way of saying, "I know what you suckers have been up to all summer." When the beers arrived, we tipped them toward our coach, and he raised his glass of Diet Coke. What a long, strange, exhilarating, perfect summer it had been.

The following morning we met in the lobby to board the bus to the airport for the long flight to Los Angeles. By then we each had at least a dozen bags, giveaway duffels from games and tournaments we'd played for months, filled with baseball gear and random junk accumulated at what seemed like a thousand stops.

We'd spend those final twelve hours together dozing, recalling the games that had come and gone, regretting the gold medal defeat at the World Championships, but celebrating every inch of the victory in Seoul. Many of us had left on this odyssey as college juniors and seniors and were returning as the property of major-league franchises. As of August 3, when I signed, I was a California Angel, Benes was a San Diego Padre, Griffin a Chicago Cub, Ventura a Chicago White Sox, Martinez a Seattle Mariner, Nagy a Cleveland Indian, Sprague a Toronto Blue Jay, Ted Wood a San Francisco Giant, Jeff Branson a Cincinnati Red, Slusarski an Oakland A, Fiore a St. Louis Cardinal, Mickey Morandini a Philadelphia Phillie, and Silvestri and Scott Servais were Houston Astros.

Most of us sensed we'd grown plenty as ballplayers, and maybe a little as men. We were sore and tired, glad to be going home, slightly nervous about our reentry into the real world, and curious about the coming experiences of pro ball. In some cases, bonus checks would be waiting at home, the first real money we'd make outside of our hometown supermarkets or restaurants or construction sites or farms. So we announced what cars we'd buy or vacations we'd take. And we argued over the best stereo systems, fishing boats, and hunting rifles.

In Los Angeles, we assembled for one final meal, a groggy twenty or thirty minutes spent over breakfast. Then someone would check his watch, stand and gather his bags, and disappear down the LAX concourse. One by one, we waved and smiled and found our flights home, until Team USA had scattered again across the country.

"All right," Sprague had said, "I'll see you . . . whenever."

And he, too, was gone, along with Fiore. They were headed to Instructional League in Florida, where they'd stay with Tino Martinez's grandmother in Clearwater.

On the flight to Detroit, I was taken by the quiet. I sat alone for the first time in months. Spring training waited on the other side of winter. I figured I'd spend some time in Ann Arbor, buy that black Jeep Grand Cherokee I had to have, maybe squeeze a few more weeks out of college. The lifestyle, if not the classrooms. Maybe I'd help my dad on his route, stock some shelves, spend a little time with him, Mom, and Chad. Heck, how did an Olympic gold medalist kill time? I laughed. I'd made some of the best friends I ever would make. I'd seen the world, some of it from a pitcher's mound, most of it alongside a bunch of guys just like me.

Just like me, I mused.

Mom and Dad were at the gate. I told them I was tired but okay, that it was great to see them and great to be home. We gathered my bags and went outside, where a long black limousine took up most of the curb. Police cars idled nearby. I eyed them, fighting the urge to explain I had nothing to do with the meat-throwing or glass-exploding incidents.

The limo was for me. For us. So were the police, who, their cars lit up, would clear our way to Flint.

Dusk was falling as we passed through Detroit and into its northwestern suburbs. Twenty-one years before, Mom and Dad had taken a similar route, in the other direction, him driving a borrowed Impala and her in full labor in the backseat.

Past the exit for Aunt Katie's and the hospital, along a highway whose neighborhoods were failing just like Flint's, Dad finally had the police escort he'd hoped for more than two decades ago. Except now we weren't in any real hurry.

The limousine drove to downtown Flint, to an outdoor pavilion, which was lit up on what had become a perfect and warm fall night. Wearing a blue Olympic jacket and Olympic sweats and with the gold medal still hanging from my neck, I swung open the rear door of the long car and friends, family, and local officials cheered. The mayor, Matt Collier, had arranged most of the homecoming celebration. He looked barely older than me. And now this was his town and these were his people, and I was one of them again.

Since leaving for Ann Arbor after high school, and then spending so much of the summers traveling, I hadn't seen much of Flint. There were times I felt sad for what had once been a robust city, then one suffocated by a blizzard of pink slips, many provided by GM. The young mayor had come to Flint's aid, as a public servant and when Michael Moore's documentary *Roger & Me* threatened to strip Flint of its dignity. Barely more than a year after I'd returned, he'd tell *Time* magazine, "Anyone who knows Flint can't help realizing the film is fiction. If this is a documentary, I wonder about all those PBS shows on whales and dolphins." He was still in there fighting for Flint, which I admired.

Back at home and greeted by hundreds of people, I was surprised by the enthusiasm. All those time zones away, it was hard to know if the Olympics had resonated here. While I wasn't much for being the center of attention, the sentiment was touching. It was good to be home. These were the people who had treated me so well when I was growing up, the teachers and Little League coaches and neighbors and friends who'd cut through my insecurities. They'd believed in me when I wasn't sure there was all that much to believe in.

They were proud of me. And I was proud of that. So, while a few folks stood up and said some nice things about me and our team, and as I fidgeted uncomfortably because they'd gone through so much trouble for all this, I was pleased they were pleased, that I'd honored their belief in me by going out and doing something worthwhile. A lot of really good athletes had come from their schools, from these streets and playgrounds, many of whom I'd looked up to as a boy. I didn't know how I could ever live up to those men and women, but this seemed a start.

Looking out at the familiar faces, seeing how happy they were for me and for the city—and it was true we both had our flaws—I was soothed by familiar warmth. It had come when I'd earned my way into the pickup games at Burroughs Park. And on the first days of Little League, when Mark Conover's dad gave me third base and a place in the batting order. And when Bob Holec had chosen me for the varsity, the day I became One-Point-Five. And when I stood in the old locker room at Atwood Stadium, pounding the shoulder pads of my fellow Central Indians, and then going out and winning a football game.

I belonged.

Bleary-eyed, thrilled to be home, and overwhelmed by the reception, I remember the following weeks as a bit of a daze. We'd retired after the downtown reception to our house, where I rehashed for my parents, Chad, and friends, the stories of the summer, the epic games against Cuba, and the Olympic experience. I'd turned twenty-one a month before, so I shared a beer with Dad. We gorged ourselves on Angelo's Coney dogs well after fatigue had set in, and we talked and laughed some more, sitting around the same table where Dad had left his note to me. "Proud of you son," he'd written, and I felt it again.

A couple days later, rested and settled, I walked into a Flint car dealership and bought that black Jeep Grand Cherokee. It came with black leather, gold rims, and some misgivings; Jeeps weren't made in Flint, as people undoubtedly would note, in a place where that still mattered. I paid twenty grand in cash, straight out of my signing bonus, didn't even haggle. That car meant freedom.

(It also would come to mean trouble. The car was stolen a couple months later and, when returned, had been all but totaled. Six months after that, a friend borrowed the car and proceeded to drive it into a deer, which nearly totaled it again. On the bright side, I once picked up a lovely young lady in that car for a first date, managed not to run into anything, and she became my wife. I'm thinking it was the gold rims.)

For the next few months, and for the first time I could recall, I belonged to no one. I stood on no lines. I was on no schedule. There was no baseball to be played. I existed somewhere between the afterglow of the Olympics and the promise of pro ball. I spent some time in Ann Arbor, but wasn't a student anymore, which I found really wasn't a bad way to do college.

Finally, I returned to Flint to bide my time until spring training, and prepared for another summer of bus trips and buffet food, all the minor leagues had to offer. As spring drew near, excited as I was, I began to wonder what the next step would bring.

I wondered if I could belong there, too.

CHAPTER 12

U p there in those rows of blue seats, among those 27,000 faces, those hopes and expectations, Dana sat behind home plate, twenty rows up, to the first-base side. I'd left her on the Upper East Side hours ago, and she'd made her way to the ballpark by game time, which she always did when I pitched.

I never looked up, never found her, but always sensed when she was there, and was grateful for it. I knew she wanted desperately for me to win, which, of course, made two of us. On television, Tony Kubek introduced the sixth inning by saying, "The Indians do not yet have a base hit," but that hadn't really crossed my mind, or Dana's. I was looking at the other "o," the one in the "runs" category, and the growing stack of water cups.

Three months earlier, on another Saturday afternoon—that one sunny and warm—in the Bronx, I'd taken a no-hitter into the eighth inning against the Chicago White Sox. I was sitting where I was now and Dana was where she was that day, when Bo Jackson came up with an out in the eighth, me five outs from the unthinkable. I'd made a good pitch and Bo flared a single to center. Then I'd made another good pitch and Ron Karkovice homered down the left-field line, and so we both remained sore enough from that emotional whiplash to be quite and totally satisfied with victory.

Now ahead 4–0—Velarde had homered to lead off the bottom of the fifth—I was thinking "win," and Dana was, too, and the Indians probably were wondering where that guy from six days ago had gone.

Jim Thome led off the sixth inning. He had this very flat swing that stayed in the strike zone for a very long time, which meant I couldn't have my curveball or cutter stay on the same plane for very long. I needed to pitch downhill, a term my pitching coach with the Angels, Marcel Lachemann, so often used, so that the ball arrived in the vicinity of Thome's bat on an angle. Though he'd not been in the league long, I recalled he'd hit some balls hard to left—his opposite field—against me before. Sure enough, on a two-ball, one-strike pitch, he lined a curveball to shortstop that Velarde gloved near his right shin. I'd take the out, even a loud one.

Then, before I'd run into the top of the Indians' order, I walked Junior Ortiz. Ortiz, you might recall, was the Indians' number nine hitter, and he arrived batting .239. I not only walked him, by the way, but walked him on four pitches, causing me to scream something very loud into my glove that, even from a couple hundred feet away, might have made Bronx denizens blush.

Kenny Lofton came up, took a strike, fouled off the next two pitches, then took a fastball up. Now, by the time I was done, only two hitters would have as many or more plate appearances against me than Lofton and hit for a better average against me than Lofton. Mike Devereaux batted .441 in forty-four plate appearances and Edgar Martinez batted .422 in forty-nine plate appearances. Lofton in thirty-nine hit .412, which is why I was so disappointed when one of my best curveballs of the game started at his right shoulder, dropped down and through the strike zone, and went unrecognized by plate umpire Ted Hendry. And why I was so pleased when the next pitch, a curveball away, was hit on a fly to left and caught easily by Dion James.

That over with, Felix Fermin hit the first pitch, an inside cutter, to Boggs at third. A routine play. Like that, I was six innings in. I was a comfortable eighty-four pitches along. I was winning. Dana, brought to the front edge of her seat by the walk and my unhappiness with it, eased against the backrest.

Up in the broadcast booth, Kubek sent the viewers into commercial break.

"The Indians," he said calmly, "are still hitless."

CHAPTER 13

The Angels were a snakebitten franchise. Since their inception in 1961, their seasons either had ended glumly or—on three occasions, just to mix it up—in paralyzing despair. In the eighties, they'd won two American League West titles. In the championship series that followed they played six games that, had they won any of them, would have sent them to their first World Series and signaled the arrival of Gene Autry's beloved franchise. They lost all six.

Their history showed they'd averaged a new manager every couple years, allowed Nolan Ryan to leave in free agency, spent millions on other free agents, and generally found ways to lose by a lot or lose by a little or lose in the most heart-wrenching way ever.

As if that weren't enough, they played their games an hour's drive from Dodger Stadium, and the shadow of the Dodgers was cast at least to Anaheim. The Dodgers had had only two managers—Walter Alston and Tommy Lasorda—since 1954. Their owner—Peter O'Malley—was a baseball blueblood. They were L.A.'s team, Hollywood's team, occasionally America's team. And while they arrived in Southern California only three years before the Angels had, the

Dodgers oozed stability and composure. They'd won two World Series in the eighties, including in 1988, a season in which the Angels
lost eighty-seven games, finished twenty-nine games out of first
place in the AL West, and fired a manager.

Because of Autry, however, the Angels had a lovable quality. They
were often underdogs, but they were dashing underdogs on a horse
named Champion, humming "Back in the Saddle Again," and wearing a big cowboy hat. Everyone loved Mr. Autry.

What I knew about the Angels beyond that was limited. Lance
Parrish, their new catcher, was one of my favorite players growing
up, because of his Tigers lineage. (One of my enduring memories of
baseball was Parrish's mitt, ringed in orange, guiding a young Jack
Morris, or a younger Dan Petry.) Wally Joyner, the first baseman,
was nearly Rookie of the Year three years before. The starting rotation was old-ish at the top (Bert Blyleven) and young-ish at the bottom (Chuck Finley), and the bullpen featured a similar blend of old
(Bob McClure and Greg Minton) and young (Bryan Harvey, Willie
Fraser).

Of course, little of the major-league team's makeup would matter
to me beyond spring training. At some point in March, I'd slide over
to the minor-league side and begin preparations for a season in the
sticks. I figured it would be like my summers with Team USA, only
longer and probably hotter. Maybe the buses would be nicer. There'd
be no medal waiting at the end.

It wasn't that I was a long shot to make the Angels, to become one
of the few modern-day players to go from a college campus to a
major-league roster. The fact was, I had no shot. I was going to start
the season in Midland, Texas, Double-A ball, get my bearings,
sharpen up my curveball, learn to be a pro. The decision had been
made. In the early meetings leading to camp—manager Doug Rader,

pitching coach Marcel Lachemann, bullpen coach Joe Coleman, general manager Mike Port would convene often—my name would not come up. I was going to the minor leagues.

By February 1989, I'd signed for $200,000 (exactly what Don Welke had recommended to the Blue Jays three years earlier), skipped my senior season at Michigan, and won a gold medal in the Olympics. And then I'd show up in spring training to a major-league clubhouse with not just something to prove, but everything to prove. I was starting over.

From Flint, I packed a single suitcase and flew to Orange County, checked into a hotel across from Anaheim Stadium, did a press conference in which the questions included, "So, Jim, any other handicaps in the family?" and then reported to the bullpen in right field, where maybe a dozen of Lachemann's pitchers were preparing for camp. The field had been prepped for a motocross event, giving the experience a Mad Max vibe.

Blyleven was there, along with Finley, Kirk McCaskill, Harvey, Fraser, Stew Cliburn, some others. For two weeks, we'd throw, work out, and then I'd walk back across the street and play Donkey Kong on Nintendo until I fell asleep. I had no car, no friends, and nowhere else to go. One afternoon I was invited to join Harvey, Fraser, and Cliburn for an afternoon in Newport Beach, where Finley had a condo. Harvey was from North Carolina by way of Soddy-Daisy, Tennessee. Cliburn was from Jackson, Mississippi. Finley was from Monroe, Louisiana. When they got to talking, I couldn't understand anything they said. They pretty much lost me at, "Son, . . ." And that was the extent of my field trips.

By the time I was picking up a word here and there, we'd driven to Mesa, Arizona, for spring training. Gene Autry Park had three full fields, a half-field where the writers played Wiffle ball at dusk, a bare locker room, a small building for the front-office staff, and a mobile home for the beat writers. The major-league players dressed toward the front of the locker room, where the lockers were large enough to store their gear. In the back, the rest of us made do with narrower lockers. More like large cubbies, actually, which we shared with another guy. I did my best to keep my head down and my mouth closed and my sweaty stuff away from my locker mate's, then I went home in the afternoons to the Rodeway Inn, where I roomed with the bullpen catcher.

The Angels, it turned out, were a fascinating, bizarre, intimidating, impressive amalgam of baseball personalities, like nothing I'd ever seen. McClure, one of many in that small, muggy room who would come to have a profound influence on my life, one morning noted my bemusement with it all and said, "Look around, kid. It may never be this good in your career again. And you will never have a manager like this again."

He was right. I hoped I made it to the big leagues one day so I could be part of it.

The manager, Doug Rader, was an imposing cigarette-smoking, snuff-dipping, Machiavelli-reading, gruff old soul who laughed loud, sometimes growled louder, and trusted his men to be men. Baseball men.

The pitching coach, Marcel Lachemann, was part father figure, part friend, part pitching guru, part gray-eyed taskmaster. When he talked about pitching, I felt like I should chisel his words into stone and drag the tablets to the mound with me.

The hitting coach, Deron Johnson, was a well-forearmed former power hitter who delivered batting tips in gravelly whispers from one side of his mouth, and pulled on a cigarette from the other, even after he'd been diagnosed with cancer.

The future Hall of Famer Bert Blyleven seemed so old I—at twenty-one—could barely believe it. His face was old. His body was older. He was irreverent, bawdy, brilliant, caring to the point of being sweet and, as soon as you believed that, he'd set your shoe on fire. As a pitcher and as a prankster, he knew every trick. I assumed it was because he'd been around so long he'd invented at least half of them.

The part-time coach, Jimmie Reese, had played three major-league seasons in the early 1930s with the Yankees, where he was a teammate of Lou Gehrig's and a roommate of Babe Ruth's. He'd wryly correct that he actually was a roommate of Ruth's *luggage*. A generous man and storyteller, he possessed a personality that transcended generations and—in his late eighties—wielded a fungo bat with a sharpshooter's precision.

The general manager, Mike Port, was so gravely earnest I avoided him in order to limit the intensely awkward conversations. Yet, later in my career he sent warm notes saying how proud he was of me.

The public relations man, Tim Mead, was a hardworking and loyal confidant to every man in the room, who bled whatever colors the Angels were wearing that year, whose human touch extended from owners to sportswriters to fans, and whose heart wouldn't have fit in one of those little lockers.

The veteran, McClure, was a Harley-riding hardball philosopher whose left-handedness extended to his sense of humor and view of the world. He feared nothing and no one.

The Chief, Chuck Finley, was called "Chief" because that's what he called everybody. With a wit as sharp as his split-fingered fastball, he accumulated strikeouts at about the same rate he did interest from women.

The designated hitter, Brian Downing, was a tough, quiet, muscled, hard-swinging guy who had almost no interest in young play-ers. Not surprisingly, we didn't hang out much. He scared me a little.

The catcher, Parrish, was an amazingly large man—who, it should be noted, preferred one of those old-school metal cups. That, too, was large. In fact, it reminded me of a tractor seat.

The ace, Mike Witt, was the All-Star pitcher, an intense guy who'd won 100 games by then, once threw a perfect game, and whose signature curveball was christened—by none other than Reggie Jackson—as "The Mercedes Bends."

And Kirk McCaskill became my best friend. A wonderful athlete, he poured all he had into everything he did. As my career progressed, along with my life, I'd often ask myself, "What would Mac do here?" Even if it didn't turn out well, I'd know I did the right thing. Though he'd pitched for only four seasons in the big leagues, McCaskill was mature and thoughtful. Over dinner, he felt like a big brother. At the ballpark, he was closer to a mentor.

At the moment, though, they were guys I hardly knew. They were laughter from the other side of the room, and inside jokes I didn't get, and holders of knowledge that came with long columns of sta-tistics on the backs of their baseball cards, some of which I still had in a cardboard box back in Flint.

The experience—everything from sharing their fielding drills to standing in line with them for morning cereal—was overwhelming. They were so sure of themselves. And my presence there was a curi-osity. Some veteran pitchers were skeptical of the Angels' decision to have me in camp, but were kind enough to keep it to themselves. A gold medal didn't rate here and neither did a big signing bonus. Paying one's dues did. Getting big leaguers out did.

On day one, I was assigned a very blue uniform with the number

60 on the back, some very red spikes and, eventually, a pitcher's mound in the bullpen, where I threw first not to Lance Parrish or any of the other catchers in camp, but to Lachemann's brother, Bill, a very nice, very capable fifty-four-year-old man. The veteran pitchers got loose and searched for their mechanics and began their progression toward Opening Day. Further down the line of mounds, I was airing it out, throwing as hard as I could, justifying the first-round decision with every fastball, and trying to make Bill's old, over-stuffed mitt pop authoritatively, which it didn't, no matter how hard I tried. The thing looked—and sounded—like a throw pillow.

When I was done, Bill nodded curtly and went off looking for Marcel, who he found near the locker room.

"That son of a bitch!" Bill sputtered.

"Who?" Marcel asked.

"Abbott," Bill answered. "What the hell you trying to do to me?"

"What's the matter?"

"It's about ninety-four and it's *cuttin'*!"

And Bill held up his arm, where welts were raising on his wrist and forearm.

Marcel smiled.

"Well," he said, "maybe we've got something here."

Maybe I'd overdone it by a little. I was too busy trying to impress the coaches and the big leaguers to notice. Not only did my little locker have to fit all my belongings (along with my locker pal's belongings), it seemed I'd also brought a few extras to camp. Questions, mostly. *Was my stuff good enough? Did I have to elevate my game? Did I need new pitches? Better pitches? Where did I stand next to all these guys, these great hitters and established pitchers who were playing a game I suspected was more refined than mine?*

I kept throwing, lapped up every suggestion from Lach, and threw again. In between, I'd report to the media mobile home and do my duty there, as well. The place was getting crowded. So eager was I, when a reporter—Jerome Holtzman, the veteran baseball writer from the *Chicago Tribune*—rather bluntly informed me I was not physically equipped to execute rundowns, I dedicated hours to practicing rundowns. Fortunately, the security guard at the clubhouse entrance offered no tips; I'd have been on the field all day.

I was eventually assigned to Parrish, which I considered a kind of promotion. I threw well. My cutter was firm and sailing. Twice when the ball ran harder than he anticipated, Parrish sprang from his squat, scraped off his mitt, and shook his howling left thumb. Generally, bullpen sessions rate just above shoe polishing when it comes to spring training events. This, however, was affirming. The cutter— its velocity and late run—was unusual here, in big-league camp, too. When the Angels began their exhibition schedule, when we bused to Yuma, Arizona, and carloads of reporters and photographers trailed behind, I pitched a morning B game, bringing another revelation. The cutter was going to be better against professional wood than it had been against college aluminum. The hitters were better and stronger, but their bats were not. I broke a few bats that morning, then four or five in my next game. Right-handed hitters couldn't keep the cutter off their hands, so I kept throwing it, and rode it deeper into spring training.

Near the end of camp, one starter was injured. Another wasn't pitching well. When the Angels picked up and moved to Palm Springs to finish their spring schedule, Lach had an idea what Rader was thinking. He suggested they not rush the Abbott kid, to allow some time for the curveball and slider to come, to at least let him get a feel for the pro game.

"Bullshit," Rader told him. "Let's see what he can do. What's he going to learn that he hasn't? What's he going to learn in the minor leagues? Is he emotionally resilient? Is he physically capable? What other prerequisites do you have to have to pitch at the major-league level? So, all spring he's in Jose Canseco's kitchen and Mark Mc-Gwire's kitchen. What more do you want?"

The unthinkable was unfolding.

THE TELEPHONE RANG just after breakfast in my room at the Gene Autry Hotel. It was Lach. He asked me to meet him in the lobby. Kind but firm, Lach could be counted on to do the right thing, and generally not the risky thing. He had been a relief pitcher in the major leagues back around the time I was born and clearly knew what he was talking about and understood the mind of the pitcher. The older guys respected him and the younger guys—Finley, Harvey, McCaskill—adored him. I'd grown to share their loyalty to him. All I knew was that he was waiting. When I turned the corner he looked serious. I wondered how many players had been sent to the minor leagues in this very lobby. I sat down. He leaned toward me, elbows on his knees.

I'd begin the 1989 season in the major leagues, he said, in the starting rotation, behind Blyleven, Mike Witt, McCaskill, and Finley. He said I'd made the team on ability, not to sell tickets for a starved franchise that had rarely measured up to the Dodgers up north. He said the team was put together to win, and that's why I'd be on it. He said that no matter what happened, good or bad, that I should not panic, because the club wouldn't. I refrained from hugging him down there in the lobby in front of all those people. Lach, a sentimental guy, looked closer to tears than I was.

I walked to my room a big leaguer.

Floated, actually.

All those levels, from the playground, to Little League, to high school, to college, to the Olympic team, like my mother said, had been gifts. From where, I didn't know. From my parents, I guessed. From the people who didn't give me a chance, and the many more who did. From this thing that I was born with, and my refusal to give in to it, or my obsession with it, or my fight for it, I didn't know which. All three, maybe.

Now there were no more levels, only big ballparks and grown men who played baseball for a living, who put roofs over their families by hitting pitchers like me.

Now there was only making something of it.

Tim Mead gave me number 25. He said Don Baylor had worn it and that he admired Baylor when he had been an Angel. Rader gave me the locker between Blyleven and McClure, so there'd be no quiet corner for me to dissolve into. When the crazy stuff happened, it would splatter all over me. Finley gave me the spare room in his Newport Beach condo. A car dealer gave me a Toyota to drive to the ballpark, a somewhat boxy sedan that more than once earned the observation "That your dad's car?" More often, then, we took Finley's Nissan 300ZX.

Anaheim was a bit of a circus.

The idea that I might be a decent way to sell tickets wasn't new. The media had us surrounded on that topic. No one from the club mentioned it to me, and when reporters questioned Rader, he was pointed in his response. First, he was angry at the callousness of the accusation. Then he got madder.

"Never," he said, "never has that been brought up. Never. What a bunch of crap that is. He is better than anything we have. He is one of our top five starters. So, start him."

My first Opening Day, Chicago White Sox and Angels, Anaheim Stadium, and I was captivated by the sun (96 degrees at game time), the crowd (nearly 34,000 in the old ballpark), the matchup (veterans Mike Witt versus Jerry Reuss), and the start of my professional career, which for the moment meant soaking in all the cool stuff going on, digging my first big-league uniform, casually scanning the stands for hot girls, and occasionally keeping one eye on the game.

So I'd been pretty distracted when, confronted by White Sox catcher and tough guy Carlton Fisk three hours later, I was unsure if I was supposed to punch him, grab him and hope somebody else punched him, or go find a middle infielder and rethink the whole thing.

It all happened fast. One minute we were in a close game, the next we weren't, and then White Sox cleanup hitter Ivan Calderon was heaving his helmet and charging the mound, where McClure waited.

With a frantic clamor, and led by Rader, teammates raced past me and onto the field. I obediently followed. There, we met an equal number of White Sox, as their dugout—and both bullpens—had also cleared out. It was in that crowd near the mound where I met Fisk, who seemed cranky, and I quickly decided to do nothing that would provoke him. Meantime, Rader was in the middle of everything, and not as a peacemaker. That, as I learned, was his nature. There was only one way to play the game—and only one way to conduct yourself. Rader would defend both to his last breath. I'd never played for such a man.

McClure had taken the ball in the ninth inning. We were down, 4–2. The top of our order would be up in the bottom of the ninth. We had hope. But the White Sox scored five runs against McClure. He'd seen a lot of baseball, been in every situation, and had his own ideas about hardball decorum. The White Sox were taking some good rips against him, the last being Harold Baines's long home run to right field. Mac believed their hitters had become a touch comfortable in the batter's box. Actually, "they were swinging out of their asses" is the way he put it. So, he reared back and threw a fastball that hit Calderon square in the back. And all hell broke loose.

We had more brawls that season under Rader than I had in the rest of my career combined, probably. Maybe he was establishing a team demeanor. Maybe he had a group that leaned toward violence, or maybe we simply built a reputation for it. But it kept happening, and Rader kept leading us out there, and a team that wasn't supposed to do much spent some time in first place that summer and stayed in contention to the end of September.

They gave me the ball on April 8, on a Saturday night at Anaheim Stadium.

Without a day in the minor leagues, in a clubhouse of strong-willed veterans and big personalities who would have significant and lasting influences on my life and my pitching, I embarked on a big-league career that few could have seen coming. Certainly I hadn't, and certainly not this soon. In defiance of Rader, it would be written that I was a publicity stunt, that I was on the opening-day roster to juice the gate, that the Angels needed a gimmick.

I didn't believe it and the Angels denied it and no one in the clubhouse seemed to think so. Even so, there certainly was a lot of interest. Nearly 47,000 people piled into Anaheim Stadium for my debut, which was against the Seattle Mariners. I lost, which didn't seem to matter to anyone but my teammates and me. The club had credentialed 150 writers. Photographers trailed me to the bullpen and policemen stood guard outside the gate while I warmed up. I didn't pitch well—the Mariners had six hits, drew three walks, forced us into a couple errors—and didn't make it out of the fifth inning.

Mark Langston—who a year later would be a teammate—shut us out for nine innings.

We lost, 7–0, and yet I had to sit in front of all those writers and television cameras afterward and be the story, which I hated. The elevator doors opened on the third floor and the area outside the press conference room was crowded with cameras and reporters and security guards holding them back, all to get a glimpse of the guy who'd given up six runs in 4 2/3 innings. I smiled the best I could, but told Tim Mead, "I lost. Here I am going to do a postgame press conference."

I'd been so excited. Against its reputation as a late arriver, the Anaheim crowd had been thick and loud before the first pitch. Cameras had flashed everywhere.

I made it, I'd thought. Four years before, I'd been a senior at Central, all elbows and knees and spotty mechanics. Now I was on a big-league mound, in a ballpark so big and crowded I couldn't find my parents, grandparents, Chad, anyone who'd come see me pitch, for all the others who'd come see me pitch. By the time I'd meet with them postgame, I'd already discovered that playing in the majors was beyond satisfying, but that losing in the majors was a dark and very humbling experience. So Mom and Dad smiled and I smiled and none of us really believed in the others' smiles. I was mad I wasn't better.

The experience changed me, or at least changed what baseball was for me, except I had no idea at the time. I'd walked in naive enough to believe that the pages of the script would keep turning and the story would remain happy. Fourteen outs later, I'd walked out carrying not just a glove and some regrets, but an urgency to succeed like I'd never felt before. Because I wanted to stay. I'd lost before, sometimes bitterly, but the taste was more pungent here.

Strangely, in a game I'd played for what seemed forever, everything had felt off. My emotions had been out of balance. I was overwhelmed by the day, by what it meant, by the expectations of the people who came to see the new kid, so at times it seemed I was outside of my body, watching like everyone else. Worse, *hoping* like everyone else.

The game moved too fast for my brain to translate, a blur from the other side of a train window, and nothing I did would slow it down. I knew I was heaving the ball with no touch and no plan, what we called "gorilla pitching," muscling the ball to the glove. I'd pitched big games in big moments, and this felt like those, up until I got up on the mound and tried to get an out. Then, I was inexplicably in a game that was beyond my ability. My focus was shot, my thoughts and strategies spun out of control, and I spent the better part of ninety minutes begging for the ball to find the strike zone, then hoping batted balls would at least aim themselves at somebody.

During spring training, I'd been amazed at how indifferent players were to the games' outcomes. When I mentioned it to my roommate, the bullpen catcher Rick Turner, he'd been amazed at my amazement.

"They're just getting their work in, Jim," he had said, and I wondered just how different the games would be come April. So far, they were very different, mostly because I'd been a wreck.

From the days of camp, when my cutter was boring in on the winter-rusted bats of the Cansecos and McGwires, suddenly I'd felt like a one-pitch pitcher, maybe two. My slow curve was mediocre. Same with the changeup. The slider was okay, but for one night it looked an awful lot like my cutter.

As I sat in that press conference, sounding resilient, eager for the

ball again, what I was really thinking was, "Man, I gotta lot to learn."
I had to get back out there.

It was a while before the swirl slowed long enough for me to process the details, in part because the attention made more of my starts
than I would have liked. After two of them, my record was 0-2. The
offense hadn't scored a single run. The defense had committed four
errors. My earned-run average was greater than 4. My third start,
which would have been at Chicago's old Comiskey Park, was snowed
out. Lach told me I wouldn't be bumped to the next night, but
skipped entirely. I wouldn't pitch for another six days. With a friend
in town, I needed to take a breath, and went for a beer on Division
Street, in an old-school, peanut-shells-on-the-floor joint called The
Lodge, and stayed for more.

Some lessons come cheap. This wasn't one of those.

Chicago is a late town and I shut it down. When I opened my eyes
again in the hotel room, the clock said it was coming up on four.

P.M.

I looked again, squinting at the tiny red letters.

P.M.

My head hurt. My stomach rolled. My hands shook. And the last
team bus to the ballpark would leave in eight minutes.

Alert enough to recall we'd be flying out after the game, and as
gently as I could while still hurrying, I threw anything that looked
familiar into my suitcase, pulled a pink shirt over my head, covered
myself in a multicolored sport coat that, admittedly, looked more
like a horse blanket, and stumbled toward the lobby. Outside, where
a cold rain fell, there was only traffic where a bus should have been.

Two weeks into my big-league career, having been handed the
greatest responsibility of my life, I stood on the curb on Michigan

Avenue hungover, matted by rain, and hoping not to throw up. There wasn't a cab in sight.

"Mr. Abbott?"

A voice from somewhere.

"Could I have your autograph?"

Trying to hold it together, I signed.

"I think you missed your bus."

It was a boy, maybe thirteen.

"My mom's here. Want a ride?"

I nodded, gently as I could.

A Jaguar pulled to the curb. The boy helped me with my suitcase and he climbed into the backseat with it. I gutted through a smile of thanks to his mother and we started toward the South Side.

My sweat smelled like beer and cigars. Had I smoked a cigar? I don't even like cigars. The windows fogged, I assumed because of all the sweating. The heat from the defroster was making me sweat more, and the more I sweated, the more the windows fogged, and the higher the kid's mom turned the defroster. If the cycle continued, I thought I might pass out.

A mile from the ballpark, I spoke.

"Ma'am," I said thinly, "would you mind pulling over?"

I opened the door, leaned into the gutter, threw up, drew myself back into the car, pulled the door shut, and wiped my mouth with the sleeve of my horse blanket.

The boy's mom said, "Are you sick or did you have too much of the Chicago pop?"

The Chicago pop. I'd never heard that.

"Pop," I gurgled.

She sighed. I sighed.

At the players' entrance to Comiskey, I thanked the boy and his mom for the rescue, muttered something about being sorry for the vomit thing, hoisted my bag from the backseat, and headed for the slaughter. I was late. I was sick. I smelled like the men's room floor at The Lodge. And I was thoroughly humiliated.

My teammates were spread in a circle on the floor of the clubhouse, stretching. Through the quiet, I stepped over a leg or two, dropped my bag at the locker, and gently crawled into my uniform. I considered joining everyone on the floor, but instead made for the bathroom, weakly explaining it must have been a bad cigar or something. From the clubhouse, a man lying on the carpet—stretching, say—could see straight into the bathroom, under the stalls, clear to the other side. What all my new teammates saw were my toes, facing the toilet, curling in anguish.

I retired to a table in the trainer's room. When I opened my eyes, Rader was standing over me.

"Cigar," I said.

I couldn't fool a mom driving a Jag. I had no chance with Rader.

"Son"—*uh-oh*—"you don't have to do that with me. I know Rush Street. And I know The Lodge. A cigar. Uh-huh."

That went well.

On his way out, Rader brushed past Blyleven. I was about to tell Bert it was nice of him to come check on me but I'd be all right, when he lit up a cigar and blew a plume of smoke into my face.

I ran to the bathroom. I felt awful, but at least I was running again.

On the bench that night during a game I could hardly see, Dan Petry sat beside me. I just wanted to take it all back and I wanted to feel like myself again and, mostly, I wanted to stop throwing up.

Petry shook his head.

"We don't do that," he said. "This isn't college. Act like a pro."

I grimaced. What a bitter lesson it was. What a fool I'd been. From then on, I'd generally stick to dinners with the other pitchers. Blyleven would take me out and pay every time. When we dined as a group, the bill would be decided by credit card roulette. My card—it was red, and I figured it must have given off heat—was blindly chosen by the waitress from a breadbasket every time. Affectionately, that card became known as Big Red.

Yeah, there was a lot to take in. And sometimes, I even pitched.

By my third start, the attendance at Anaheim Stadium was about half of what it was for my debut. I pitched a decent six innings and beat the Baltimore Orioles. The game had quieted in my head some. The baseball began to feel more familiar, the strategies clearer, and I was able to disappear—a little—into a clubhouse where I badly wanted to be one of the guys. It was April 24. Frank Robinson, the Hall of Famer, was the Orioles' manager. Cal Ripken was the shortstop. I'd given up a couple runs early and was behind, 2–1, when in the fifth inning Parrish homered and Johnny Ray drove in Claudell Washington with a grounder. I pitched a scoreless sixth inning, Minton got five outs and Harvey got four.

Afterward, I went into the trainers' room and asked if I could use the phone. It was late in Anaheim, two hours later in Michigan, but I knew my dad would be awake. I pulled the door closed behind me as the phone rang on Maxine Street in Flint.

Dad picked up. I could tell he knew it would be me.

"I won," I told him. "I won."

"Jim," he said, "I'm so happy for you, so proud of you."

He hung up the phone and told Mom, "If it all ends tomorrow, he can say, 'I won a major-league game.' How about that? Another threshold. He sounded good."

I won some and lost some, shut out the Boston Red Sox in the middle of May, and two weeks later beat the Milwaukee Brewers on a night where I pitched seven innings and McClure got the save. We were in first place that night, I'd won five games so far, and Mc-Caskill had a couple of us to his hotel room to burn off some energy. McClure was there. Amid the laughs, he became serious.

He looked at me and asked how much longer I intended to go on like this, surviving on a pitch or two. I thought I knew where he was headed. He'd counseled me before about the changeup and the curveball, about the difference between surviving and winning, about hitters who'd figure me out. And about *staying.* Didn't I want to *stay?*

"You're not as good as you should be," he said in a room that had gone quiet but for his voice. "You're not living up to your ability."

I looked at him without expression. Nobody had said that to me before.

As much as I hated what it implied, perhaps I'd come to agree when people wrote and said I'd long ago outdistanced my natural abilities. They'd meant I'd done a lot for a guy without a hand. Mc-Clure looked through that, maybe in ways I couldn't.

I was shaken by his honesty. It occurred to me I'd survived that night's game but might not get out of this hotel room.

We'd had conversations before about pitching. He'd urged more off-speed pitches then. We'd be in the back of a bus and we'd get to talking about the art of pitching. With his rebel spirit and tough-love challenges, he reminded me in some ways of my father. Mac, like Dad, was going to send me back out to the playground.

"Quit fighting it," he'd say. "Learn to throw that pitch. Someday you're going to throw a changeup and you're going to get it. You have the power fastball. But there's other ways."

Invariably, I'd ask, "When do you know when to take something off a pitch?"

He'd say, "I don't know. You just know."

"What?" I'd say. "I don't get that."

"There's no answer, Jim. No right answer."

So I'd get off the bus thinking about the answer to the unanswerable question, to the question that wouldn't be asked, or whatever it was Mac had said.

Idling away a night in Milwaukee, we'd left the arena of pitch selection and entered into something deeply personal. I worked hard. I wanted to win so badly. I *was* winning, mostly. Wasn't I doing all I could? Wasn't I?

"Learn how to pitch," McClure said.

Like that, he'd changed my view of how others might perceive me. I'd so wanted to be seen and judged purely by the way I pitched, and by the results of my pitching. McClure, without having been asked, complied. And it made me . . . uncomfortable.

Could I endure that examination? What was I without the back-story? Was I the man who, in victory, welcomed the appraisals, but believed them harsh in defeat? How honest did I expect people to be?

I hardly slept that night and didn't do much better the night after.

McClure was relentless, and I worked with Lach on developing a pitch that wasn't hard and a plan when to throw it, and some days it came and others it didn't. Mostly, I threw the cutter and the slider, became more proficient at throwing to the left and right sides of the plate, and pushed through toward the end of the season. We endured two late losing streaks, spent one final day in late August in first place, and finished in third, eight games behind the Oakland A's.

My record was 12-12, which was about what I deserved. The

team, I thought, deserved better, but there was no questioning our fight. In fact, it had become a trademark of ours.

We were in Chicago, falling out of contention, when we found ourselves in another shoving match with the White Sox, not quite as heartfelt as the one on Opening Day, but still potentially damaging. It only takes one guy to change the emotional dynamic of fifty men on an infield, and on this day he found Rader. As the teams were separating peacefully, a man from over our dugout screamed, "What the fuck are you gonna do with one hand, Abbott?" I, of course, had heard that kind of thing before. In moments like that I almost expected it.

Rader didn't.

He tore after the heckler, three Angels holding him back, the fan retreating up the steps to the concourse. Rader shouted after him, "Bad things are going to happen to you! Bad things! You'll burn in hell!"

I loved Rader.

He was, however, up against a fight I had too much experience with, and one that would never go away. Just two months after Opening Day, I'd hit the Brewers' second baseman, Gus Polidor, with a pitch during a game in Milwaukee. Polidor, a slight Venezuelan, took exception and raced toward the mound shouting angrily in Spanish. I had no idea what he was saying, but as he was pointing aggressively toward his own right hand, I guessed it was something about mine. He pulled up short of the mound, turned toward our dugout, and got into it with Rader, who'd started toward the mound himself. It ended peacefully, fortunately for Polidor.

But for all of that, my rookie year was not entirely about pitching mechanics, bench-clearing melees, Jaguar rides, and various big-league sniff tests. In fact, some of that season wasn't really about baseball at all.

I HAD AN idea—an inaccurate one, it turned out—that reaching the major leagues would be a personal finish line. I was never going to have two hands, but I assumed the story would grow old, and some other sparkly object would come along to catch the eye of the sports world and, anyway, by then I would have proven the game was not so different for me. I'd just be a guy on a roster, trying to be special, but owed nothing of the sort.

I was wrong. The attention from the media was, at times, stifling. The labels remained. The headlines in the local papers in every city we played were unchanged. I was, first, the one-handed pitcher. Away from my teammates, I'd tell my story over and over, because people wanted me to and because I wanted the organization to be proud of its choice to believe in me. And because I had the hardest time saying no, even when I would have preferred to be a kid learning to pitch in the big leagues and nothing more.

And even that wasn't what I was so completely wrong about.

I was wrong about the children. I didn't see them coming, not in the numbers they did. I didn't expect the stories they told, or the distance they traveled to tell them, or the desperation revealed in them.

They were shy and beautiful, and they were loud and funny, and they were, like me, somehow imperfectly built. And, like me, they had parents nearby, parents who willed themselves to believe that this accident of circumstance or nature was not a life sentence, and that the spirits inside these tiny bodies were greater than the sums of their hands and feet.

The letters and phone calls began in spring training. First, there were a couple letters at a time, and Tim Mead would bring them by my locker, and we'd write back something supportive and personal. Soon, there were requests to come to camp for a meeting, and we'd schedule fifteen minutes in a day. By the time we got to Anaheim, a couple letters had become dozens, and during the season became hundreds. I read every letter, and Tim and I answered every one, because I knew these kids and I knew how far a little boy or girl could run with fifty words of reassurance.

The letters became lines of families at the doorways of clubhouses from Fenway Park to Yankee Stadium to Comiskey Park to the Kingdome, and tiny, quiet tears in dugouts from Arlington Stadium to Kauffman Stadium to SkyDome to Anaheim Stadium.

Some we knew were coming. Others just showed up. And Tim would catch my eye, point his thumb toward the door, and I'd excuse myself from the card game. At times, I was conflicted. I did not want to leave the clubhouse or teammates I was just then getting to know. Every time I stood up—"Back in fifteen minutes"—I was announcing again my difference, confirming how I was viewed, not that there was any missing it. Every photo that ran with magazine and newspaper articles featured my right hand. That is, when I wasn't covering it with my left hand. The *Life* magazine photographer Neil Leifer followed me for three days, and the result was a lot of pictures of my right arm.

Apparently, that was who I was to them, to most everyone, including the children.

And yet, I could hardly decline.

When I was a boy, a ballplayer from Flint—Ron Pruitt—had made it to the big leagues. Dad knew him a little. So when he came to Detroit with the Cleveland Indians, Dad took me to Tiger Stadium and Pruitt shook my hand and gave me a ball, and the experience meant the world. Years later, Rick Leach, a Michigan guy and Detroit Tiger, helped recruit me to Ann Arbor, and I could barely hear what he was saying over the screaming in my head, *That's Rick Leach!*

I knew what it meant to brush up against a major leaguer. I had no idea what it might have meant to meet a major leaguer who looked like me.

So I found my glove and followed Tim through a tunnel and into the dugout, where another family was waiting with another story. And then I'd be moved by both. The parents would be kind and appreciative, and their little boy would stare out with wide, yearning eyes, and he would be missing an arm, so that one sleeve of his baseball jersey would flop all over, and it wouldn't seem to bother him at all.

"Hey," I'd say, "you play baseball?"

"Yeah."

"Show me how you do your glove."

And the little boy would hoist this massive glove head high, waiting for an imaginary throw, determination spread across his face.

"What position do you play?"

"Pitcher, like you."

"Aw, don't be a pitcher," I'd say. "Be a shortstop. They get to play every day. All right, now show me how you hold the bat."

The parents, standing nearby, would laugh along. I know they wanted to know, exactly, "How?" How had I made it work? How could they? How would their little boy grow up to be whatever he wanted to be? How would he endure?

I would tell them about my parents. They'd made me feel special for what I was, and yet treated me like I was every other kid from the neighborhood. I would tell them about my frustrations, and their words, "This is something to be lived up to." I asked them to see that that, and so much else, were possible, and amazing things could happen. My parents had done that for me, and they could do the same for their boy.

The connections lasted five minutes, maybe ten. I felt better leaving every single one. I hoped they did, too.

A little boy named Adam came to see me at Comiskey Park. He stood with his mom and dad outside the clubhouse before batting practice. Tim opened the door and Adam, who was five, stepped back against his mom's legs, across the concourse. He was missing a hand.

His mom leaned into his ear. "There he is," she said. "You can go talk to him."

Adam looked again to his mom, gathered his courage and ran to me, wrapping his arms around me when he arrived.

As the meetings accumulated, and as I was touched by every single little boy and girl—when some literally would reach out to confirm that my defect was as real as theirs—the experiences shifted my perspective from me and my condition to a broader recognition of all of these other people and their conditions. I hadn't known, hadn't even considered really, how many people were like me.

I'd lived their young lives already. Now they were waiting on kindness. They were waiting on the one thing that came along that they loved so much, they would never put it down. Baseball was powerful like that. The game drew me to it, and now it drew them to me. In a few quiet minutes orchestrated by Tim and the elements of right time and right place, this child and I would stand inside the cathedrals of baseball, passed by clattering spikes on cement, and convince each other that anything was possible, still.

The meetings weren't always so formal, and then they'd be a voice from behind the dugout, or from the hotel lobby, or from a sidewalk half a block back.

Along the rail in foul territory, before a game, I'd inch toward the dugout, signing as I went. A ball here, a baseball card there, a cap or a glove. And then there would be a little boy, not asking for anything, just standing with his arms out, one hand absent.

See? his eyes pleaded. *I'm like you.*

"Hey, pal, how you doing? Play ball? Good for you."

Or a little girl, shyly gripping a ball, too shy to actually push it out over the rail. In the moment of eye contact, I could always tell she was special.

"Show him your hand, honey," her mom would say. She wanted me to see.

And the little girl would draw her arm from her coat pocket, showing no hand at all. I knew what she felt. I had kept my hand in my coat pocket, too.

It was powerful. These were the people who'd come to the ballpark early, fought through the professional autograph hounds, worked their way to the rail, and hoped.

Stop, their eyes said. *Don't go.*

I never felt like I did enough. The letters I wrote, the ten minutes I spent before batting practice, the hours over a course of a series, it wasn't enough. I couldn't convey what I wanted to share, the belief that so much is possible. Not for what I'd done, but for what they would do. For what they could do, if they believed, too.

Some came with their own tales of achievement. They were playing baseball. They were playing hockey. They were getting straight A's, or learning to drive, or in the band, and they came to tell me their stories. They wanted me to know they were doing great, too, that they were hopeful and upbeat and unsinkable, too.

There was a boy, maybe fourteen. His arm was to be amputated. I didn't know why. He wanted to come see me pitch, but when he was healthy enough to go to the ballpark, I wasn't healthy enough to pitch. I was on the disabled list. We just missed each other. I'd met him. He was a good kid, and scared.

Tim Mead called on a Saturday morning. The boy had suffered a stroke. I drove to Anaheim and together we went to the hospital. We entered the room and the boy, upset that I was there, ashamed I would see him hurt and vulnerable, began to cry. His mother began to cry. I couldn't help but cry.

I sat on the bed and we talked about courage, and about getting better, and about believing in himself.

We left him in that room. Then, in silence, we drove back to Anaheim.

Tim left me at my car, climbed the stairs to his office, and pulled the door closed. Then he began to cry.

There were so many out there like that boy.

I was inspired. They pushed me back onto the field and into my own battles. I was going to be just like them.

CHAPTER 14

The zero, the one everyone was staring at, had been on that old scoreboard for so long it was getting hard to ignore. The yellowed lights, while burning a perfect and comforting rectangle into a gloomy Saturday afternoon, by the moment grew more electrifying and more difficult to live up to.

As I returned to the mound for the seventh inning, thinking about a first-pitch strike to Carlos Baerga and surviving the middle of the Indians' lineup another time, it hung somewhere over my right shoulder, glowing expectantly.

Zero hits.

Had there been a chance I didn't know, I could have read it in the ballpark. There was something new in the crowd's tone, like a living thing. Day games started slow, the august place sleeping off the night before. Teammates who might have mentioned a pitch here or there, grunted something about a good or crummy play, commented on another score in another town, began to keep those observations to themselves.

Three innings is still a very long time, plenty long enough for something to go wrong. If it was perspective I sought, I'd need to go back only those six days, when the Indians required three innings to score seven runs and send me stomping into the Cleveland night.

I'd thrown eighty-four pitches through six innings, which wasn't too many. I could get to 120 or so without too much trouble. And I began to feel a push. I didn't feel alone at all. In fact, I couldn't help but begin to enjoy what was happening. Not the result—which again, who knows?—but the process. These nine guys—ten with the DH—trying to do this ridiculously difficult thing. For nine more outs I'd let go of the ball, then stand back and watch it all unfold.

Carlos Baerga, still batting left-handed, led off the seventh inning. Nokes set up away for a cutter, but not just away: beyond-the-head-of-Baerga's-bat away. The pitch was down and, indeed, away. Baerga, aggressive as usual, went after it and got just the top of the ball, which bounced once in front of the plate and again about half-way to first base. I busted a few steps toward the bag, and slowed when Don Mattingly gloved the chopper and waved me away. My momentum carried me at a jog toward the bag and, after recording the out, Mattingly poked me in the gut with his mitt before turning and firing the ball to Randy Velarde.

About then it occurred to me, *He knew. They all knew.* And they were beginning to think about it, too, counting down the outs, feeling the crowd, glancing now and again at the scoreboard, confirming that zero still hanging there. Mattingly's gesture was his way of encouraging me, his way of saying *We're all here for you, trust us and keep it going.*

Two pitches later it was clear how right he was. After fouling off a cutter, Albert Belle pulled a grounder crisply and dangerously wide of third base. Nokes had asked for something down and in and I'd left it up half a foot, and I'd watched the grounder zip past me toward the hole. Velarde went deep to his backhand side, along the cut of the outfield grass. If the ball got to him, he'd have no chance to throw out Belle.

Wade Boggs, in his first season with the Yankees after all those seasons in Boston, had at that point not won a Gold Glove, but there were two in his future, and when he got them I'd think of what happened next. Boggs took a couple jabby steps and lunged to his left, half-smothering and half-spearing that three-hopper just as it nearly skidded past him. In a cloud of dust, he leaped to his feet and made a hard throw to Mattingly, just as Belle crossed the bag. First-base umpire Jim Evans raised his fist, the crowd roared, and I turned and nodded at Boggs.

From that play, acknowledgment came from the stands. The quiet etiquette of the ballpark had evaporated in those four seconds—from the crackle of bat on ball, to the snap of ball in glove, to the silence as the ball raced Belle across the diamond, to the cascade of approval from Yankees fans—we were all connected. It was on.

It's one thing to be pitching a no-hitter in the seventh inning. It's another to believe that maybe it could happen. At that moment, with the way the fans were cheering, the way the guys were playing behind me, the way the Indians' hitters kept finding gloves, I began to believe there might be something special out there. I mean, I couldn't utter the words, of course. I could still hardly fathom them. But that was a hell of a play Boggs had made, and I wasn't the only one feeling it, and with one more pitch—Randy Milligan hit a soft chopper to Boggs at third, a routine play if somewhat close at first base—I was through the three-four-five hitters and into the eighth inning, six outs left.

As I approached the first-base line, I picked up my head and spotted Jimmy Key, a really good, smart pitcher I'd become friends with, and Scott Kamieniecki, another former University of Michigan pitcher I liked a lot. They were on the bench and, as usual, having a pretty good time. Bursting with excitement and anticipation, I smiled at them and—before those 27,000-plus and the television cameras and anyone else who might be looking in—broke into my imitation of Kamieniecki's typically exaggerated jog from the mound. It was heavy-legged and loose-armed, and bent slightly at the waist and, of course, more than a little goofy. And I just felt like doing it, like I needed to let out a laugh and so did everybody else.

As I descended the stairs into the dugout, Nokes rapped me on the butt with his mask. Key laughed and gave me a high five, not because I was pitching so great, but because I'd dogged Kamieniecki. As I pulled the navy jacket around my shoulders again, I couldn't help but grin again toward Key, who was still smiling about my lope off the field. I liked those guys and I was having fun, even amid the pressure of winning a game and then winning it like this. I'd never pitched in the playoffs, but I imagined every game felt just like it.

Among the guys in our clubhouse, that dugout, there was a bunker mentality, and generations of Yankees players before and after us would admit the same. There had to be, given the pressures from ownership, the manager, media, and fans. Under Showalter, in particular, players were cautious because conspiracy theories abounded. There was a sense that anything you did or said, every eye roll, might have been reported to Steinbrenner or Showalter. We covered ourselves because, with only a few exceptions—Mattingly, for one—everyone was expendable. The Yankees had the money to cover their mistakes and go get the next guy. The coaches were especially vulnerable; they made hardly any money and so were easily disposed of. Showalter was so guarded, always seeming to talk out of the side of his mouth, like it was top-secret stuff. Honestly, I'd nod my head, but could barely make out what he was saying.

Though my own struggles undoubtedly added to my perception of clubhouse suspicions, many of my teammates admitted their uneasiness, the nature of the Yankee beast. Had I pitched better, maybe it would have seemed different. As it was, I sensed the Yankees were disappointed with me, that teammates might have unconsciously distanced themselves from me because of it, and that made the clubhouse kind of a lonely place. Still, along with a deep respect for sturdy veterans Mattingly, Gallego, O'Neill, and Stanley, and a fun friendship with Pat Kelly, who lived in the city with his wife, Rebecca, I really enjoyed my fellow pitchers, guys like Key, Kamieniecki, and Mike Witt. Pitchers seemed to get one another, which was good, because so few others got us.

I drew some water from the big bucket and found my regular place on the bench, back in the moment. Again I swung my foot over the floor, clearing the debris of exhilaration just as I would disappointment. I cleared my head and ran through what was next. Manny Ramirez would lead off the eighth inning. Out there, just outside my scope, the bottom of the seventh inning ended when Paul O'Neill flied to left field. Splashing the dugout floor with what was left on the bottom of the cup, I turned and placed it on the stack. There were seven.

CHAPTER 15

B y the end of a warm afternoon in Oakland, on the final weekend of April 1991, two seasons and a month in the major
leagues had my record at 22-30, my ERA at 4.34. For 1991 alone,
I'd made four starts and lost them all. My ERA was 6.

On the bright side, my quest to be recognized as simply a pitcher
was fulfilled.

The fresh public angle on Jim Abbott was that he was in over his
head. More specifically, my command was poor, my curveball was
spotty and, as a result, hitters had figured me out, primarily because
two years before I'd been rushed from college to the big leagues.
There were, however, fewer questions about how many hands I had.

Nice story, decent guy, not getting enough outs. I'd given up
more hits than anyone in baseball in 1990 and lost 14 games.

After the promise of '89, the Angels had fallen into mediocrity.
We weren't pitching or scoring runs like we once had, the team was
aging faster than the calendar could keep up, and management answered by acquiring veterans past their primes. We were getting
older, not younger, and worse, not better.

By 1991, we were headed for a last-place finish in the AL West. Doug Rader would be fired in late August and replaced by Buck Rodgers. It was then I first considered the cold side of the game, when Rader—wearing a cowboy hat and a forced smile—returned as the former manager and hugged every man in the clubhouse. He'd believed in me. In late spring, I wasn't winning. The issues that led to 246 hits allowed and 14 losses the season before hadn't dissipated. In the club's front office, serious consideration was given to sending me to the minor leagues.

Asked his opinion, Marcel Lachemann told the baseball operations staff, "Well, that's a bunch of bull. There's no way he deserves to be sent out. In fact, you send this kid out, you send me with him."

Years later, Lach recalled, "I think they thought I was kidding, because they never put me to the test. When I left the meeting I thought, 'What did I just say?' But, it never came to that."

The game can be moody. It is cool and then comforting, warm and then entirely unjust. For no apparent reason, it began to like me again. There was no explanation, and I didn't ask for one.

Over the next five months, I was 18-7 with a 2.55 ERA. I shut out the New York Yankees in the Bronx in mid-May, shut out the Milwaukee Brewers over seven innings in mid-June, beat the eventual World Series champion Minnesota Twins twice in August, and won 9 of my last 12 starts. My curveball was effective. I worked the outside half of the plate to righties. I'd never been better.

In the midst of coming back from 0-4, I told *Sports Illustrated,* "It was the toughest thing I've gone through, baseball-wise, in a long time. In the back of your mind you think, 'Maybe I just don't have it. Maybe every lousy pitcher thinks that someday he's going to get good.' And then all of a sudden, your worst fears are out in the open, in public debate."

I still had Lach on my side, McClure in my ear, a developing feel for pitching on my fingertips and, if any of that failed, Harvey Dorfman in my head.

Harvey was a sports psychologist. He was in his mid-fifties when Boras, intrigued by advances in the mental side of baseball, introduced us after my rookie year. By then, Harvey had served on the Oakland A's staff for six years, as the brain coach sitting on the bench not far from the hitting and pitching coaches. Before that, he was an educator and coach and before that a soccer player and before that a child so stricken with asthma he could barely get out of bed to play with the other children.

I didn't know why Boras came to believe I was in need of a sports psychologist. When he suggested I go see Harvey, I looked at him so blankly he assumed he'd offended me. In fact, Boras had been considering bringing Harvey and me together for more than a year. Standing just off to the side of my first season in the majors, Boras had watched the stadiums fill when I pitched, he had watched the media swarm and the fans rush to me when I entered a hotel lobby. It was daunting, and it wasn't commensurate with my performance so far. And Boras believed I'd be tested one day, when my performance did not match the expectations of the public or myself.

On the night of my very first start, he'd looked around Anaheim Stadium and thought, *Oh my God, how is he going to be able to put this in perspective?*

Performance fluctuates. Results fluctuate.

As long as he's on top of his game, Boras thought, *all this works. What happens when he's not? What happens when life gets serious? He was so strong climbing up the mountain. What happens when he gets to the top and has to look down?*

Eighteen wins looked to Boras like the top of the mountain.

Harvey and I met over lunch. A month later, I flew to Phoenix, where Harvey picked me up at the airport, two hours south of his home in Prescott, a small town in the Bradshaw Mountains. I'd spend the weekend with him.

Harvey wasn't one of those touchy-feely therapists. We drove an hour before he pulled into a diner where he could get a bowl of chili, and by the time we left I could tell he would never ask me what kind of tree I'd be and I wouldn't be writing haikus describing my childhood. If he was sympathetic to the way I was born, he hid it behind the edginess of a New Yorker (he was born in the Bronx) and the demeanor of a coach (his old job).

Harvey thought I was too nice. I knew that because he said, "You're too nice."

When we returned to the car I told him, "You have made me talk more in an hour about my hand than I have in my entire life."

"Isn't that why you're here?" he said.

We pulled out of the parking lot and Harvey shot me a look that said, *That's the freakin' problem, pal.*

I couldn't help but smile.

For two days Harvey asked questions, I answered, and he took notes. He'd arrived at the sessions knowing what I was and what I'd done, if not who I was. He assumed the weekend would be more painful for me than it was for him, and he was correct.

He asked if, as a kid, I'd ever been in a fight. When I said I hadn't, he nodded as if he'd already known the answer. I'd been mugged in a stairwell in high school. And there were fights I should have taken up that I didn't. I wasn't proud of it.

His observation: "You would do nothing to antagonize anybody into a confrontation. The last thing you wanted to hear was, 'Ah,

screw you, you stump-handed kid.' You did not want to be dispar-
aged. You placated people so there would be no name-calling. You
didn't want to hear the words."

I nodded, even if I wasn't sure I agreed, which probably was his
point.

"There are a couple things to consider," Harvey continued. "One,
you can't please everybody. Two, if you believe this perception of you
is valid, you are living your life based on what other people believe
you to be. You wear the mask long enough, it becomes your face."

Harvey had a lot of clients. More than a few had asked him to
teach them to be jerks. It was the baseball thing, the competitor
thing, the killer-instinct thing.

But he and I talked about balance, about being strong without
being insensitive, compassionate without being weak. My need to be
liked, he determined, was so ingrained I'd become deferential to everyone. Had I continued on that course, he believed, I might have
taken to deferring to hitters, as well. Even hitters. Imagine.

We all have a sense of our own vulnerability, he said, and to that
end we fake it till we make it. I couldn't fake mine, he pointed out,
because my vulnerability extended beyond my shirtsleeve. The best
I could do was to put my hand in my pocket. By doing so, of course,
I drew more attention to it, to the fact I was hoping to hide it.

I hid my hand a lot, maybe unconsciously. I believed everybody
was looking. And they probably weren't. If so, maybe momentarily.
But, I struggled with it. In nearly every photo from childhood, I'd
buried my right hand in my pocket, or covered it with my left hand.
Not even my parents had noticed. Even in childhood, I'd have rather
avoided the subject, ducked the questions, and eliminated the expressions of pity.

Harvey was right about these talks. They were painful. I hadn't thought I was faking anything. I guess I thought of it as "coping." Or "overcoming." Or just *pitching.*

Prodding, Harvey was continuously drawn to my tendency to, as he said, "Give myself away"—that is, to ignore the insults and slights of others. He concluded that such a lack of self-esteem could manifest itself in the amount of trust I took to the mound. He was right, though I wasn't completely adrift. With the ball in my hand, I felt I had a direction—to show people I wouldn't give in to my quite obvious vulnerability. It was not forward thinking, but a regular and reliable ambition. I didn't understand it. It just was.

The level I strove for as a boy and the challenges I took on through college, by the big leagues I wondered at times if they were enough. I wondered again if I belonged. Those voices might sink in over time, along with those questions, and I might be in serious danger of answering, "I don't know." I think that's what Harvey was getting at. Whether I was 10-14 or 18-11, did I trust I was good enough? Did I have the conviction? Would I continue to believe in myself come those times when the greater of two wills would win?

I liked Harvey. My career had sped off so quickly over the previous couple years I'd barely had a moment to make sense of it, and that's when Harvey came along. He seemed a wise man who possessed a broad sense of the world and an ability to place baseball within it. Being twenty-two, I was searching for myself and looking in all the usual places, hoping to stumble into a truth by pulling random books from library shelves. None of it was deep enough for Harvey. But he provided an ideal outlet for points of investigation and discovery.

It was just easier for me to sacrifice my self-interests if that meant peace and harmony—mine, my parents', my teammates', anyone's.

Of the messages I took away from Prescott, not the least was that I did not have to apologize for the way I was born, least of all to myself. And it was not for me to comfort others because of it.

Harvey's lessons would be easy to conjure in the few days immediately following our visits, but nearly out of reach amid the rigors of a baseball season. To that end, we stayed connected through books he'd recommend. Harvey was exceedingly literate and a bibliophile, and over the years he sent me dozens of books, or handwritten lists of works he believed worthwhile. I'd read them, at times searching for Harvey's coded messages reinforcing the conversations we'd had. I'd grin at the passages clearly intended for me, such as the Cormac McCarthy line "It is always himself that the coward abandoned first." Or another McCarthyism: ". . . those who have endured some misfortune will always be set apart but . . . it is just that misfortune which is their gift and which is their strength."

I was all over the place, thinking something would make sense somewhere.

Harvey enjoyed my discoveries, even if he'd not intended a direct hit at all.

"Sometimes," he told me, "I use the musket mentality."

Where we diverged, however, was at the pitcher's mound. Years after I'd earned my way onto it, I would not yield to those who tried to knock me off. Baseball still gave me the venue to fight back against all the other stuff in my head, and against what I assumed to be in other people's heads. If anything, I evaluated my performances through the prism of my insecurities. I did believe I was letting people down when I didn't win. And I did take losses hard, though not much harder than pitchers with two hands. I'd once heard of a pitcher who'd lost badly and afterward sat at his locker, silently carving up a baseball with a hunting knife. A little disappointment and reflection—a run through downtown Cleveland, say—seemed tame by comparison.

I returned from the weekend feeling somewhat raw but unburdened, and I continued the self-examination. Maybe I was too nice, and maybe that was unusual in professional sports. But, maybe it wasn't an act—or a mask—but a way to make me happier. Harvey probably wouldn't buy it. Later, I sent him a photo. He hung it on his office wall at his home, alongside those of other athletes he'd counseled. I wrote, "Harvey, thanks. You are an inspiration to me." And, of course, that made him laugh.

"It was nice," Harvey once said. "But, me? Inspirational? I appreciate it, of course. But, the choice of words. Say thank you. Can that other stuff."

He'd inspired me to think of who I was and what I wanted to be in ways I'd never thought of before. He inspired me to think of people and the journeys they have taken. He recognized that sports, to me, were validation. He told me, "You don't need to validate who you are. You don't need that. This is who you are without this." I don't think he even cared much about the pitching.

So, yes, he was an inspiration. Sometimes where he saw "other stuff," I saw genuine feeling. That would piss him off, too, probably.

I maintained my relationship with Harvey through the rest of my career, and until he passed away in the spring of 2011, mostly through our love of books, sometimes when I needed a kick in the rear end, and occasionally just to say hello. But I carried that weekend in Prescott with me, and maybe it was coincidence and maybe it wasn't, but in the period of my life leading into and through my times with Harvey, I met my future wife. She just didn't know it at the time.

DANA DOUTY WAS a senior at UC Irvine, a college basketball player
and a person grounded enough to be dubious of the whole professional baseball player thing. She came from a family of firefighters.
Her brother had been a college pitcher who, two years before, was
drafted by the Philadelphia Phillies.

I should have been at spring training, but a labor impasse resulted
in the owners' lockout of the players until early March. So, I was at
a party—hosted by a friend of a friend of Chuck Finley's—instead.
Dana was smart and beautiful and athletic, all of which had me quite
nervous for our first date, dinner a few nights later with those somewhat mutual friends. It went well enough that I was somewhat torn
when the lockout ended the following day. I packed up that morning, drove to Arizona for my second spring training, and the moment I returned asked Dana for a second date. We shared childhood
and family experiences; we both saw the world as a good place, and I
realized early on that she was far too decent of a person for me.

She never asked about my hand. In that, I felt her strength, her
certainty. Maybe she believed in me, but I translated it as a belief in
herself. I admired her acceptance of it, and me. As I fell in love—it
took moments—I became thankful she would take it on, to endure
the second glances, to wonder what our children might have to overcome, and to make my life ours. Love, as a concept, to me means
personal concessions. In our case, Dana did nearly all of the conced-
ing. She wanted to come along, but not to nurse me; to stand alongside me. In many ways, she embodied the person Harvey was trying
to teach me to become. I liked that in her, and I believed I was closer
to being that person with her.

I proposed—originally enough—on Valentine's Day in 1991 and we were married after that season.

In many ways that year was perfect. Dana's love, and her company, and her calm, helped me to believe in myself. My pitching matured with the rest of my life. I won 18 games and finished third for the American League Cy Young Award. People were talking about my ability to pitch again, this time not to opine that I was terrible and should be sent to the minors, but to say I stood with the best pitchers in the league.

The best part of it was not the validation of me (though I didn't hate that), but the vindication for those who stayed with me: Rader, Lachemann, Finley, McCaskill, even Jimmie Reese, who—whether I'd won or lost—would drag his fungo bat into the outfield the next afternoon and hit me a hundred more. I recall every one of those afternoons as sunny and warm, the two of us camped in right field, me standing between two baseball caps and him sixty feet away, a half-dozen baseballs at his feet. It was Jimmie who transformed me from a decent fielder to a better one. He'd draw two batting gloves over his hands and give me a nod. I'd pantomime my delivery to the plate and with perfect timing he'd snap toward me a ground ball—crisp, like he'd hit the sweet spot of the bat every time. In his day, they'd say, Jimmie could pitch batting practice with that fungo bat. It was in these sessions I developed a greater rhythm for transferring the glove from my right hand to my left, and I was proud of the work we did. Jimmie would try to shoot balls inside the ball caps and past me. He bet me cans of Coke he could. I think maybe he owes me a six-pack or two.

Rader used to say that Jimmie and I were put on earth to meet each other. Jimmie hung around almost ninety years to make it happen, and by then he was stooped and frail and angular, like he'd been carved from the very lathe he kept in his Westwood workshop. There, he made picture frames—he framed almost everything he came across—and his own fungo bats, cleaving them the length of the barrel so they were flat on one side and rounded on the other. Jimmie helped me to assimilate into the big leagues, then to survive them once I was there. I'd sit next to him on the bench during games, which he'd chart for Lach and the pitching staff. And in the spare moments Blyleven wasn't sliding under the bench to hotfoot him or spitting sunflower seeds on the chart so Jimmie would have to tear it up and start over, we became friends. When I told him I'd become serious about a girl, he insisted on meeting Dana, afterward saying, "Beautiful smile, kid. Beautiful smile. Nice teeth." He was kind and made me laugh and paid for every early-bird buffet meal we ever had together, during which he would remind me to watch my money and to invest in T-bills. He loved the T-bills.

Jimmie died in 1994, at ninety-two. Because he hadn't much family, I always thought of him as being survived by baseball. I didn't keep much from my career, but I have two of his handmade fungoes, one signed to me, the other to Dana.

The beauty of Jimmie, he was the same gentleman in 1991 as he had been the season before, when I lost 14, and was the same guy in 1992, when I pitched as well as I ever had and was 7-15, and the same again in 1993, when I was no longer an Angel.

I'd miss him.

From the moment I was drafted, I figured I'd be an Angel forever, like Al Kaline was a Tiger forever, and Alan Trammell and Lou Whitaker certainly would be. Growing up in Michigan in the era of free agency and Marvin Miller and rising salaries, I admired players such as Trammell who played for one team. I never heard about his contract negotiations. And every Opening Day he ran out to shortstop like there was no place else he could ever be. On the back of his baseball card, under TEAM, there was just a tall, endless stack of TIGERS. I wanted to be that guy, to be that reliable. Yet after my fourth season with the Angels I was in the middle of a very public contract negotiation and being portrayed as another greedy ballplayer rejecting money most people couldn't fathom. Heck, *I* couldn't fathom the money.

It was the winter after the 1992 season, in which I'd lowered my ERA from my 18-win season and still lost 15 games. The Angels' offense finished last in the American League in nearly every important category: we lost 90 games, finished 24 games out of the lead in the AL West and clearly were in transition. So, I wasn't alone on the staff. As a team we had the third-best ERA in the league and yet Mark Langston lost 14 games and Chuck Finley and Bert Blyleven each lost 12 games. Little had gone right. Rader had been fired in late August the season before and the organization was finding its way under Buck Rodgers, a popular former Angel with a big personality who'd managed the Expos for a half-dozen seasons. Even a bus trip down the New Jersey Turnpike proved too much of a challenge for those Angels. In late May the first of two buses carrying the club from New York to Baltimore crashed into the woods, seriously injuring Rodgers and battering and bruising a dozen players and team personnel. I'd pitched into the eighth inning that night at Yankee Stadium, allowing only one run, and we lost anyway, and I left the Bronx thinking things could hardly get worse. Two hours later we were pulling guys out of a bus that was on two wheels and threatening to tumble sideways down a hill, the manager was moaning in pain, the second baseman's ankle was the size of an ice bucket, the traveling secretary's ribs were cracked, the bullpen catcher was bleeding like crazy, and the right fielder had punched the bus driver in the jaw.

We were never in the race. The season ended, mercifully, but over the summer team general manager Whitey Herzog, Boras, and I had begun discussing a contract extension, two years before I would become a free agent. Boras was by nature opposed to contract extensions—he preferred the free-agent market, where teams drove up the cost of players on one another—but it was my desire to remain in Anaheim, and there was no harm in negotiating. We'd seemed to settle on the contract extending for four years, which would cover two arbitration years and two years of free agency. Now it was about the money. When the team was in Baltimore in late August, Herzog placed a piece of paper in my locker, folded once. I opened it. He'd written, "$16 million." At the time I would have been the highest-paid four-year player in the history of the game. I should have accepted.

Just a couple weeks earlier, we—Boras, Herzog, co–general manager Dan O'Brien, and I—met for lunch and to decide my future, at McCormick & Schmick's, a seafood place on Main Street in Irvine. Officially—and, it seemed, confidently—Herzog offered $16 million over four years. I nearly choked, it was so much money. Boras was somewhat cooler. He responded by sliding several pages of statistics across the table and countering at $19 million. It wasn't what Whitey was hoping for, though I'm sure he half expected it. He barely looked at the packet Scott had prepared before tossing it dismissively back at him.

"This type of shit," Herzog announced to the table, "is what's wrong with baseball nowadays."

That didn't sound too good to me, but I left the meeting believing we were close, that a deal was likely, that we'd settle at $17.5 million, that I'd still be an Angel forever. I was thrilled and rushed home to tell Dana about it. Turned out, the Angels weren't negotiating. They'd given us their best—and only—offer. I had no idea, but we'd way overshot what owner Gene Autry would pay and what Herzog had the patience for.

After the note from Herzog in the clubhouse and lunch in Irvine, I would never again hear from the Angels about that contract. The season went on, September passed, and it hung in the air, neither agreed upon nor dismissed. And on a rainy night in early December, that contract was the furthest thing from my mind when Dana and I stood curbside at LAX, watching Dana's mother approach in her car. We'd been in Hawaii on vacation. We were exhausted from the long flight. The weather was terrible. When I opened the car door, I knew something was wrong. Something had happened. Dana's mom had been crying.

"You've been traded," she said.

In a hotel room in Louisville, Kentucky, where baseball's annual winter meetings were being held, Tim Mead opened his window and felt the cold air whip against his face. Before he would write the press release Herzog had ordered him to write, Mead screamed his frustration into the night, a primal profanity that jarred loose his own tears. As he sat at an unfamiliar desk and typed the words—Jim Abbott . . . Yankees . . . pitchers Jerry Nielsen and Russ Springer, first baseman J. T. Snow—his phone rang. He said hello. I asked if it was true. He said it was.

I was stunned. Dana and I both were. And hurt. It wasn't about going to the Yankees yet, it was about leaving the Angels. I rolled it all around in my head countless times—the faces of my teammates, my friends, Dana's family, her mom, the contract negotiations, Herzog's biting words. I didn't think we had rejected their offer and they never actually said, "Sign it or you're gone." I would have signed it. I would have stayed.

The following days were muddled, an eddy of regret and anger that eventually slowed and then stilled, leaving acceptance. Mead set up a press conference so I could answer some questions, which I showed up for and immediately regretted. As hard as I tried to keep it upbeat, I felt I'd sounded whiny about the failed negotiations and the trade. It all seemed so terribly wrong, like first I'd gone along with Boras's negotiation strategy and then with Mead's media strategy, and they'd both meant well, but I should have known better. Not only would I not be an Angel forever, but it was ending disgracefully. Instead of keeping my mouth shut and moving on, I kept trying to justify the negotiations, trying to get Angel fans to like and forgive me.

When I arrived late morning there were twenty-five reporters in a small ballroom at the Doubletree Hotel, a few blocks from Anaheim Stadium. Mead believed the fans needed to hear from me, that it was the right thing to do. "Closure," he kept saying. "People need closure."

He felt so strongly about it that he organized the media event without the Angels' permission, and he was scolded by senior management when the morning newspapers carried the accounts of it.

A few days later the letters to the editor in the *L.A. Times* were so hurtful. To the people who'd penned them, I'd become the player I never wanted to be. I was greedy and selfish and ungrateful.

Jackie Autry, owner Gene Autry's wife, called a few nights later. It was late and it seemed she had been crying, blaming it all on Boras, saying she and Gene didn't like him very much, which put them in the majority of baseball owners.

I had chosen Boras when I was twenty, when all that was guaranteed was that very first check. Fairly new to the industry, he'd negotiated a big bonus for Cris Carpenter, a right-hander out of Georgia, in the 1987 draft. The first pick of that draft—Ken Griffey Jr.— signed with the Seattle Mariners for $160,000. Carpenter, taken fourteenth overall by the St. Louis Cardinals, also received $160,000. That was good enough for me.

But this seemed wrong.

Later on, Boras's style sometimes bothered me. As he built his firm and reputation, there came clubhouse talk about his aggressiveness both at the negotiating table and in pursuit of other clients. I defended him. Almost immediately the Autry-owned Angels had problems with him and hinted I was wrong for employing him. Boras called their tactics "the oldest trick in the book," but I wasn't so sure. I know that I probably disappointed Boras, too. His refusal, I believed, to consider what other people thought of him (or me) didn't match up with my hypersensitivity. In the end what attracted me to him—the unyielding toughness that bordered on antagonism— also pushed me away. And maybe that's why he thought I needed Harvey.

While I was right that he cared little for how he was perceived (it wasn't, after all, his job to be liked), Boras was disappointed in himself for the way he played the negotiations. For one of the few times in a career that would continue long after I retired, Boras had become emotionally attached to a player, and therefore an outcome. He believed the Angels—Herzog, O'Brien, the Autrys—had mistreated me through their hard-line negotiations. Boras saw people in the seats and on the concession lines. He saw a community that fawned over me. And he saw a good pitcher, which he equated to value for a franchise. And he believed that was worth more than a take-it-or-leave-it offer.

In the hours after negotiations failed and I was traded, Boras regretted his tactics, which were driven by anger. He wished he had done better by me, that he could have looked above what he considered to be deplorable conduct by the Angels, and kept me in Anaheim.

Herzog had called him in the final hours and told him, "Look, you better take it or we're going to trade him."

Boras did not think Herzog was bluffing. He simply got mad.

"What?" he said aloud when he put down the phone. "Move Jim Abbott? What are you thinking?"

Even as he became less popular with teams, his results were so good I couldn't complain. Indeed, in some ways I don't think I was ever fair to Boras, because I never let on about my discomfort with his ambition. Swallowing potential issues until they became full-blown crises was a lifelong habit of mine, and on this occasion it got me traded to the Yankees. While I was sure Boras and I viewed the world differently—*very* differently at times—he was incredibly loyal. He thought I was a better pitcher than I thought I was, for one, which could be inspiring. He surrounded himself with the kind of bright and savvy baseball people—vice president and former Olympic teammate of mine Mike Fiore, Harvey, conditioning director Steve Odgers—that suggested to me he understood his own weaknesses.

None of that mattered to Jackie Autry, who told me Herzog had talked Gene and her into the $16 million offer, but then came to believe we would never sign a long-term contract. Again and again she said she didn't like "the people you have working for you," that I should hire a different agent—Dennis Gilbert, she said—instead. And she'd begged Herzog to trade me to Toronto, away from the "vicious media" in New York, but Whitey told her he couldn't get the same players from the Blue Jays. She finished by warning that you should never turn down your first million dollars (though I'd made more than that the previous season) and intimating that I'd been angling to get myself back to Detroit. It wasn't true.

I couldn't dismiss Jackie so easily. The Autrys had come to my wedding. I loved Mr. Autry. I once had him autograph a ball for my grandmother, who adored him. He would recall visiting Flint while on tour and he loved sharing the story with me. To have things play out this way was difficult and demoralizing. The Angels were all I knew; they were my baseball family.

Boras had also called. His focus was New York and how the city and the Yankees were great opportunities for me. Beyond the new lifestyle and the new team, he said he easily could get a contract offer comparable to the Angels'. As it turned out, we went to salary arbitration and lost, the hearing being my first real encounter with the Yankees. So, instead of being surrounded by friends and family with the Angels for $16 million over four years, I was introducing myself around and looking for a place to live in New York, and for a lot less money in a one-year contract. I wouldn't regret the move to New York, but I didn't know it at the time. What I did know, what I did think about, was how there are decisions in our times that are truly life-changing, but at the moment they seem like they can be put off for another day. Then, suddenly and regretfully, you find that circumstances—or somebody else—has made the decision for you.

After considering the suburbs of New Jersey, Connecticut, and Westchester County, Dana and I slowly turned our attention to New York City. We found an apartment on the Upper East Side, and during spring training Dana returned to furnish the place. Intimidated—

but slightly exhilarated—by the commotion of Manhattan, and convinced that everyone but she knew exactly where they were going, she waved down a cab, headed downtown, and with some relief reached a store that rented furniture. She paid her fare and stepped out of the cab, straight into two men who'd taken their fistfight into the street.

"Where *am* I?" she thought, clutching her purse tight and hurrying into the shop.

We were far from Orange County, for one, far from the familiar faces at the market, from the family dinners on Sunday evenings. After the initial shock and sadness, we'd talked ourselves into the adventure of New York City and the Yankees. Dana was determined to put her head down, walk fast, be decisive, turn her wedding stone inward toward her palm, and get on with it. I was determined to restart my career for a team that, if not as homey as the Angels, certainly would win more baseball games.

The first time I was on an airplane it was to visit Princeton when I was a senior in high school. My parents were behind that. I had no chance of being accepted. My host drove a few of us to New York City, where we gaped at the skyline, ate pizza, marveled as the waiter brought four high school kids beers without hesitation, and watched all the people try, and fail, to stay out of one another's way. I fell in love with the place.

The second time I was on a plane was for *The Phil Donahue Show*, and the third time was for *Good Morning America*. I stayed in Midtown hotels with marble floors and soaring ceilings, had long black cars pick me up at the curb, and then went on television. New York was a darned fine place, as far as I was concerned.

Of course, it was one thing to visit, another to be kicked to one of those curbs by the only organization I'd known. Fortunately, I wouldn't be alone. I had Dana. And over five weeks after the 1992 season, the Yankees traded for Paul O'Neill, traded for me, signed Spike Owen, and Jimmy Key. For a four-headed press conference, the club put us up in a suite at The Plaza and heralded the return of the late great Yankees, and it struck me that playing for this team in this city would be a glamorous life.

For a short time, it seemed like it was meant to be.

The Yankees were the Yankees, even when they weren't. They hadn't been to a World Series in twelve years and hadn't won one in fifteen years. Yet, they remained the team of Ruth and DiMaggio and Mantle. Thurman Munson had died fourteen summers before, but in the Yankee Stadium clubhouse his locker—the one nearest the trainer's room—remained unoccupied. The old place still bore the fine footprints of the greatest the game had ever seen, along with the rattling footfalls of George Steinbrenner. Even at a time when they had gone four years without a winning season and were routinely outplayed and outdrawn by the crosstown Mets, the Yankees were special. My heart leapt every time I walked along that dim corridor and turned right into the clubhouse.

I hoped there was something to a fresh start. Unlike the Angels, who were on the decline, the Yankees had a chance to be competitive, and then to recapture the city. The general manager, Gene Michael, was building a good team. Don Mattingly, who in my mind stood with some of the franchise's greats, was optimistic about the changes. After serving two and a half years of a lifetime ban for spying on Dave Winfield, Steinbrenner was in charge again, and loud about it. He'd come off the suspended list declaring, "Jim Abbott has to be a hero in New York," the kind of thing all the players would chuckle about, except the guy who had to wear it around for

a week. I had a feeling that were I ever to be traded from the Yankees, I would never get a weepy phone call from George.

Barely a month later, not only wasn't I a hero, I wasn't winning a
lot of baseball games. A headline in one of the morning papers read,
ABBOTT'S STILL UNDERWHELMING. In another: ABBOTT'S PROBLEM:
A MINOR LEAGUE FASTBALL.

That was about the time Dana started hiding the newspapers and
magazines.

I liked New York, its energy, its demands for accountability. It
was a lot to handle, sure. But, cast from the insular world of the Angels and Orange County, Dana and I to some extent *found ourselves* in
New York. There was nothing quite like being in that place, in those
years, in that fishbowl, with a whole career ahead of us.

It would have been great to bring a fastball along. That certainly
would have softened the edges of the expectations carried by Steinbrenner and the city, and healed the jarring experience of salary arbitration that had me wondering why the Yankees had even traded for
me, and eased the creeping sense that the pennant race—the first in
the Bronx in seven seasons—had gone off without me.

Buck Showalter, the Yankees manager, used to say New York is a
"snowball town, both ways." The trick was to keep it tumbling in
the right direction, and to somehow keep from being swallowed up
in it. The guys who'd been there awhile looked right through the
noise and clutter. The rest of us tried.

The season, and Dana's and my life in it, swung in all sorts of directions. At home, we embraced the city and its people, at least the
ones who didn't shout critical things at me from the street corners.
I'd underestimated how difficult it was to be anonymous in a place
with seven million people. Everybody—*everybody*—had a comment.
Sometimes it was nice, other times not so nice. And it was incessant.

On the field, I could be very precise with my pitches or very hittable because of them, depending on the night. The Yankees hadn't traded for me to be erratic, and that's what I'd become. I was supposed to be a number one starter, or at least a number two to Key's number one. I was having a difficult time getting lefties out, and I wasn't winning on the road. At the end of April I was 1-4, and by the end of summer I was 9-11, and the Yankees were growing in their disappointment with me.

Michael became alarmed at my lack of velocity and my inability to throw a straight fastball. He would pull Showalter aside and complain, "Buck, he's throwing all cutters. You guys have to get him off the cutter. He's got to throw some straight fastballs to keep the hitters honest. The hitters are thinking in. They're all looking in. They're all off the plate and they're *giving* him the outside part of the plate."

For his crusty exterior, Showalter actually felt bad for me. He felt the snowball coming. I discovered later he wasn't even that mad at me for leaving the clubhouse in Cleveland, but rather worried for me. He, like the rest of the Yankees, and like me, had counted on more. When Michael came to him, Showalter simply shrugged. Their radar guns had my fastball at 85 mph. I'd lost almost 10 mph and couldn't get it back.

"He doesn't have the bullets in his arsenal," he told the GM. "He's not defenseless, but there's no margin for error. The secondary pitch just isn't there."

They were frustrated, and it wasn't long before the media began to feed on that. On a morning in late August, at a time I was pitching reasonably well but needed to win more if we were to stay close to the Blue Jays, *The New York Times* ran a story—it was more like a graphic, really, headlined, A PENNANT TRIES TO GROW IN THE

BRONX—that combined my season with fellow starter Melido Perez's and read, "The excuses are growing old. Solid starts and games
that could have or should have been won by these two underachiev-
ers are no longer important; only victories are."

I read through it again. *Underachiever?*

It wasn't a word I was comfortable with.

The piece was written by Jack Curry, a young and talented writer
who had a solid reputation in the clubhouse.

I waited by my locker for the writers to arrive. Usually there were
dozens of them. At 3:30 exactly they'd stream through the heavy
metal door, searching for stories for their early deadlines, eager to
hound the guy swinging a hot bat or to corner the lost soul in a hor-
rific slump.

When he walked in, I was holding the morning *Times* in my hand.

"Jack," I said.

Reporters knew when a story they'd written would bring a confrontation. Some aimed for it. Curry wasn't an instigator. But the
sight of me clutching the newspaper told him all he'd needed to
know.

"What is *this*?" My voice raised as I held up the newspaper.

Other reporters, standing a few yards away, watched and listened.
The sight of one of their own in an altercation was great theater, of
course, and carried the potential of a story.

Curry explained it was an article about who needed to perform
better if the Yankees were going to catch the Blue Jays.

" 'Underachiever'?" I quoted.

Curry understood: I wasn't being defensive about the season so
much as I was about my life.

"You always told me you wanted to be treated like everybody
else," he said. "I used that word to describe your season."

I hated confrontation, probably because I wasn't very good at it. I was embarrassed that my feelings had been hurt. I tried to keep the red out of my face. And then I had no idea how to end what I'd started.

I left the newspaper at my locker, shook my head at Curry to show how deeply I was offended, and stalked off to the refuge of the trainer's room.

When I was gone and the scene still hung in the room, a fellow writer told Curry he should have known better, that if he was going to rip a player in the *Times,* he should have ripped one who didn't read the *Times.* Most guys, the writers believed, read the *Post* or the *Daily News,* if anything.

But Curry was reassessing his word choice.

"Did I go too far?" he wondered.

I hadn't gotten to the trainer's room before regretting the confrontation. Curry's assessment was accurate. And I was wrong to be angry with him. Though Harvey might have applauded the courage to defend myself, he wouldn't have approved of its motivation.

The fact was, I—my pitching, my results—was a disappointment to the Yankees and their fans. But I was the last to see it. Kirk McCaskill and I played regular rounds of golf in the winters. He'd once observed that when you miss a putt, of all the people on the green, you are the last to recognize the ball isn't going in. Spread over months, even over two seasons, I think I was the last in New York to realize this ball wasn't rolling in the right direction.

I naively assumed my past efforts and record would be factored in to an analysis of how I had performed, and then what could be expected out of future performance. And then I was too immature to understand how illogical that was. Harvey would have told me to toughen up. New York got to me.

The game is about results. I thought about the inspiration I derived from the kids who came to visit me in those stadiums, and their refusal to let the circumstances of their lives become an excuse. Because of the temptation in my own life to use my hand as both a shield and sword, the examples being set by those children were unforgiving. In that way, I didn't always measure up to them. The choice to use my hand as a defense against someone who was fairly calling me an underachiever was too easy. And in the first few strides, leaving Curry standing at my locker, I was already disappointed in myself. He was fair. And simply because I was trying as hard as I thought I could, I should not have held myself above the criticism. For all the credit I'd been given over the years for being tough, maybe I wasn't.

I never apologized to Curry. It's strange how you feel about the writers who cover your team. I liked most of them. And yet because of the inherent terms of the relationship, I could never be close with them. As ballplayers, we held an automatic posture, a defensive one, even when the reporters were right. Especially, perhaps, when they were right.

On that day, I'd given in. I had used my hand as justification for expecting a kind review, and my conscience stung. All this talk of being a role model, all this talk about rising above the challenge, and when the scrutiny became intense I ducked for cover. I carried that day for a long time.

I finished the season 11-14, and we finished seven games behind the Blue Jays.

After a second—and mediocre—season with the Yankees that began much like the first and ended in August because of the player strike, Dana and I were ready to go. The promise of adventure in New York had become rather heavy on our lives, the mood of which was predicated on me winning baseball games, which wasn't happening often enough.

We packed with a good idea I wouldn't return and with no idea of where we would be next. Dana flew to California. I drove cross-country with Billy, a springer spaniel pup I named for Yankees coach Billy Connors. My previous dog had been hit by a car and Connors found another like it, presenting it to me while the team was in Anaheim. Billy—the dog—returned to New York on the team charter, and as he flitted about the aisle, I thought this was probably the only dog to ever fly aboard a Yankees plane. George Steinbrenner might have disagreed.

Free agency was a player's reward after six years of major-league service time and was in Boras's wheelhouse. For me, after two uneven seasons with the Yankees, free agency meant I didn't have a job, and I'd have to wait at least through the strike, which lasted eight months, to get one. And some team out there was going to have to believe in me again.

When the strike ended in late March 1995, I met with the Angels in a conference room at Anaheim Stadium, Boras and I on one side, general manager Bill Bavasi and Mead, promoted from public relations to assistant general manager, on the other. Boras, as he had almost three years earlier, slid a folded piece of paper across the table. Bavasi, as Herzog had almost three years earlier, unfolded the paper and, ultimately, passed.

I had an offer from the Cleveland Indians. And I got a call from the Chicago White Sox, though not from the general manager. Robin Ventura and Kirk McCaskill had reported to spring training with the White Sox. Ventura, my Olympics teammate, was their starting third baseman. McCaskill had become a full-time reliever for the White Sox the season before, but had been assured an opportunity in camp to become a starter again.

They called from the clubhouse. Would I come? What if they talked to management? How much money would it take? They hung up and in their spikes and uniforms walked to the office of assistant general manager Danny Evans.

"Jim Abbott's still out there," McCaskill told Evans. "He'd love to come. You have the money for him?"

The next day, I was on a flight for Florida, for spring training, for a team willing to take a chance on me and into a clubhouse of friends. McCaskill, who'd gone to camp eager for a place in the rotation, not only found me a job, he found me his job.

I desperately wanted to pitch well again. In the three seasons since I'd won 18 games for the Angels, I'd become average. No matter how I prepared, how many hours I toiled in the weight room, how many mechanical adjustments I made, how many scouting reports I memorized, how hard I tried to throw my fastball, I'd become a guy who was barely making it. I couldn't get it right. Six years in, twenty-seven years old, I wasn't the player I wanted to be. I couldn't believe how difficult it had become to win a baseball game. Fastballs come and go, but not at twenty-seven, and not in an arm that felt loose and strong.

Determined to take my career back, and unsure exactly how to do it, I went to the row of spring training mounds and threw a pitch. And then another. When the exhibition games came, I went to those mounds, and threw more pitches.

And still couldn't get anybody out.

Rick Peterson was the bullpen coach of the White Sox. Or, more accurately, the pitching coach of the relievers, something general manager Ron Schueler, pitching coach Jackie Brown, and Peterson had worked out.

During one of my failed spring outings, Schueler stood beside Peterson and said, "What do you think?"

"You know what, Ron, until I get this on film, I'm not going to know for sure," Peterson said, "but with the naked eye, he's got his glove on his hand before the ball's going through the hitting zone. That's not just the cut fastball now. He's cutting pitches off."

"Okay," Schueler said. "Why?"

"I don't know. But, if I had to guess, he's been smoked. He's scared to death of the ball coming back. There's no way he can throw a ninety-plus-mile-an-hour fastball and put that glove on his hand before the ball gets in the zone. He's not finishing."

Almost a year before, in a game against the White Sox at Yankee Stadium, I'd thrown a fastball to Frank Thomas. Seemingly as the pitch cleared my fingertips, pain bolted from high on my left thigh. I'd never seen the line drive. When Thomas returned to the dugout he told McCaskill he'd never hit a ball harder. The next day the bruise started at my thigh and ended at my ankle.

I'd never really thought about defending myself on the mound. That was for other people to worry about. The ball Thomas hit, had it been a couple feet higher, might have killed me. But, if I was shortening my delivery as a result, going for the glove too soon and cutting off my momentum to the plate, it was subconscious. It was instinct. It was survival.

Peterson sat me down. He was an interesting guy and a good pitching coach.

"Let me ask you this question," he said. "Do you know how many guys have ever died on a baseball field?"

I said I didn't, but seemed to remember one, Ray Chapman, who in the early 1920s was hit in the head by a pitch and died hours later. Peterson made a circle with his five fingers.

"None," he said.

I wasn't going to argue the technicality.

"So, if it happened to you, you'd go right to the Hall of Fame. They'd take your uniform right off and ship it to the Hall of Fame. I know that. They'd entomb you in the Hall of Fame."

There was that.

"If you need to transfer that glove to your hand before that ball goes through the hitting zone, I'd suggest you go home and stop playing, because you've got no chance at competing at this level. You're going to have to give this up and overcome this fear."

So, he said, I had to finish every pitch, complete my delivery, and when I did the ball would have more life. And if, as a result of following through, I would be left defenseless, then I could be bloodied and wheeled away to the Hall of Fame. Either, I figured, would be preferable to what I was already doing.

If nothing else, it gave me something to work toward and believe in, and that by itself was more than I had had to hold on to for months.

By late July, I was 6-4. My ERA was 3.36, more than a run better than the season before. From the end of May through the middle of summer, my ERA was under 3. Under Brown and Peterson, I developed some consistency with the curve, cutter, slider, and a baby changeup—variety and speed changes I hadn't always had. In terms of velocity, I wasn't Nolan Ryan, but neither was I defenseless. I could be aggressive, and it was exhilarating. I'd wondered if I would be that guy again, and now I was, and in Chicago, surrounded by good friends. Dana and I were where we wanted to be. We could breathe again. And we should have known it wouldn't be that easy.

On July 27, I was traded back to the Angels in a six-player trade. The White Sox were out of the race. The Angels had an eight-game lead in the AL West. While I was somewhat conflicted over leaving Chicago, the Angels by all appearances were going to the playoffs. And it was home, still. And maybe the hard feelings and misunderstandings of three years before would be lost in the homecoming and in a pennant. Maybe it could be easy again.

When I took the ball for the first time back in that uniform, I beat the Milwaukee Brewers on a Saturday night in Milwaukee. The Angels led the division by ten games. Three weeks later, by the middle of August, we led by 10½ games. The team had grown up in the time I was gone. Lach was the manager. The lineup was laced with strong young players—J. T. Snow, Garret Anderson, Jim Edmonds, Tim Salmon, Gary DiSarcina—and the veterans Chili Davis and Tony Phillips. Chuck Finley and Mark Langston were formidable at the top of the rotation, as were Lee Smith and Troy Percival at the back of the bullpen.

After years of grasping at roster-building philosophies, the Angels had discovered something that worked for them, and we were running off with the AL West. We thought so.

A month later, we were in second place. Two nine-game losing streaks, a lot of lopsided scores, and a near miraculous four-game sweep of the Oakland A's over the final long weekend of the season put us in a one-game playoff against the Seattle Mariners and Randy Johnson in the Kingdome. If we won, I had the start the following day in New York against the Yankees in the division series. We lost, 9-1. The collapse was complete.

As horrifically as the season had ended—and the flight home from Seattle was among the dreariest three hours I'd ever spent—I was encouraged. I was proud of my pitching again. The team was young and seemed to have many contending years in front of it. Soon, the Angels would sign me to a three-year contract extension. After three years away, I was comfortable. I was going to be in the right place at the right time again. I was so sure of it, Dana and I decided we were settled and grown up enough to start a family.

FOR GOING ON thirty years, I'd not asked my parents what happened to me. I sensed from an early age there would be no answer, or nothing to be gained from an answer. I was born this way, and that would be enough of an explanation. It would have to be. My duty was to figure it out from there.

Dana and I were considering having a child, however. For better or worse, I had accepted my disability. I wasn't sure if I had the authority—or the courage—to accept a disability for a son or daughter, too.

When Dana mused about a little boy or girl, and I warmed at the thought of her as a mother and me as a father, I became ever more fearful that I carried a genetic predisposition for physical imperfection. I'd managed, but what if our child couldn't? What if the condition was worse? I would be responsible for that. Would it be selfish to bring into the world a child who would be so challenged?

There were times when I met children who had such challenges and for a moment I'd have to catch my breath, just imagining their daily fight.

I believed ardently that disabilities do not confine our lives to struggle. I also was unsure if I would knowingly take the risk. The guilt I would have felt for my child and for my wife would be so hard to bear. I didn't know if I was strong enough for that. I'd accepted it once. Twice, I just didn't know.

So I called my mother and asked her what she knew. There were no answers, she said.

Then, in a quiet moment in the Anaheim Stadium clubhouse, as our season was faltering, I approached the team physician, Dr. Lewis Yocum, the renowned orthopedist. I told him what I'd been thinking about, starting a family, being sure. He recommended a genetic specialist at UC Irvine.

The day of the appointment, I could barely keep food down for the nerves. I continually looked at Dana, so in love with her for facing my insecurities with me. We sat before the doctor, a stranger who studied me like the doctors of my own childhood had. Her questions were pointed, my answers vague. And near the end of what I feared would be a terrible, heartbreaking day, the doctor nodded at us reassuringly and said, "These things happen. I don't think you're at any risk of passing this on."

By March, Dana was pregnant with a girl we'd call Maddy.

In early summer, Dana had her first ultrasound examination. Studying the monitor, to myself I counted to ten. Over and over, I counted to ten. By the time I was done, I struggled to hold back tears. I wished to hide from Dana how close I was to fear. She looked at me, took my hand, and smiled.

CHAPTER 16

The flagpole at the old Yankee Stadium—the tallest one with the American flag on it—was in left-center field, where it rose out of and towered over Monument Park.

In there, monuments to Lou Gehrig, Babe Ruth, Mickey Mantle, Joe DiMaggio, and Miller Huggins were on red marble slabs, while other legends were depicted on reverential plaques. Not only was it a nice place to visit, it was a pretty good place to pitch to. The fence was almost four hundred feet from the plate and the ball didn't carry well to left-center field, which is why left-handed pitchers were at something of an advantage: More right-handed hitters meant fewer lefties knocking pop-ups into the right-field bleachers.

Just beyond the outfield fence, the pole stood in front of the frieze and the banners spaced perfectly along the top rim of the ballpark and the buildings of the Bronx beyond that. There were scoreboards and advertisements on the back wall, and pennants whipping in the breeze—a lot to meet the eye.

But with two out in the eighth inning, a runner at first base and a little time to kill, it was the flagpole that drew my attention—or, more precisely, the golden ball at the top of it. In that moment, with the crowd crying out and clenching its fists, with so much seemingly at stake and four outs to go and Sandy Alomar Jr. taking forever to pine-tar and resin his bat and then take his warm-up swings, I reassured myself in a place fifty feet in the air. This was my habit. When my confidence ebbed or I found myself giving the hitter or the situation more than I should, I would step off the rubber and find that focal point, imagining the word TRUST written confidently in sturdy block letters across the golden ball. It was a reminder to myself to return to my strengths, to what I do best. It was about presence and awareness, being in the moment, living with the result because the process and the journey were sound and pure.

Anyway, it had always made sense to me.

Ten minutes before, I'd dropped a seventh water cup on my dugout stack, laid my jacket on the bench, and exhaled hard. This was the inning I'd lost my no-hitter to Bo on an elevated cutter he flared into center field. I wanted to win. I wanted the no-hitter.

So I went after Manny Ramirez with cutters early, which got me to a 2-and-2 count. The crowd groaned every time plate umpire Ted Hendry ruled a ball and applauded every strike and shrieked at every swing whether the ball was put in play or not, all of which was fun and scary and so thrilling.

I was trying to stay in the game, trying to keep my mind on executing every pitch. I was thinking, "Outs. Just get outs," which is a little broad, but better than having my thoughts dart all over the place. Throughout my career, a no-hitter almost never entered my mind because I didn't have what baseball people would think of as classic no-hit stuff. I gave up hits and then I got ground balls and double plays and moved the game along that way. But, you come a certain distance, you get twenty-one outs, and you might as well go get it. So I threw a changeup Ramirez swung over the top of and got my twenty-second out, which led to an odd moment. Ramirez's follow-through was long and, because he'd been fooled on the pitch, a bit wild. The bat crashed into Nokes's left shoulder. Nokes winced and rolled to the ground, and I, thinking the ball had gotten free on the strikeout, dashed toward him before realizing the ball was in his mitt. Okay, so I was jumpy.

By then, pockets of fans were standing and shouting for every pitch. And so a first-pitch strike to Candy Maldonado, a cutter that sliced through the middle of the strike zone, brought thundering applause. The next pitch—another cutter, this one up and in— jammed Maldonado, who fisted a routine grounder to Randy Velarde at shortstop.

There were two out. Four to go, starting with Jim Thome, the dangerous left-handed hitter. He took two cutters, both away, the first a strike and the second a ball. On the third pitch, thinking Thome had already hit the ball hard once against me and was look- ing kind of comfortable, I dropped my arm angle to three-quarters for a fastball that Thome missed by six inches. I hadn't used that near-sidearm delivery for the previous twenty-five hitters and would do it only once more, but it seemed right for Thome. Ahead 1 and 2, I missed with two cutters and then with a curveball, none all that close, so I walked him, which bothered me, because I'd followed the best pitch of the day with three that lacked faith or precision, that lacked trust.

The moment, I knew, had crept into my head, alongside hope. Hope would do me no good. Because he'd hit a line drive in the sixth inning, Thome was a threat. I pitched to miss his bat, so I had be- come a contact pitcher pitching away from contact, deserting the aggressiveness that had gotten me this far.

Which was when I found the golden ball. Junior Ortiz wasn't going to hit. Sandy Alomar Jr. was. Alomar came out of the dugout and slathered up his bat. Waiting, I stood off to the side of the mound, seeing TRUST across that ball in the sky. It seemed so easy. The plan was the same, to throw the ball to the strike zone and let its natural movement carry it to the end of the bat, or toward the handle. Yes, trust.

When Alomar was ready and I was again on the mound, I took one more look at the flagpole, turned, got the sign from Nokes—curveball—and threw a good one that Hendry must have thought was high. Alomar then fouled off a cutter, took another curve for a ball, and then hit a cutter toward third base. Wade Boggs snared it on an in-between second hop and threw to Mattingly. I was again headed to the bench, again untouched. I broke into my Kamieniecki routine again, because I needed everyone to laugh, myself included. I sat down and thought, *Here it is.* For the first time, I think ever, I rooted for the team not to score. I wanted to get back out there.

CHAPTER 17

Once, when I'd known I'd let down the Angels and the people who wanted to believe in me because I couldn't get enough outs, when I was so frustrated I no longer could pretend I believed in the next pitch or the next start or the next anything, I took a baseball bat in my hands and beat an inanimate object until I reached exhaustion.

The heavy bag, the kind boxers practice on, hung in the tunnel behind the home dugout at Anaheim Stadium. It was soft from years of abuse, and it was red like the faces of those who abused it.

When the bat splintered, I flung it to the ground, found a second bat, and continued to thrash until that splintered, too. Then I got a third bat, which died similarly, in a rage I'd never felt before.

I'd pitched poorly before and would again. I'd gotten hit and misplaced the strike zone and lost before. But sometimes a guy has to beat something, because hitting myself with the bat would have looked foolish. I was finished in the fifth inning that day.

Head down, legs heavy, Lachemann had come for the baseball.

And I went for the bat rack. Then to the heavy bag. I stopped because my reaction was an embarrassing display of immaturity and selfishness, and because it could have been construed as showing up Lach, and because it went against all that my father had instilled in me in childhood about dignity and composure. And because I couldn't find a fourth bat.

That was September of 1995.

The following season was worse. Every day was worse. Every game, every restaurant meal, every night I came home to a quiet house, every time the phone rang, it was worse.

The promise of the previous season—heavy bag excluded—ran off in spring, in the Arizona desert, and never really did return, not for long enough.

There is perhaps no better job in the world than being a ballplayer, and no better position than starting pitcher. In fact, professionally speaking, if I had to live one day every day for the rest of my life, it might be the day after a win. Any win. The sun is warmer and the laughs are easier. The clock is meaningless. Lunch stays down. The next day of work is forever away.

Lose, however, and I would have rather done anything else. Lose, and the next day my arm didn't feel quite right, and the traffic to the ballpark was exasperating, and all those guys getting ready to play again were the lucky ones. Lose, and the four-day wait for redemption was interminable.

Lose a bunch, and the impatience to win again becomes the very grounds to lose again. Rather than concentrating on executing a single pitch, the focus becomes winning a ballgame or three, and that's far too big. Or, actually, it becomes not losing another ballgame. The cycle can be murderous to a baseball season, then to a career.

Lach used to tell us, "Trust your stuff." Believe in your pitch and throw it to the mitt, he said, and think of nothing else. In a losing streak, however, the single thought in a pitcher's head—at least this pitcher's—was, "Don't lose." Sometimes, "*Please* don't lose." I'd get a perfectly good sign from the catcher and risk it by thinking, "Don't let this be the pitch that beats me."

Obviously, that's not conducive to pitching well. And I didn't.

I lost 20 games in 1996, 18 of them in the big leagues, two of them when the Angels had seen enough and sent me to the minor leagues. Unlike the last time team management considered demoting me, no one put his career on the line and threatened to go with me.

It wasn't simply a bad season. It was an epically, historically, hide-the-women-and-children bad season. On May 1, I was already 0-4. From the middle of May to late June, just to take one particularly imprecise period, I was 0-6 with a 12.72 ERA. By August 10, I was 1-15. I was losing by football scores.

By the time they counted up the big-league numbers at the end of the season, all based on at least 141 innings pitched (which I somehow managed to accumulate), my win-loss percentage (.100) was the ninth-worst in history. And my 7.48 ERA—again, based on at least 141 innings over a season—was the worst ever. Those numbers don't come by accident. There aren't that many bad breaks in a season.

At twenty-eight years old, and feeling mostly strong and healthy, I had perhaps the ugliest season in baseball's modern era, which spanned thousands of pitchers over three-quarters of a century.

Generally, I viewed my seasons in the context of the areas that could have gone better. Even the good seasons—12-12 in '89, 18-11 in '91, 11-8 in '95—I tended toward underselling the high points, at least to myself.

There was no underselling 2-18. I was 0-8 in Anaheim, in front of

Angels fans, family, and people who mattered the most to me. And they were so nice about it. I'd walk off the field down five runs in the fourth inning, and get an ovation for it. It was painful.

Left-handed hitters batted .347. I couldn't keep the ball away from their bat barrels. Had they been one guy, they would have finished third—behind only Alex Rodriguez and Frank Thomas—in the American League batting race. And when there were runners on base, when I really tried not to lose rather than simply making a pitch of some passable quality, the league batted .358 against me. And, speaking to my dearth of confidence, I walked 78 batters, the most in my career, and five more than I'd walked in 1991, when I'd pitched 101 more innings. I even threw 13 wild pitches, none of which, it should be noted, were hit off the left-field wall for a two-run double.

As a pitcher, the season had been a breakdown of body, mind, and, hard as I fought it, spirit.

Tim Mead would find me after games in the weight room. A sweat puddle chased me from machine to machine. We'd stand there looking at each other and I'd ask, "What would you do?"

What would anyone do?

Remarkably, Lach and general manager Billy Bavasi stuck with me for as long as they did. Second-most-remarkably: Dana stuck with me all summer without making me sleep in the garage. Hard as I tried, I often failed to leave the hurt and frustration of the season at the ballpark.

I lifted more weights, threw more bullpens, threw more fastballs. When that didn't work, I lifted fewer weights, threw fewer bullpens, and threw fewer fastballs. Then I'd start over. I couldn't figure it out, and neither could Lach or his pitching coach, Chuck Hernandez.

Without a good fastball, my secondary pitches were not effective enough to get me through a game. Bob McClure was right, all those years ago. He'd told me I had to learn to pitch, that I wouldn't have a fastball forever, and now it was gone and I had nothing to turn to. From the days of softball-toss competitions in elementary school, I'd always been able to throw hard; I'd assumed I always would.

For the first time, Dana and I discussed the possibility that my career was over, or discussed what we'd do when it was over. Something was wrong that couldn't be fixed, and maybe I would not have the twenty-year career—and the lifestyle that came with it—we had assumed. Dana, ever protective, dragged these notions out of me. When I was home, I couldn't talk about the games, because my failure in them was consuming. I couldn't face old friends, people who shared a baseball connection, because they, I was sure, would want to help, or—worse—feel sorry for me. Going to dinner was torture. When I walked into a restaurant, I thought people saw not Jim Abbott, but the guy who was approaching 2-18, like a neon sign was hung over my head. Back in Orange County, I believed my entire world was wrapped up in my struggle. I tried to balance the joy and uncertainty of Dana's pregnancy against my job, but never did. The pit in my stomach that came as I left for the ballpark was as painful as it was relentless.

On August 4 I lost my fourteenth game. The next day, Lach, among the most decent men I'd ever met and someone who'd once risked his career for mine, was fired by the Angels. Among my many mistakes was in allowing the losses to become personal, not only to me, but to Lach, Billy, Tim. Every day I looked into their eyes and felt I'd let them down. Even by that standard, August 5 was a terrible day.

The Angels held a press conference, where Lach glumly answered questions about what went wrong. He was, as ever, a picture of dignity and resilience. I sat in the back of the room and watched my coach, my friend, bear the weight of a season lost and a franchise suffering. I thought it should have been me up there.

A week later, after nearly eight full major-league seasons, I was sent to the minor leagues. The organization hoped a gentler environment might clear my cluttered head and develop those elusive secondary pitches. The plan was to rebuild my psyche and let my career follow, to facilitate my transition from a power pitcher to a finesse pitcher, the latter being what they call pitchers without a fastball. That, and a minor leaguer.

In spite of Bavasi's sound reasoning, and in spite of the preponderance of evidence supporting his decision, I viewed the demotion not as a chance at a fresh start, but as the final stage of a complete breakdown.

My home games wouldn't be in Anaheim, but in Vancouver. I had a pregnant wife at home. There were hundreds—no, thousands—out there like me, grown men with families who'd gone off to pursue baseball careers, aiming to advance through minor-league systems and one day stand in a big-league ballpark. I was moving in the other direction. Our paths crossed in the Pacific Coast League.

I had struggled with the Yankees, but that didn't feel like outright failure. That was temporary. Success was a couple miles per hour away, a little more depth on my curveball, slightly more tilt on my slider. Success was within reach. It was four days away.

The minor leagues were outright failure, and it wasn't all about how hard I would throw a baseball.

The Vancouver Trappers were playing a series in Tucson, Arizona.

I pulled open the clubhouse door, lugged my duffel bag across the threshold, and became a minor leaguer for the first time, after 1,535 major-league innings. In that moment I joined the many who were scraping and clawing their way to the majors. Some would get there. The rest would stop here, agonizingly close to all they'd ever played for.

Some of the faces were familiar, the ones that had come through Anaheim for short periods or had been in spring training. Mostly, however, they were kids, earnest kids who'd worked their way through the system and wore some of the weariness of baseball summers. They were, however, still enjoying themselves, still young and grateful enough for that anyway. I even laughed some that first night, something I hadn't been doing a lot of in Anaheim.

The next morning was cool and sunny. I awoke to the chatter of families in the parking lot, the clicks and slams of car doors, and the rough stirring of engines. Gone were the trappings of the majors— the cozy beds, the room service breakfasts, even the quiet of morning. I'd pitched myself into a roadside motel in Tucson and woke up to the scent of bygone travelers and old cigarette smoke, and to a career in distress. In a dim light cast through thready drapes, the fall from hardball grace ended on an orangey-brownish carpet, and knocked the wind from me.

I saw myself as a ballplayer first, and as a worthwhile person because of it. Who was I without a fastball? What was I without a major-league uniform?

I'd built a life on a foundation of athletic achievement, beginning in places where the bases were toppled lawn chairs and salaries were paid in grilled cheese sandwiches and apple cider. My self-image came with a baseball cap, a roaring fastball, and a crowd on its feet, applauding strike three. If I was special, or as special as some people thought I was, it was the game that made me so. How could anyone like me if I wasn't a good baseball player?

Twenty years after I'd been handed my first uniform, near dawn and a few yards from the growl of semis on Interstate 10, I mourned the decline of that person. I searched my life for signs of what else I could be, of *who* else I could be. When nothing came but blankness and indecision, I sat on the end of the bed and questioned how it was—with so many blessings in my life, including and especially a wonderful wife and a daughter on the way—that failure on the base-ball field could bring me to absolute misery. Nothing—not Dana or family or friends or money—offered more than temporary comfort, which only heightened my pangs of selfishness. The money least of all. In fact, the weight of the contract enhanced my despair: I was not just disappointing people, but cheating them, too.

I was a little dark that day. It wouldn't be the last day like it or the worst day like it. But, it was the first of such depth. Fortunately, soon I got to pitch again. And, turned out, I had a little fun. The atmosphere with the Trappers was more relaxed. The spotlight was dimmer. Dana visited Vancouver, and with lighter hearts one morn-ing we drove the ninety miles to Whistler. In just a few weeks, Southern California and the big leagues seemed a long ways away.

I returned to the Angels in early September, through Miami, where Harvey was working for the Florida Marlins. Scott Boras and Billy Bavasi worked out the details, all quite clandestine considering Harvey was employed by another club. Harvey and I spent a day together.

He reminded me that I was not my job, that the way I pitched did not define me, not when I was bad and not when I was good. Believing I was a good person because I was pitching well, of course, was not the current issue.

As he'd done before, and would again, Harvey looked me in the eye and in that crackling New York accent said, "So, what are you going to do about it?"

Harvey had little patience for self-pity.

I'd tried just about everything. In fact, I asked over and over, what *hadn't* I done about it?

Just being around Harvey was good for me. I met the team in Minnesota, won a game against the Twins, pitched in three more games and lost all three of them, numbers sixteen, seventeen, and eighteen. Like I said, historically bad.

The Angels lost 91 games and finished in last place in the AL West. We'd gone through three managers (John McNamara followed Lach, and then Joe Maddon followed McNamara). The season ended and I was glad for it. I needed to get out from under those eighteen losses, to clear my head so I could get on with saving my career, and it wasn't going to happen as long as I was dragging 1996 around with me.

The year ended just as it should have, with a fresh and hopeful beginning. Maddy was born in December. She was healthy and happy and came into the world with a full complement of fingers, toes, and innocence. She was a blessing in every way. Having her in our lives allowed us a measure of perspective in an uncertain time. By herself, Maddy diluted my pain. Maddy's timing was perfect. For her, I felt a renewal of purpose. I was going to pitch long enough for her to know her dad's story, to witness at least a part of it. Every morning of that winter I left the house seeking to banish 2-18 to some other place than my head and my conscience. I ran, and I lifted weights, and I threw. And when I returned home to Dana and Maddy, exhausted and wrung with sweat, I was convinced I'd taken back another inch toward repairing my name and my game.

Confident again, I was strong and, at twenty-nine, in my prime. By spring training, and in spite of the debacle of the season before, I was sure of myself. I'd done the work. I'd pushed the uncertainty away. I had more to pitch for.

Then I could barely get an out.

As though there'd been no five-month break, no morning workouts, no dedication to fulfilling my contract, I could barely throw a strike.

I made a few starts. The last was in Tucson, which meant a two-hour bus ride on a Saturday morning to face the Colorado Rockies. Nobody wanted to be on that bus, and few of the veterans were. I'd been knocked around by the Oakland A's five days before, so I was eager to get on with my comeback, even if it meant 230 miles roundtrip. Close enough to that minor-league hotel room that I could almost smell it, I pitched an inning.

I couldn't find the strike zone, like my arm wasn't even part of my body anymore. Jim Leyritz was the catcher and he'd set up wherever he set up—in, away, down the middle—and I wasn't ever close. It was gruesome. I'm sure it was pathetic to watch from the dugout, the stands, and the press box. It was worse from the mound, I could have assured them. Over the course of three outs, I'd given up walks, given up hits, even been struck on the shin by a rather firm one-hopper.

When I did finally get out of the inning I went straight to Lach, who had returned as manager Terry Collins's pitching coach, and asked for another inning. "Just one more," I said. When he said no, I begged for another inning, pleaded for another chance.

"You're not going out there again," Lach said. "You're done."

Back in the clubhouse where months before I'd managed to muster a laugh in the face of demotion, I couldn't put the pieces together. Here I was, a veteran player, familiar with the game and its routines, and yet my career was hanging by a thread.

Something that had been there my whole life—the ability to throw hard, to throw near the plate and with movement—was gone. I wasn't even thirty. Hours later, the bus drove north past that same motel, back across the desert to Tempe, dragging my career behind it.

The following morning Bavasi called me into his office. My head spun, thoughts of forging ahead mixing with ideas that I should make life easier for everyone by walking away. I was hoping for a pep talk. Keep working, hang in there, we'll get this right, that sort of thing. Instead, his eyes were hard and his words pointed.

"If I had your stuff," he said, "I wouldn't throw strikes, either."

It was not going to be a pep talk. He laid into me. I put my head down and took it like I deserved it. After 14 2/3 innings, and with the regular season a week away, my ERA was 13.50, almost twice the ugliness of the season before.

"You're not going to make this team," Bavasi said. "Here is your choice: Go back to the minors and work your way back or take your release."

I'd gotten to the ballpark early that day, said my hellos, and changed into my uniform. Then I sat across from Bavasi wishing it were different, wishing I had a fastball to defend myself with, and wishing I wasn't wearing the uniform. It seemed out of place, like a Halloween costume in March.

The choice was Triple-A or unemployment, neither of which sounded like an attractive career move. He'd stated the obvious, that it just wasn't getting any better, maybe it was best to move on, or stick around and serve the organization as a coach or consultant or something. I kept thinking I was too young for that. For any of this. Two years remained on my contract and I desperately wanted to make good on it.

Telling him I'd think it over, I left his office and returned to the clubhouse, where I laced on my spikes, put on my cap, and picked up my glove. Maybe somebody would give me the ball.

Tim Mead, a wonderful friend who'd been through so much with me, put his hand on my shoulder and asked if I wanted to take a walk. We found ourselves in center field and sat down, our backs to the outfield wall. I talked about all that had led me there, the pressure, my stinkin' fastball that needed miles per hour and direction. Tim had seen me at my worst—the nights I'd lose and punish myself emotionally in front of my locker, or physically in the weight room— and at my best. Here we were at another crossroad, only this time my career was in jeopardy. We talked about family, about financial security, about moving on without the game, finding a purpose beyond baseball.

I think he knew I wasn't going back to the minors and starting over, especially with Maddy at home. After a while, we stood and headed back across the field. The rest of the team was coming out to stretch, and I walked through the group, literally going in separate directions. I paused to say good-bye to Chuck Finley and Mark Langston. My world was ending, I thought, and theirs was going on. As they reached for something meaningful to say, I fought back tears and gave them a little wave, then left to find Bavasi. I was a wreck. The conversation came and went, jagged because it was unpracticed.

"I'll take my release," I told him.

"Are you sure?" he asked. "Maybe you can figure it out."

"It seems like these things, I don't know, aren't going to go away," I said.

Billy stared. I reached for more.

"They're a distraction to you and a burden on me," I said.

He wasn't disagreeing. I'd hoped he might.

"It would only continue the drama," I said, and after a breath, added, "I'm through."

He nodded again. Neither of us knew who was supposed to talk next. I was stunned by the finality of it, and maybe Billy was, too. I wanted to leave, but didn't know how. He wanted me to leave, too. So I nodded back. And as I turned to find the door, he said something about the two years remaining on my contract, that the team would "seek relief" or something, but I wasn't listening anymore.

I left my uniform in the laundry bin, packed nothing important into a cardboard box, and hugged a few former teammates. I was so jealous of them, being able to play still. In my truck, I drove to a lower field looking for Lach. This, I thought, is what it feels like when a career ends: standing in the outfield of a minor-league field holding nothing but disappointment. If Lach said anything, I didn't hear it. He had been there through so much, had shown so much faith in me, and had endured the disappointments with such great compassion. The only kind of good-bye to a man such as Lach was the terrible and wrenching kind.

Then I drove home to California, listening to Willie Nelson and barely comprehending that the game, the Angels, all of it would go on without me. There'd always been an answer to the struggles before. More effort. More focus. Throw harder. Throw softer. Throw more curveballs, or fewer. But now this was it. All I could do was drive faster, to get home and to get away. My family, I decided, needed me.

As I rode westbound on I-10, Willie's song "Your Memory Won't Die in My Grave" seeped into my head. "Baby's taking a trip," he said, "but she ain't taking me."

By the time I cleared the state line late Sunday morning, clubhouse attendants had cleaned out my locker and removed the nameplate from above it, like I'd never been there.

In the afternoon, reporters found Langston shaken by the morning's news.

"This," he told them, "is a very difficult, a very emotional time. Jim is like a brother to me, and I guarantee you no one in this clubhouse worked harder than he did this winter. That's why this is so disappointing. I don't know what's going to happen, but I know this is not what he wanted."

"I want what's best for Jim," Lach said. "I love him like a son. I told him I can answer any questions he has, but I can't make the decision for him. It has to come from him."

Of course, I'd already made my decision. I was going home, and already halfway there. The game goes on, I thought. I wasn't part of it. I thought there would be relief. There wasn't.

Dana was at the door and I had nothing to say. She looked at me kindly, glad to have me, and all I could think about was all the people I'd let down, starting with her. At least Maddy would have a full-time dad.

Dana viewed the homecoming as an end to the suffering. While she held me and assured me we'd find something to do with the rest of our lives, she was thinking it had been too hard for too long, that perhaps one good hug for both of us would leave baseball behind. The game—at least my struggles in it—had hung around our necks for long enough.

I needed to talk to Harvey. The answering machine in my office held twenty-three messages. Most were from friends, teammates, and family. One was from Boras. Another was from the Angels' financial officer. I'd kept a spiral-bound notebook on a bookshelf, in among signed baseballs from Mickey Mantle ("To Jim, My best wishes. Stay hot. Mickey Mantle"), my boyhood idol Mark Fidrych, Ronald Reagan, and Bruce Springsteen. On the first clean page I wrote the names of those who called. I turned that page and dialed Harvey's number. I found a pencil and transcribed as quickly as I could, writing the words just large enough so I could go back and read them, and just small enough that they wouldn't sting, Still, he filled a couple pages.

"Using your family as a way out," he said, was a "cop out."

"See, Jim," he said, "we invent motives for our behavior. You use the separation from family in one context and not the other? Does that make sense? If you were pitching well, you'd still live for your family."

I underlined "family."

"To what extent will you regret this?" he searched. "What about in five years? Can you live with it appropriately? Use all the info, then you'll have no regret. Until then, it may be what you feel, but true is better."

I lingered on "true." The truth was, my fastball was gone, and it would still be gone in the minor leagues. The truth was, it was humiliating. The truth was the Angels didn't want me anymore.

"It's a bitch," he said, "to get released by beating yourself. Have you given the best to the Angels? Do you owe them Triple-A?"

I honestly didn't know.

Harvey kept going. I kept scribbling.

"The issue rests with you. Can you live with it? If you have to bury this, then it's wrong. If you're tired, then there you go. Do you have the energy or inclination to continue? If you enjoy it, then continue fighting, because an environment like this will never challenge you again."

Was I done with baseball? Does baseball decide? Or do I decide?

"The ordeal"—Harvey's word for "life"—"will be a quiet, solitary one."

I said good-bye, put down the phone, closed the notebook.

Dana was relieved. When I couldn't wander the house wishing I was at the ballpark any longer, we took Maddy to Hawaii. And when we returned, I did what any out-of-work twenty-nine-year-old would do. I gathered the family and took off for a cabin in Good Hart, Michigan, my favorite place in the world, bought a twenty-one-foot Boston Whaler, and tooled around Lake Michigan all summer.

Even then, weeks after my final spring training game, a bruise lingered on my shin, a yellow-green-purple reminder of the come-backer I couldn't glove against the Rockies. Into summer, it still hurt to the touch, the last evidence that I was once a player. It seemed strange to be out of the game so quickly that a superficial injury would follow me into retirement, if that's what this was to be. When the sun set over the lake I'd turn on the television and watch my teammates play baseball, still sore from when they really were my teammates.

I so missed it I ached.

The feeling wasn't mutual, apparently. A stray letter from former Dodgers, Angels, and Padres executive—and Bill's father—Buzzie Bavasi, who encouraged me to return to the game wherever I could, was the only correspondence I received with that message. I'd pitched myself out of the game. No team was going to invite me back in.

Had the year been 2007—2002, even—and I'd pitched until I

had nothing left but fifteen years of big-league memories, a winning record, and an empty jar of Advil, the wind against my face would have smelled of contentment.

I knew my career would end in Good Hart, retirement guided by Little Traverse Light, a speck of glowing green in the gloaming. It is a town of fewer than five hundred people near the top of the Michigan mitt, twenty-five miles or so from the Straits of Mackinac and the Mackinac Bridge, which spans the meeting place of the Great Lakes Michigan and Huron. Of the seven or eight businesses in downtown Good Hart, five—the general store, bakery, deli, and real estate and post offices—are in a single one-story building. Fords vacationed not far away, as did Wrigleys. I had a place big enough for a bedroom, a loft, and a few regrets.

But I'd have my family nearby, splashing in the shore water in the mornings and building campfires at night. In between, we'd sand and paint the old cottage, built only twenty-five years before but worn by the hard winters of the North Woods.

And while Dana, Maddy, and I filled our days just so, I was not satisfied. Maybe it was the contract or my age or the feeling I'd left something undone, but I spent the summer with one eye on the baseball on television and the other on the calendar. I'd decided I didn't deserve to be there, in my idea of paradise, watching a baseball season disappear with the whitecaps over the horizon.

The contract gnawed at my sense of fairness. I'd signed for three seasons and pitched one of them, and the one was a disaster. Now that I was sitting on a patio twenty feet above the shoreline in Northern Michigan watching my little girl wobble around, I worried I was taking money I didn't deserve, or that other people thought I was taking money I didn't deserve, which is sort of what I thought. I talked to Dana, Boras, and my accountant, all of whom said they understood yet looked at me like I was overly sentimental and foolish. The standard argument—had I won twenty games, the Angels would not have insisted I take a raise—came up often. The logic rang hollow.

It wasn't something I was proud of, and I wish I'd been that person who could have stood up and said, "No, this isn't right, you keep the money."

But I wasn't. Maddy's future was in those paychecks. So was all the work I'd done to earn the contract.

Maybe, had Gene Autry still owned the club, I would have felt different. But Disney did. The club sent a lawyer to meet with Boras, a conversation that went no further than Boras's refusal to negotiate a buyout.

So, from May until September, from early in the season when the harbor was nearly devoid of boats until the harbor nearly emptied again at the end of the season, I—we—avoided tomorrow the best we could. I'd never really captained a boat before, never mind something as unwieldy as a twenty-one-footer, and my trips to Harbor Point and back usually ended with some mooring drama. It wasn't long before the other boat owners in the marina would see me coming and dash along the dock, grabbing ropes, offering rubber fenders, shouting instructions, whatever they could to save their own boats. At that point, I might have been a better pitcher than a boat driver.

The solitude was good for all of us. The cottage was in the woods, away from the road, reachable only by a small electric trolley on a track that plunged 180 feet to the front door. The place was as rustic as it got, made of fieldstone and board-and-batten siding; inside a fieldstone fireplace, one bedroom, and a loft. From the back patio I could kick a rock into the water. Mom and Dad came around that summer and we'd sit out back and not talk about baseball. The summer before, when I couldn't win, I'd driven from Cleveland to spend a day with Dad and he'd had his say then.

"If this is it for you," he'd said, "I'm proud of you and what you've done."

He knew I was hurting.

He added, "Remember where you're from."

The distance I'd come, he meant. That I'd done more than most, maybe a little more than some might have expected. It wasn't enough for me, of course. Not near enough. But I understood what he was saying. And a year later, sitting lakeside near the end of an idle summer—the first of my life—he didn't give me that Dad look and order me back onto the playground. Instead, we shared a couple beers, laughed with Maddy, watched the sun go down, and ignored the fact I'd washed out at twenty-nine.

Before we knew it, the afternoons weren't warming with the sun anymore and the fireplace was lit round the clock and it was time to come out of seclusion. Dana and I packed up, locked down the cottage for winter, and boarded a flight to L.A.

I never did name the boat.

The phone rang in early spring, or about the time I assumed my next game of catch would be with Maddy. Buck Rodgers, who'd managed the Angels for parts of five seasons and was a notable bus-crash casualty in that time, wanted to know about the family, and how I was feeling, and after a while he was talking me into a comeback. Rodgers had been fired by the Angels almost four years before, but stayed close to the game, had some ties to independent teams, and knew his baseball.

At least I hoped so. A few times a week I'd leave the house—Dana would watch out of the corner of her eye, wary as to where this was headed—meet Rodgers at a local junior college, and throw. He said if I could learn a split-fingered fastball, I could throw that off my fastball and have the off-speed pitch I'd been searching for.

It was a reach. But, it was good to stand on a mound again, and good to have someone believe in me. Though I'd opted for my release over the minor leagues the spring before, turned out I'd never been ready to quit. Actually, it felt more like the game had quit on me, and not unjustifiably. I could be hopeful again, I was sure. Maybe the year off, a new team, a reset away from the Angels, maybe I could try. So it hadn't taken Rodgers long to convince me that one more shot wouldn't do any harm, and six weeks later I was on another mound, this one in Chicago, at Comiskey Park, in a tryout. I didn't have a splitter, but, after twelve months off, my arm—I must say—felt pretty good. Robin Ventura and Frank Thomas, Olympic teammates from a decade before, watched nearby. Magglio Ordonez, a rookie in '98, stood in and took some swings. Ron Schueler, the general manager of the White Sox, had one eye on me and another on a radar gun.

When I was done, Schueler told me he'd give me a chance. I nodded, ecstatic. I was getting my career back. Maybe.

I'd start in Class A, in Hickory, North Carolina, he said. We'd go from there. He promised not to lose track of me.

I'd be a Crawdad. At thirty. With a bunch of nineteen-year-olds as teammates, like I was the dad at a T-ball game.

I couldn't wait.

Dana wasn't so sure. She'd long before thought baseball was supposed to be more fun, rather than engender such regular heartache. While sympathetic to my four-day mood cycles after losses, as well as to my inability to walk away from the game before it was taken away, she'd grown weary of the defeats, of sharing our relationship with them. Yet, she went along with the minor-league experiment, half expecting me to walk back through the door in two weeks.

I never did, at least not that season, though I did call home plenty, wondering what I was doing out there on the blue highways, hanging out with teammates who couldn't buy a beer without a fake I.D., and searching for velocity in a dozen new places. And I couldn't shake the guilt of being off on my own, chasing what was now a vague and seemingly impossible dream, while Dana alone raised our little girl.

From the perspective of a rickety folding chair, surrounded by fast-food wrappers and pizza boxes, wondering what sort of flesh-eating something was living on the floor of the nearby shower, watching a major-league game on television in a minor-league clubhouse is about as far away from that dream as I could have been.

The uniform, however, was real. The games meant something to me, as did the path on which they sent me. Before long, I graduated from the A-ball Hickory Crawdads to the high-A Winston-Salem Warthogs, made four starts there, and became a Double-A Birmingham Baron.

This was my summer of 150 teammates, of thousands of hard miles, of catchers whose names I couldn't remember, of lunch eaten off my lap on a bench seat bound for somewhere else. On the days I didn't pitch, I'd sit in the bleachers and chart someone else's pitches. And I'd sweat. One night in Chattanooga a scout looked at me, leaned over, and said, "What the hellya doin'? Need more money?"

I laughed and thought, *Damned good question, pal.*

He wouldn't have understood—or maybe he would have—but I just wanted to play again. I wanted to finish better, if being finished was what I was. And I wanted to see if the weight of everything in Anaheim had become too much to bear, if maybe the ability that had leaked out of me might be sopped up and recycled.

A few nights later, with Dana and Maddy in the stands in Birmingham, I was bombed and gone after two innings. When they boarded a plane for Michigan the next morning, Dana struggling to corral Maddy and their luggage and the stroller and get them all on the plane together, I fought the urge to get on the plane with them. I nearly quit the next day, but Roger McDowell, the pitching coach, wouldn't allow it.

"You're closer than you think," he said.

I doubt it, I thought, and found a seat on a bus—the one Michael Jordan had bought for his own minor-league ride—bound for Huntsville.

Slowly, I began to pitch better. Well enough, in fact, that after eight starts in Birmingham, Schueler moved me to Triple-A Calgary.

"Good news, Dana!" I shouted over the phone. "I'm going to be a Cannon!"

The air was cool enough to feel like baseball weather. My velocity was better. Not what it once was, but better. I was getting outs. I was gaining confidence. When I'd made five starts, Schueler came to me in the clubhouse and held out his hand.

"A jersey with twenty-five on it is waiting for you in Chicago," he said. "You've got the Yankees Saturday night."

The Yankees would win 114 games in '98. They'd come a long way since I'd been there, winning a World Series in '96 and poised to run off three more in a row. But I didn't care. Two years had passed since I pitched in the major leagues.

From Lake Michigan to Hickory to Winston-Salem to Birmingham to Calgary to Chicago, each level, again, felt a little like a gift.

With the Yankees of Derek Jeter and Paul O'Neill and Tino Martinez and Bernie Williams laid before me, Dana in a box seat behind home plate, the grass of a major-league infield under my feet, and the lights of a major-league ballpark over my head, the moment—and the journey back—seemed almost unfathomable.

I pitched into the seventh inning. On a meaningless September night for a White Sox team that would finish well out of first place, I'd had few prouder experiences on a baseball field. We beat the Yankees. And no matter what happened from there, I'd finished things differently.

I won five games for the White Sox in September. I pitched okay over those five starts. The White Sox scored forty-one runs in them, which helped. I was encouraged enough to sign that winter with the Milwaukee Brewers, as they assured me a place in their rotation, which seemed important.

It didn't work. This time I knew it wouldn't ever again. This ordeal would be less solitary.

I retired mid-summer 1999, a little more than a decade after it all began. I was thirty-one, in my prime. I was also in Milwaukee, pitching out of the bullpen for the Brewers, and not very well. My ERA was around 7. My cutter was neither hard nor quick. Over the years I'd heard older teammates say the hitters would tell them when they were done and, well, it was becoming unanimous. Again.

I'd made it all the way back and that, at least, was meaningful. Well, some of the way back.

I should have stayed in Chicago, with a team and people I knew. Instead, I went to the Brewers, figured I was ready to resume my big-league career, and was wrong. I was so wrong I couldn't wait to get away.

I retired with eighty-seven wins and wondering why it all ended so abruptly. Where were the next ten years? How could I be sent away now, with a body so young? Wasn't I going to do this forever? I'd left the game once before, been run off before, but my head and my heart told me then it was not permanent.

This was going to be permanent.

I wish I could have gone on pitching. Maybe I could have for somebody, in some role, and found a way to get outs. To survive. Maybe I could have remade myself as a pitcher, come up with a way to throw a ball to the outside corner against right-handers, become a side-armer, developed that splitter Rodgers was always talking about, something. Maybe, if I kept working at it.

But I was miserable again, and not just as a ballplayer. As a person, the unhappiness had resurfaced, crept up on me like that kid from North Carolina off third base so many years ago. I needed to cast it away forever, the part of my life that was hurting me. Amazingly again, that was baseball. I wasn't who I wanted to be anymore. The failure—it just never stopped—was exhausting and agonizing. In Milwaukee, I wasn't contributing. I was the last man on the bench for the Brewers, who weren't winning, who weren't competing, who played in a lousy stadium where nobody came. I had almost no connection with my teammates. I mean, I liked them, but my head was somewhere else. I was wishing I'd stayed with the White Sox, or was back in Anaheim, or on my nameless boat on Lake Michigan, anywhere but in Milwaukee. I didn't care how much money I was making, it wasn't worth this bottomless hurt. I couldn't endure it again.

It was my job, so I took the ball one last time in the ninth inning of a game at decrepit Milwaukee County Stadium. We were losing, 4–0. This was the very definition of mop-up duty. I pitched to nine batters, gave up three runs, and got off the mound by striking out

Jim Poole, a relief pitcher who'd bat .125 over eleven seasons, with the last cutter I ever threw.

By then, retirement had been coming for a while. I walked off the field after that last game embarrassed and frustrated. Milwaukee was such a strange experience. Sal Bando, the general manager, was terrific and so was Phil Garner, the manager. But it was disheartening to play for a team that didn't really have a chance at winning, worse to be among the reasons for it. About halfway through the season I was taken out of the rotation and assigned to the bullpen, so it was obvious they had no plans for me, and I really never enjoyed relieving. In the final month, I sensed it was my last go-around, and lingered especially one afternoon on the field of my youth, old Tiger Stadium in Detroit. I took one final, long look around. I tried to smell it and taste it. My trips as a kid to the old ballpark on Michigan Avenue had helped cement my aspirations. They'd become real there.

I'd been to the lake over the All-Star break. The Brewers would open the second half in Milwaukee against the Royals. I didn't want to go back. I wanted to stay with Dana and Maddy. But, I trudged away and put my uniform back on and tried to pitch when I knew I couldn't. Dana and I had so many late-night talks; I was frustrated and fearful that regular life (whatever that was) seemed so appealing.

So I walked off the field, hung around through the bottom of the ninth and waited for the writers to clear out of Garner's office. I went in, closed the door, and told him I was willing to take my release if it made things better for the club. Not surprisingly he thought it would.

A couple days later the team went off to Florida—the bus that would take it to the airport idled nearby—and I went the other direction, to California, where Dana and Maddy were, where the rest of my life was. I rolled my suitcase through the concrete corridors of County Stadium, through the stray cups and wrappers of the last baseball game I'd play, searching for a pay phone to call Dana and let her know the flight I'd be on. I was alone. A cab was waiting outside. As difficult as it was to go willingly, I did. The pervasive cloud of disappointment began to lift. Just to be physically away from the team, the game, felt like freedom. Strange, bittersweet, frightening freedom.

As the days put distance between me and my decision, I found contentment. I'd had long talks with my dad and with close friends such as Kirk McCaskill. They knew my pain. They felt the time had come, too. Once, I'd left the game believing I'd beaten myself, that my failures had been self-inflicted, that maybe I hadn't given enough of myself to become great. Not this time. The hitters said it was time. My body and mind agreed. I wouldn't ever be good enough again. I could have told Harvey that now.

Boras, meantime, knew I was in turmoil. He'd flown to Miami and waited at the team hotel there, thinking I'd be on the plane. He was going to convince me to keep at it, to learn to become a reliever. He was disappointed.

I'd have second thoughts. A little pang here or there. Maybe I should have hung in there longer. I'd seen plenty of players hanging on because they needed the paycheck or had nowhere else to go. I didn't admire them. I still loved baseball, of course, but my love for my place in it was gone. To push onward seemed motivated by money, or desperation, neither of which seemed honest. I'd made enough money. I thought I'd done enough hanging on. I thought I could be happy. So, at thirty-one, I moved on with life. I was frightened, but I also felt blessed that the game had given me such a great head start.

Like my mom said, every step, every new level, was supposed to have been a gift. And it was. You know, maybe I'd go throw a ball off the bricks in Flint again. Maybe that's where all of this was to end.

CHAPTER 18

A s I gathered my thoughts and composure in the dugout one final time, my breath came in jagged wisps.

I laid my jacket on the bench, stacked the eighth and final cup with the others, took comfort in the process, and had a fleeting recollection of another time like it. Five years before, there was a ninth inning in Seoul, South Korea, an Olympic gold medal waiting beyond three more outs. The ballpark was just that loud and I was just that nervous, just that excited.

I'd been through it, thrown strikes, finished it in a pile of teammates. Maybe I could get there again. Maybe we could.

Still, stooping to pick up the baseball on the mound, I was haunted by a familiar thought: With my heart hammering like this, how was I going to throw a single pitch, let alone get a big-league hitter out?

I found Nokes and threw a warm-up pitch. A few more. I forced a deep breath. My chest felt heavy, but I was okay, not at all fatigued, and the ball was behaving, leaving my hand smoothly. This is it, I thought. Trust, I thought. Let's throw a strike. Let's throw a no-hitter.

Kenny Lofton stood in from the left side. Nokes, still on our plan, wanted a slider. I threw it with confidence, toward the middle of the plate, believing the break would carry it away from Lofton's bat barrel. All that happened, except Lofton turned, slid his left hand up the bat and jabbed at the pitch. More than a tenth of his hits that season were bunt hits. And yet in that moment I'd not given the bunt a single thought. I'm not sure anyone had. I wasn't ready for it. No one was. The ball skittered down the third-base line, foul.

The crowd booed. Lofton grimaced. Wade Boggs moved in a few steps from third, Don Mattingly crept in from first base. This was Lofton's game, granted. And of course his first thought was to win the ballgame. We were ahead only 4–0. Breaking up a no-hitter in the final couple innings with a bunt, however, is considered bad form. I wasn't sure about that, but I was sure I would have hated to lose eight innings' worth of no-hitter on a thirty-five-foot hit. Also, Lofton generally killed me; he certainly didn't need to bunt to get on base.

Nokes said nothing to Lofton directly. He didn't have to. He shouted out to Boggs and Mattingly to keep an eye on that, saying it in a tone like, *Can you believe this guy?* By then I was relieved I'd thrown a slider instead of a fastball, which Lofton might have timed better, and relieved the ball had spun foul, and relieved to be still pitching for a no-hitter.

I took another ball from Nokes, forced another long breath. We were a single pitch into the ninth inning, and already we'd had a defiant play, a near miss, a gust of anger, and a do-over resolution. Man, I thought, this is fun, and excruciating. So, we reset. Three outs suddenly seemed a long way away. Nokes settled back in behind the plate, Boggs and Mattingly leaned a little forward, the fans stirred again loudly, Lee Smith resumed warming in the bullpen,

Buck Showalter and Tony Cloninger recrossed their arms in the dugout, the bunt no longer a near miss or an emotional flare-up but a strike. Strike one.

Believing Lofton wouldn't try that again, Nokes wanted a cutter. Lofton didn't try it again. Instead, he took strike two on the outside corner. Now we'd eliminated the bunt entirely. We went to the slider on 0 and 2, sweeping it away, and just as I had on Thome, I went to a three-quarter arm slot, figuring there was no reason to hold anything back. It ran well off the plate and Lofton held his swing. So we went back to the cutter, Lofton swung, and for the second time in the at-bat I believed the no-hitter was probably gone. The ball bounded over my head and up the middle toward second base. I gave a little jump, swiped at the air, but had no chance. I turned, half expecting to see the ball rolling into center field.

Instead, I saw Mike Gallego swooping in from the right. I'd worked Lofton away and Gallego had played him up the middle. Like Boggs earlier, and Velarde earlier, and Gallego himself earlier, we were in the right place again. He took the ball on two hops on his backhand side, threw across his body on the run and the ball beat Lofton to the bag by a half-step.

The ballpark shook like it was full. I tried to pull one long, calm breath, and it came as if filtered by the noise and anticipation. So much for that. I'd settle for a strike to Felix Fermin. Fortunately, I was still throwing off-speed pitches in the strike zone, got a called first strike, and got to 2 and 2 before leaving a curveball over the plate. Fermin, who would go on to hit four home runs in more than 5,500 professional plate appearances, crushed it to left-center field. Thankfully to left-center field, where the ballpark goes on forever.

As the game had progressed through the middle innings, Dana, who arrived by cab well before the first pitch, had wondered where all her friends had gone. She'd sit with some of the other wives and girlfriends—Pat Kelly's wife, Rebecca; Danny Tartabull's wife, Kelly; Wade Boggs's wife, Debbie; and Scott Kamieniecki's wife, Rita, were often at the games, and they'd be clustered together on the field level, twenty rows up and just to the left of home plate. They had a good time.

She'd always just wanted something good to happen, knowing how hard I'd take the alternative. She dared not hope for anything like this, only for a good game and a win, then maybe some contentment.

By this ninth inning, Dana was alone. None of the other wives wanted to be the one who said something to jinx the no-hitter, so one by one they'd gone off to the restroom or for a soda and never come back. Dana's brother had played some college baseball, so she'd grown up with the game and its etiquette. She'd also known the disappointment of having Bo Jackson break up my last shot at it, so she sat on the edge of her box seat and didn't eat, didn't drink, and barely moved, as desperately as she too needed to run to the restroom. She also knew enough about the game to think Fermin had gotten an awful lot of that curveball. In fact, she thought it was a home run. Me? I was thinking double. There was a groan from the crowd. That ball, everyone thought, was going to get down.

Along came Bernie Williams. Running hard from straightaway center field, Bernie, a middle-distance sprinter in his youth in Puerto Rico, appeared to be in mid-440. With his right hand extended behind him feeling for the fence, he caught the ball coasting onto the warning track. Fermin, robbed by Gallego five innings before, had lost another hit.

One more out.

The place was going crazy. Really crazy. So was my head, my heart.

Thirty-seven years before, Don Larsen had thrown a perfect game in this very ballpark, from this very spot, in the World Series. Bob Feller threw a no-hitter here for the Indians. Allie Reynolds had a no-hitter. A decade ago, another lefty, Dave Righetti, threw his no-hitter here, won 4–0, then had sweetly and memorably laid his head on the shoulder of his catcher, Butch Wynegar.

I knew the feeling. These are not solo flights.

Carlos Baerga stood in, the switch-hitter still batting left, still defending against the cutter. Gene Michael, the Yankees GM who'd traded for me, stood up in his box behind home plate, no longer able to sit still. Willie Randolph sat to his right. Brian Cashman stood to his left. From the television booth, the voices of Dewayne Staats and Tony Kubek tightened. Dana gripped the bottom of her chair.

My brother, Chad, twisted the volume knob on the radio of Mom's Honda Accord, straining to hear the play-by-play above the ambient crowd noise. He was in Harbor Springs, Michigan, in the driveway of my parents' condominium, the car key turned to accessory. One of his college friends was in the passenger seat, another in the backseat. A family acquaintance had called the condo from Flint in the seventh inning, asking if they'd heard what was happening that afternoon at Yankee Stadium, and Chad and his buddies had dashed into the driveway in search of a radio.

With each of the last nine outs, he'd yell to Dad. Eight more! Seven more! Finally, one more!

In the stands, the middle-inning lines at the pay phones—people calling their dads and sons and friends to turn on the TV—had thinned to nothing.

Behind me, Mattingly worked the dirt at first base with his spikes, scraping at it like a hockey goalie would the ice in front of his net. The energetic Gallego bounced on the balls of his feet near second base. Boggs, whose defensive plays had helped get me here, pounded his glove expectantly at third. At shortstop, Velarde shook his legs. They felt heavy, a little sluggish. The grind of the game, day game after a night game, had settled in his thighs. *Don't hit it to me,* he thought.

They'd only just gotten over the Fermin scare when I threw the first pitch to Baerga, the next-to-last pitch of my afternoon, a slider. He couldn't have seen many breaking balls from the left side all year. He took it for a strike, then gestured with his left hand like the pitch was too high. From there, the up-and-in slider, we went down-and-away with the same pitch. Baerga pounded it toward shortstop and Velarde. He rolled forward off those tired legs and gathered up the ball. *Hit him in the chest,* I thought from memory. *Hit him in the chest.* Velarde threw to first, hard and true.

At first base, Mattingly caught the baseball with a hard *thwack* and raised his arms.

"He did it!" Staats cried from the booth.

The crowd, all those people, rejoiced. Dana stood among them. Michael, his tie loosened, Randolph, and Cashman exchanged handshakes and fist pumps.

Cloninger and Showalter jumped to their feet, mindful of the low dugout ceiling, grinning at each other.

Nokes, who'd backed up first base on the throw from Velarde, rushed in from my left, his hands in the air. Boggs charged in from behind.

All I could think of was, *Yeah, baby! Yeah, baby!*

So I yelled it over and over. I yelled it to Nokes and toward the stands and into the gray sky. I yelled it so Dana could hear it twenty rows up, so my mom and dad would hear it in Michigan, so the Angels would hear it in Anaheim. I'd been practicing that last pitch, that last out, since my dad first knelt in the backyard, since I'd peppered that brick wall in Flint.

Taken in itself, beginning with that horrible start in Cleveland, living with it for going on a week, hating it, preparing and then sticking with a completely different plan, then living it for almost three hours, for all that, the final moment arrived with shocking suddenness.

I'd survived all the little bounces that could have changed it. We'd survived it, Nokes and I, the nine of us in all. It had come true. What remained was this very cool celebration, hugs from Nokes and Cloninger and Williams, from everyone, in a place like Yankee Stadium. It took a long time to leave the field, in part because I didn't want to. I didn't want anyone picking up the trash just yet, or hosing this moment away.

Amid all those bodies, feet stomping around, various gloves and gear strewn on the infield, I found my cap on the ground near the first-base line, randomly. I wasn't really even looking for it. I tipped it to the crowd.

"One of the most wonderful moments," Kubek was saying in the booth, "for as sweet a man as there is in any uniform in a major sport."

More important for this afternoon, I'd managed a great result from the pitcher's mound. We'd won. I'd held together and, by the ninth, was throwing the ball with conviction. I descended into the dugout, thrilled so many people were still in the park. Over the dugout, Yankee fans hugged and shouted and laughed, and I felt just like they did. Someone had scooped up my jacket. The cups were still there, stacked just so. Passing along the bench, I made a left into the tunnel that led to the clubhouse, and the cheers chased me up that narrow, dark, and musty passageway.

There would be champagne. And there would be another trip to the field, where I'd raise my arms to the people behind the dugout, and then I'd summon Nokes, who needed to share in that. He'd been so good. He'd believed.

There were writers everywhere in the clubhouse, asking questions between the phone calls, the hugs, the laughs.

In Anaheim, Tim Mead grinned. "Every time Jimmy succeeded after he left," he'd say, "I wanted to say out loud, 'Look what Jimmy Abbott did today.' I can remember all you naysayers, whoever you are, well, screw you. For all the individual accomplishments I was privileged to be around, and I wasn't around for that, I may have felt as happy for Jim Abbott doing that as for any athlete. He did it."

In Florida, Doug Rader was charmed.

"I've seen a ton of no-hitters," Rader, who then was a coach with the expansion Marlins, would say, "and I'll never forget Abby's. Most no-hitters are almost clinical. They're just so aggressive. Jim's, I don't know, it touched me emotionally."

In California, Marcel Lachemann nodded and smiled. Cloninger had come to him in spring training, wondering where my big fastball was, wondering about the velocity. Tony told him he wasn't sure I could pitch anymore.

"Next thing you knew," Lach would say, "he was throwing a no-hitter at Yankee Stadium."

In Michigan, Mike and Kathy Abbott celebrated with Chad, who'd come up from the driveway and burst through the door with the news. And in homes from Anaheim to Baltimore, in places where children wished only to be normal, to fit in, maybe the world took another step toward them, not away.

Amid the cheering and the toasts (George Steinbrenner sent the bottle), the best moment of the day came in the hallway outside the clubhouse. Normally she would wait in the family room, but Dana had been led to the big metal door. I came out in my uniform, unbuttoned to the middle of my chest. Her expression was of pride, disbelief, and joy, ultimately a reflection of all that had gone on in our lives for the past couple years.

In that dingy cement corridor, where New York sent its reinforcements to feed on the news of the day, we stood for just a few seconds alone in the swarm of lights and gazes.

"How about that?" I said, smiling.

"How about that," she whispered, smiling back.

We'd come all this way, from California to New York, from familiar to foreign, and seemed to hit every bump along the way. Now we laughed and held each other in the clamor of the hallway, and for a moment all the cameras disappeared, and it felt a lot like we'd made something of it all. I left her with a promise that I wouldn't be long.

Back in the clubhouse, twenty-five men raised plastic cups to the occasion, to the 234th no-hitter in major-league history, the eighth by a Yankee, and the sixth by a Yankee in this ballpark.

The cab ride home, back along the Major Deegan, over the Third Avenue Bridge, then to the FDR Drive and onto the surface streets of the Upper East Side, seemed less rutted and jarring than they'd been eight hours before.

In the backseat, Dana and I relived the final outs: the Lofton bunt that skewed foul, the Fermin drive that on another day and in another ballpark might have changed everything, and the clamor that chased Baerga's ball straight into Velarde's glove.

In the apartment, the red bulb on the answering machine blinked impatiently. And the phone was ringing.

"Big Jim," Chad shouted from Michigan, "with the no-no!"

We dialed the phone and shared the good news, and in between picked up the phone and apologized for the busy signals. Our view was of the East River and a sliver of the skyline downtown. Sitting twenty-seven stories high and looking out over a small slice of the city, opening another bottle of champagne, we marveled at the way the world turns over anew again every day, and then was kind enough to include us. In the clinks of our tulip glasses, we shared a wish that this was the start of something very good. Neither of us dared dampen the night with the words.

We took the two-person party downstairs and into the streets of the Upper East Side, and to Cronies, a bar that felt a little like home. Mattingly sent a bottle from across the bar, as did strangers in Yankee caps, and we celebrated as dusk turned to night. This was the New York we'd longed for, as I'm just as sure this was the Jim Abbott for which New York had yearned.

In most other cities, the people identify with the local team. They cheer and they boo and then they go home to their lives. In New York, allegiances are tauter than that. The Yankees and their fans are bound by history, by the men who wore the uniform and the fathers and grandfathers who witnessed their greatness and failures. The relationship bordered on obsession for each other, so that on special days in that ballpark, tens of thousands of people in the stands and the players on the field seemed to share a single heartbeat.

I'd had a day like that.

Not just a game, but an entire day. When we left Cronies, the streets were alive on a Saturday night. Corner vendors already were selling copies of the next morning's papers, and people called to me and waved the early editions of the *Post* and the *Daily News,* their back pages trumpeting history at The Stadium. I signed autographs as we walked, feeling for the first time that I belonged among these people—Yankee fans, New Yorkers, those who worshipped the pinstripes.

Dana and I slept that night feeling as close to New York City as we ever had, and probably ever would. It wasn't home, exactly, but a place familiar and comforting, like we were starting to fit in, like we'd justified our presence there. It was good to belong.

The alarm shrieked mid-morning. There was a game in four hours, and a flight to Texas after that. Through the mild thumping in my head, I filled a suitcase with ten days of wardrobe and supplies. No matter the game, the routine always won.

Downstairs, the doorman grinned his congratulations and nodded toward the sidewalk, where a television crew stared back through the glass. The headache kicked up a notch, maybe two. A yellow cab took me past the usual landmarks, into the Bronx, along the perimeter of the stadium and to the back gate, where more cameras waited. It hadn't occurred to me the story might creep into another day, after the box seats had been wiped down, after the mound had been regroomed. My footsteps echoed in the corridor where the afternoon before I'd had to turn sideways to navigate the mass of people. On the other side of the metal door, my locker was surrounded by reporters, some of whom had come from Philadelphia and Boston and Baltimore to sort through the day after. The Advil was all the way across the clubhouse.

I went along with the storylines because, I guess, the moment had earned them. The story for the story's sake, the one-handed pitcher making his way, I never liked. The story with achievement, however, seemed more relevant. That had been the goal—to be a good pitcher. To win games. I'd needed to earn my way, to be good enough, to hold on to the hope that more was possible. I'd wanted to lift my arms to a gray sky, to honor a victory, to feel the approval in my heart. The stories could say what they wanted, but two-handed guys or one-handed guys don't throw no-hitters. Pitchers throw them. Eight other men share them. And maybe occasionally one of those nine doesn't look exactly like the others, but the game doesn't recognize that.

Boggs kept looking at me, smiling genuinely, like he hadn't put yesterday away yet, either. He was a touch offbeat, Boggs was, but he loved the game, its history, and the way it evolved a little every day. I thought he was enjoying the memory as much as I was.

I was summoned to the trainer's room to take a call from St. Louis. On the line was Dave Righetti, whose San Francisco Giants were finishing a series against the Cardinals. A decade before, he'd no-hit the Boston Red Sox as a Yankee and in this ballpark, the first Yankee to throw a no-hitter since Don Larsen's perfect game in the 1956 World Series, and the last until the afternoon before.

Frank Albohn, the groundskeeper, asked if I had a moment, and in a side room he and his crew presented me with the pitching rubber. They'd spent the night before exhuming it from the mound, then had it signed by my teammates and the plate umpire, Ted Hendry. The groundskeepers signed the rubber as well. I was struck by their generosity, and then by the amount of work it must have taken.

Albohn was built low and wiry, like a middle infielder or a center fielder. The old-timers around the team, the ones from the neighborhood who raked the infield or mowed the grass or knocked mud from our spikes, would say that Frank indeed had been a ballplayer. He'd been fast and sure-handed, enough so that the New York Giants had had him in for a tryout. When they didn't have him back, Albohn went to work at a machine shop near Yankee Stadium. There, he'd had an accident. Years later, when he was grooming the area around home plate or meticulously laying the foul lines before a game or hustling across the field when the rains came, you'd have to look closely to see that one of those machine blades from the shop had fired unexpectedly, taking off most of Albohn's left hand.

Gradually, the clubhouse cleared, and soon there was another game. I sat on the bench with hardly a care, staring out to the field, still amazed at what had happened there just yesterday. Baseball rarely stops to consider the game before, but on that Sunday morning there was a pause, at least for me, before starting up again. We won and moved into first place, tied with the Blue Jays, for the last time that season.

Six days later, in Kansas City, I pitched again. The first batter of the bottom of the first inning, Greg Gagne, got just enough of a cutter to push it over Mattingly's head and down the right-field line. It was a decent pitch. I watched the ball roll untouched and Gagne run hard into second base, and I turned to Nokes and thought again about the game, how it honors itself in its relentlessness.

Behind the mound, I waited, my glove on my left hand. I wanted the ball. I wanted to pitch.

CHAPTER 19

My parents believed my missing hand was a responsibility to be lived up to.

I didn't always get it.

How do you honor something that doesn't exist? I searched the length of my right arm and saw emptiness.

They saw potential.

I suspected limitation.

They saw an opportunity for resiliency, of body and spirit. They saw hope for me, and then for others.

There is a white box in Tim Mead's office at Angel Stadium that once had been emptied of ten reams of copier paper. Over two decades, Mead carted it around, lugged it into new offices, cleared space for it in new closets, slid it across new carpeting and old linoleum, and nudged it into corners with his foot.

The box had grown out of a single red folder in Mead's right-hand desk drawer—a tab, center-right, labeled it ABBOTT, JIM—to what it is today, a dozen 8 ½-by-14 red folders, some yawning with crispy newspaper clippings, lustrous magazine pages, and forgotten game programs.

In those files, however, there are mostly children, boys and girls who innocently reached out and touched my hand, and who smiled, and who—I hope—dreamed. Their every new level, like mine, would be a gift.

They begin,

"Dear Mr. Abbott, I have a son who is five . . ."

"Dear Mr. Abbott, I'm writing this letter for the son of a very dear friend . . ."

"Dear Mr. Abbott, I have a daughter . . ."

"Dear Mr. Abbott, I know you're busy with baseball . . ."

And there are stories, heartbreaking stories of cerebral palsy, and accidents, and birth defects, and amputations, and a little girl who opened a toothpaste tube that had been rigged with an explosive and lost her hand.

And there are words difficult to find, because the pain is real and the fight doesn't get easier when the bandages come off and the consequences are lifelong. I couldn't make it go away in four paragraphs. I hadn't made it go away for thirty years.

I write,

"Dear Brendon . . . don't hesitate to challenge yourself."

"Dear David . . . physical handicaps have little or no control over our mental abilities."

"Dear Josh . . . your story is so special. . . ."

"Dear Jason . . . you and I both know that handicaps are only setbacks in the eyes of others."

They came to the ballparks, mostly. They stood with their parents, or just behind them. I remember their faces. I remember their hurt and their hope. I remember thinking there were so many of them, these beautiful children who'd grown scared and timid and already were tired of having to be so strong. Sometimes, I was tired, too.

Over forty years, a good part of them spent in and around the game, all of them alongside a disability I hoped was not defining me, the children were the inspirations. Those mid-afternoon taps on the shoulder from Tim, me leaving behind the comfort of the clubhouse to sit in the dugout with the young Brendons and Davids and Joshes and Jasons, the children gave me hope. They were in Anaheim and Baltimore and New York, in Chicago and Kansas City. They were poor and rich and middle-class and they were every color.

They came with stories and a little sadness, but with a preternatural capacity to endure and to fight.

A long time ago, I sat with many of them and walked with others. Some, I played catch with, and they'd maneuver their glove just the way they'd practiced in their bedrooms, in their mirrors and away from all the other kids, like I had.

Most important, we talked. I rewarmed the encouragement my parents had offered once upon a time and I repeated their stories. Mom and Dad had searched for people who rose above hardships in their lives to make extraordinary contributions. Years later I told the children about those people. And I shared with their parents the example of *my* parents, their "why not" attitude, the way they made me feel up to every challenge, as though I was not just capable in spite of being different but special for being different. Their message to me was powerful when I was young, and it became powerful in me. They believed there were many ways to navigate our worlds, and that because my way was different didn't mean it wasn't as efficient.

There I was, trying to be the kind of person my parents might have been on the lookout for, and because of that I would nod at Tim and excuse myself from the card table or remove my headphones and close my book. Honestly, there were times—many times—I'd have preferred to hunker down in the clubhouse. But I trailed Tim to the dugout, I guess because I couldn't disappoint them, and because I needed to tell them they didn't have to fall in with what people thought they could do or would become.

Indeed, what drove me were the low expectations people had for me, especially in new situations. I insisted on showing them what I could do. I could play Little League. I could play for the high school. I could go to college and win an Olympic medal and pitch in the big leagues. I might not win, but I could fight. As I continued to wage my own battles, I tried to offer more promise to the children in theirs as well, encouraging them to rise above what other people thought was possible for them. Once I saw the look in their eyes, and their parents' eyes, it would be very hard to say no anyway. How could I not make the time?

Ultimately, I think my playing was of more consequence than my words. I hated being labeled—one-armed, one-handed, disabled, whatever—and I understood how we all wanted to move beyond those kinds of perceptions, but I felt the sting of those throwaway words every day. It would take success on a major-league field to clear the path, to make even one of those kids believe. It wouldn't be enough to get by, to show up. I needed to accomplish something more tangible than participation. We all did, I thought. If I didn't last, didn't perform and produce, even my baseball would have seemed based on me being different. That's what set my jaw so tight when a couple runs scored and what cut me loose in the weight room when I lost. It's what helped bring me back when my fastball was surely gone. I adored the game first, but I owed everybody around it second.

Some of my closest friends and people I admired most in the game believed my pitching suffered because of the time I spent trying to further a cause—often one child at a time—that was so personal to me. Those in that camp—and my friends weren't the only ones— believed I carried a torch that became burdensome, both in body and mind.

After I was 11-14 with a 4.37 ERA and the Yankees missed the playoffs in my first season in New York, George Steinbrenner announced the following spring that Jim Abbott would be better off giving "100 percent of his attention to baseball."

"His agent," Steinbrenner snapped, "has to lay off for a while. So do other people to allow him to reach what he knows he can do." He later added, "I must demand total dedication to the task."

The back pages of the tabloids gave that big play, of course. Fortunately for me, the tone of the news stories and columns was, "Boss Rips Abbott for Being a Decent Human Being." As Brian Cashman, who would become general manager of the Yankees four years later, wryly observed, "If you're going to get ripped for something, you want to get ripped for that, I guess."

I would have loved to use that as an excuse. It seemed to me a few minutes on a day I wasn't pitching had little bearing on the fastball that stayed up in the zone two days later. I never felt encumbered by the meetings with families. There were days and situations when I wished I could blend in a little more, maybe not walk away from the guys in the clubhouse, or get through a hotel lobby to my room without stopping. But it never affected the way the ball came out of my hand. In fact it may have helped it, providing a drive and inspiration, a need to seize this opportunity that may not have been there otherwise.

Years after we were both retired, Doug Rader would say, "From the time Jimmy was up in the morning, he was carrying the banner for somebody—all day long, every game he pitched, every pitch he made, the whole time he was in the big leagues, and well before that. This was something he's been burdened with, and truly it is a burden. Anytime you have that much of an obligation and you have so many people pulling for you so hard and you represent a group to that extent, it has got to be very, very difficult. And I understood what Jimmy was going through. Every time he failed, he failed for everyone."

He was wrong. I did it for myself. I was driven only to be the best pitcher I could be. If there was something to be gained from that by others, then that was a fortunate—yet accidental—consequence of my efforts, which were minimal beside theirs. I did come to see there were peripheral benefits to what I tried to do, but they never drove me, and never impaired me, either. Instead, what I learned was that there will be another like me, another like them. And they won't owe themselves to anyone for it, either. They will advance in their lives unencumbered by responsibility to anything but their own inspiration. They, too, will achieve for the love of the achievement, and let the cause come along for the ride.

Those children were not burdens. Besides, what difference would it make? Would I have changed anything? Could I have? The baseball was temporary. And I raged against its impermanence. When it left me, I feared that which would remain. Just me. Imperfect me. My career would be done, but not my life. Not my hand. And not those children's lives.

I still think of Cormac McCarthy's words,

Those that have endured some misfortune will always be set apart but that it is just that misfortune which is their gift and which is their strength and they must make their way back into the common enterprise of man for without they do so it cannot go forward and they will wither in bitterness.

There was, if I'd chosen to shrink away, a very good chance of "withering in bitterness." I could not hide from it, hard as I might have tried.

I do not know if I ever came to be a person of value, but ultimately hope that I held up reasonably well in times where I was tested. I wasn't a great major-league pitcher. I experienced moments I considered great. I had a few seasons that were satisfying, and many more that were not. But, in some ways, the struggle was more important to my understanding of my hand and who I was than had I had a career with fewer obstacles. Baseball—and success in it—was so important it brought upon me a distorted view of winning and losing. The games' outcomes became personal. The perception of myself rode with the outcomes. And it wasn't until I struggled that I came to understand its destructiveness.

The examination of my faults on a baseball field in turn led me to look at my right hand differently. Instead of hiding it, I tried to develop a strength that was independent of the circumstances around me. That awkward second glance at my right arm from a passerby on the street, or that insensitive comment by a stranger, those were theirs to own, not mine.

It wasn't easy and it never ended. At forty-four, I battle it every day. I put my hand in my pocket. I recoil when a child blurts, "What happened to your hand?" Not long ago, I was a guest in a suite at Angel Stadium. Between innings of the ballgame, I went to the back of the room, got a plate of food and a cup of coffee, and returned with the saucer and cup balanced on the end of my right arm, like I'd always done. Another guest turned to an acquaintance and said, a bit too loud, "What is this, the circus?" But I can catch myself succumbing to the influences that, right then and there, once changed the way I felt about myself.

Baseball gave me many great blessings—the people I met, the places I saw, the incomparable feeling of winning a major-league baseball game. But maybe the greatest gift was that it helped me come to peace with the burden of being different. The lesson had to be learned through losing, painful as it was.

So I played on, and I helped a little where I thought I could. And when Tim Mead with the Angels or Jeff Idelson or Rob Butcher with the Yankees came along and said, "Excuse me, Jim," I knew it was time and from the moment I'd lay eyes on those children I would not regret it for a second.

And, heck, I still got to pitch.

The no-hitter was terrific. I loved it, looking around, feeling the ballpark and the fans close in, feeling teammates who wanted it at least as much as I did. But, you know, I always had looked back on it and thought about all the great plays behind me, and the five walks, and figured it was fine. Just fine. I had remembered it the way Manny Ramirez had—pitches hit hard, a few walks, some great plays behind me, and a game that happened to end with no hits.

That's where I had it, too, almost. A thrilling afternoon with my teammates, a really fun night on the town with my wife, something to talk about for a half century or so, another way to bore my daughters, and maybe that was all.

But, you know, much of a lifetime later, I wonder if it wasn't a microcosm of the way I looked at my career, maybe a little more negatively than I ought to have. Maybe there were more good things about it, that it wasn't all eighteen-loss seasons and declining fastballs and long, hard runs through the Cleveland afternoon.

At the end of every scarred road—even one as traveled as FDR Drive—there was a ballgame. There were plenty of cloudy mornings and chances for rain, but the weather held out, or someone turned on the lights, or we simply played through the rain.

September 4, 1993, was special for its collision of right time and right place, a habit of mine. The day was special for what it meant for twenty-five guys who happened to be there, and for the 27,000 or so others who were there, too, because we all left the ballpark feeling good about ourselves and our place in our corners of the world.

That wasn't just a day for me. But, taken in stages, I lived a good part of my life in those hours, and in the days preceding it, and in the afterglow of it.

From the seeds of doubt, from a place where there could have been little, along came something out of the ordinary. Along came a little something different. It wasn't even pretty. It wasn't perfect. In fact, it was quite imperfect. But a few of us believed in the notion of the story and in the idea of a happy ending, even if we weren't sure of it. We'd played enough ball to know the outcomes weren't usually as good as the stories themselves.

We showed up the next day anyway, gluttons for the game, convinced that belief begets satisfaction.

So I beat myself up over some failure, questioned it all, traversed that same stretch of uneven road, and returned to the game. It wasn't so different from my childhood, when my father ordered me back to the playground. And the people who decided I wasn't good enough, hadn't they always been there?

For one day, I was as close to perfect as I'd ever be on a baseball field, but not because of me. I was there because Tony Cloninger was there, and Matt Nokes, and Don Mattingly, and Wade Boggs, and Mike Gallego.

I was there because Dad wouldn't let me whine and quit, and because Mom was inspirational in her work ethic and resilience, and because they, too, lived together and returned to each other through their imperfections, and because Mr. Clarkson had come along, saving Buck Showalter from having to tie my shoes before the game. I was there because Mark Conover's dad issued me a uniform and a position, and Bob Holec insisted I play varsity in spite of my misgivings, and Joe Eufinger taught me how to take a snap, and Don Welke and Bud Middaugh refused to believe in absolutes. Their faith sent me to the feet of Doug Rader, Marcel Lachemann, Kirk McCaskill, and Bob McClure, to uncommon men who viewed me as physically common.

I was there because this thing wasn't going to defeat me. I'd let everyone else be surprised. Me? I'd go to Yankee Stadium on a day it was supposed to rain, and pitch for my job if that's what was called for, and believe in who I was and what I was capable of, and maybe win a ballgame.

I don't know why I lost my fastball, any more than I understood why I had it. Maybe I'd lifted too many weights and lost the flexibility of my youth, as Middaugh believed. Maybe it was all the cutters, as Michael thought. The human arm has only so much in it. Maybe mine was just done. That left arm had carried me an awfully long way.

Through it all, I never did dread taking the ball. Not late in that second season with the Yankees, when I was struggling again at Yankee Stadium and an infield grounder elicited a cry from a fan, "Run, gimpy, run!" as Dana and Chad sat nearby.

Not when I was 2-18 for the Angels, or when I spent five months in the minor leagues in 1998, or when I won five starts for the White Sox at the end of that season only to learn it was a mirage, or when I got kicked around the season after that in Milwaukee.

I was always hopeful, and almost always optimistic. Every time they took the ball I wanted it back again. Every time an inning ended I wanted another. No matter how bad it got—or looked—I always figured I'd overcome more, that I'd will and pitch my way out of it. I'd always want one more hitter. So, I'd hold up my glove, expecting someone to give me a baseball.

It had happened before. A month into the 1993 season, not five months after I'd been traded from the Angels to New York, I returned to Anaheim Stadium with the Yankees. I started against Mark Langston on a Wednesday night, both clubs having come out hot, the crowd pretty big, the usual energy pulsing through a ballpark hosting the Yankees. The Angels led, 2–0, until the top of the ninth inning, when we scored two runs against Langston. Handed a fresh game, I would face Tim Salmon, Chili Davis, and J. T. Snow in the bottom of the ninth, only I never did see Davis or Snow. Salmon hit a long home run into the left-field bleachers, ending the game. Except—out of instinct, familiarity with the ballpark, shock, regret, forgetting which team I played for, I don't know—I lifted my glove as a target for the umpire to toss me another baseball, even as the Angels celebrated and the rest of the Yankees trudged off the field. I wanted to keep pitching. I wanted to win. I wanted a chance.

We flew through that night to New York. In the morning, I didn't bother going to bed. I left the apartment and walked to Carnegie Deli, ordered a plate of food, and sat alone, then could hardly eat.

Four days later, I pitched again. That was what was important to me.

I took the ball on a patch of dirt in Flint, some would say improbably. I gave it back on a major-league diamond twenty-five years later, reluctantly. In between, I did like my career. I'm proud of it. The fact that the last few years were so filled with struggle and unending fights and disappointment, perhaps it all shaded some of the really fulfilling moments that preceded them. But still.

For me, the satisfaction of victory was never quite as intense—or lasting—as the ache of defeat. I hated losing and I fought against that more than I fought for the winning. And as much as I loved to win, my career—like my life—was always more about fending off those demons. If anything, I sometimes look back and wonder if I made the most out of it, if I got all I could out of myself. I wonder, "What more could I have done with my left hand?"

Then, maybe I could be a little more generous with what I did and how I did it. You know, maybe I did what I could.

I think about little Ella in the schoolroom. Like Maddy, like her mom, she's growing up tall and lanky and beautiful. I think about her question: "Dad, do you like your little hand?"

Really, it's not much to look at. Was I less for it? Or was I more for it? Maybe in the times I wasn't carrying it, it was carrying me. What couldn't I like about that?

Maybe I lived up to the responsibility of my little hand. I hope I did.

Acknowledgments

I didn't want to turn on a tape recorder and simply tell my story.

Whenever—and wherever—possible, I asked others for their assistance with the details so that I could re-create the past forty-some years through their eyes, as well.

First, I'd like to thank my parents, Mike and Kathy, for who they are, what they stand for, and what they tried to make of me; and my brother, Chad, for always getting back up; and my aunt Katie Norris, for being a wonderful person.

Thanks to Harvey Dorfman, for allowing me to lean on him for all those years, and then opening his files and speaking from the heart. I sure miss you, Harvey. Just so you know, I'm still working through your reading list.

I'm grateful for Tim Mead, the best PR man in the business, who saved boxes of newspaper clips, letters, and photos that twenty years later became the backbone of this book. More, I owe him for his friendship. And special thanks to V. J. Lovero, John Cordes, and Debbie Robinson.

Thank you to those who contributed hours of their lives for the interviews that filled in my memories, and for the kindness they showed while making those memories: Doug Rader, who gave me the ball; Marcel Lachemann, who taught me when and where to throw it; Bob McClure, who tried to show me the way; Mike Fiore, Ed Sprague, and the rest of the '88 Olympic team, who grew up with me over two of the greatest summers of our lives; Scott Boras, for making it personal; and Kirk McCaskill, for letting me tag along.

Thanks for believing in me, Donn Clarkson, Bob Holec, Joe Eufinger, Don Welke, Jim Schneider, Bud Middaugh, Jeff Blanchard, and Ted Mahan.

To Matt Nokes for his insights; to Billy Connors for his compassion; to Rick Peterson for his trust; to Don Mattingly for his leadership; to Mike Gallego for his passion; to Bill Lachemann for his toughness; to Brian Cashman for his help; to Buck Showalter for his determination; to Pat Courtney for his spirit; and to Jack Curry for his professionalism, I thank you.

Thanks to my East Court neighborhood friends Mark Conover, Johnny Lutton, David Cramer, Chris Ebbott, Stuart Kale, Alex Green, Danny Nathan, Pete Philpott, Howard Croft, and all the rest for letting me in the games.

This book does not happen without David Black, who loved the idea of it from the start, and Mark Tavani, who made the idea presentable, and Lilly Walters Schermerhorn, who provided the spark.

To Tim Brown I will forever be grateful. In many ways he had the impossible task of putting into words many feelings and thoughts I had been unable to adequately articulate for much of my life. With never-ending enthusiasm and empathy, he succeeded beyond what I could have hoped for, or imagined. From here on out, I look forward to being his friend, and his fan.

Thanks to the many others who helped with their memories, encouragement, and support along the way. Over the seasons and the years, I benefited greatly from the generosity of so many teammates, trainers, coaches, teachers, and team personnel. You are part of this. And thank you to the children who came to say hello. You inspired me.

I would also like to thank Pete, Jan, Dean, and D. J. Douty. Their love and support for me in any endeavor, including this book, has been unwavering.

Finally, Tim and I are forever grateful for Dana Abbott and Kelly Mullens-Brown, for their love, their words, their deeds, and their patience.

Especially their patience.

About the Authors

JIM ABBOTT was a major-league pitcher for ten seasons; an All-American at the University of Michigan; an Olympic gold medalist; and threw a no-hitter for the New York Yankees at Yankee Stadium in 1993. After retiring in 1999, he has worked with the Department of Labor's Office of Disability Employment Policy and as a motivational speaker. He and his family split time between Southern California and northern Michigan.

TIM BROWN is the award-winning national baseball columnist for Yahoo! Sports. For twenty-five years he has covered Major League Baseball for the *Los Angeles Times, Newark Star-Ledger, The Cincinnati Enquirer, Los Angeles Daily News,* and Yahoo! He studied journalism at the University of Southern California and California State–Northridge. He lives with his wife in Venice, California.

About the Type

This book was set in Garamond No. 3, a variation of the classic Garamond typeface originally designed by the Parisian type cutter Claude Garamond (1480–1561).

Claude Garamond's distinguished romans and italics first appeared in *Opera Ciceronis* in 1543–44. The Garamond types are clear, open, and elegant.